A History Of The Works Of Sir Joshua Reynolds, P.r.a

A

L+⁶

A HISTORY OF THE WORKS OF
SIR JOSHUA REYNOLDS

P. R. A.

A HISTORY OF THE WORKS

OF

IR JOSHUA REYNOLDS

P. R. A.

BY

ALGERNON GRAVES, F.S.A.

AND

WILLIAM VINE CRONIN

DEDICATED BY GRACIOUS PERMISSION TO
HER MAJESTY THE QUEEN

VOLUME II

H - L

LONDON
PUBLISHED BY SUBSCRIPTION FOR THE PROPRIETORS BY
HENRY GRAVES AND CO., LIMITED, 6, PALL MALL
MDCCCXCIX

CHISWICK PRESS :—CHARLES WHITTINGHAM AND CO.
TOOKS COURT, CHANCERY LANE, LONDON.

ILLUSTRATIONS TO VOLUME II.

DATE.	SUBJECT.	OWNER.	PAGE
1772.	SIR JOSHUA REYNOLDS, P.R.A.	Thomas H. Ismay, Esq. *Frontispiece*	
1763.	H.R.H. PRINCESS CAROLINE	Sir David Salomons, Bart.	424
1763.	LADY GORDON AND SON	H. L. Bischoffsheim, Esq.	432
1764.	MRS. BLAKE	Sir Horatio Davies, K.C.M.G., M.P.	448
1764.	KITTY FISHER	The Most Hon. the Marquess of Lansdowne, K.G.	456
1764.	GENERAL THE HON. WILLIAM KEPPEL	The Rt. Hon. the Earl of Rosebery, K.G.	464
1765.	DOROTHY, COUNTESS OF FIFE	His Grace the Duke of Fife, K.T.	480
1765.	MISS MURRAY	The Rt. Hon. the Earl of Normanton	496
1765.	MRS. POWNALL	The Rt. Hon. Lord Aldenham, F.S.A.	504
1766.	MISS FRANKS	M. T. Martin, Esq.	512
1766.	GEORGE AUGUSTUS SELWYN	The Hon. Robert Marsham-Townshend	528
1766.	MRS. SOUTHWELL	Abel Buckley, Esq.	544
1767.	JANE, DUCHESS OF GORDON	His Grace the Duke of Fife, K.T.	552
1767.	HENRY, EARL OF PEMBROKE, AND SON	The Rt. Hon. the Earl of Pembroke, G.C.V.O.	560
1767.	CHILDREN OF THE EARL OF THANET	The Rt. Hon. Lord Leconfield	568
1769.	MRS. BURKE	L. Lesser, Esq.	584
1769.	JOHN, DUKE OF DORSET	The Rt. Hon. Lord Sackville	592
1770.	THE HON. CAROLINE FOX	The Rt. Hon. the Earl of Ilchester	608
1770.	H.R.H. THE DUKE OF GLOUCESTER	The Rt. Hon. Earl Waldegrave	616
1770.	MRS. HOARE AND CHILD	The National Gallery (Wallace Collection)	632
1770.	REFLECTION	The Rt. Hon. Lord Leconfield	640
1771.	MARY, COUNTESS OF THANET	The Rt. Hon. Lord Hothfield	664
1771.	MRS. TRECOTHICK	The Rt. Hon. the Earl of Ellesmere	680
1772.	ELIZABETH, COUNTESS OF PEMBROKE	The Rt. Hon. the Earl of Pembroke, G.C.V.O.	696
1773.	MISS SARAH CHILD	The Rt. Hon. the Earl of Jersey	712
1774.	MARIA, DUCHESS OF GLOUCESTER	HER MAJESTY THE QUEEN	728
1774.	EMILIA MARY, DUCHESS OF LEINSTER	His Grace the Duke of Leinster	744
1775.	ANNE, COUNTESS OF DROGHEDA, AND CHILD	The Rt. Hon. the Earl of Drogheda	760
1775.	C. BOOTHBY SKRYMSHIRE	The Rt. Hon. Lord Leconfield	776
1776.	FRANCES, COUNTESS OF TYRCONNEL	His Grace the Duke of Rutland, K.G.	800
1776.	GIRL AND DOG	Arthur Kay, Esq.	832

Facsimile of page K from second ledger.	First payment		550
,, ,, M ,,	Second payment		628
,, ,, M ,,	,,		654
,, ,, R first ledger.	,,		787

ROYAL ACADEMY DIPLOMA OF SIR JOSHUA REYNOLDS 790

ROYAL ACADEMY ASSOCIATE DIPLOMA SIGNED BY SIR JOSHUA REYNOLDS FOR SIR THOMAS LAWRENCE 804

LETTER FROM SIR JOSHUA REYNOLDS TO ALDERMAN BOYDELL . . . 814

HADLEY, Mr.

Sat in 1762.

HAGGET, Mr., or HOGGETT.

Sat in February, 1765. Paid for, 1765, Mr. Haget, two pictures, £95.

HAGLEY, Mr.

Memo.: "1767. Mr. Hagley's small portrait to be sent to Mr. Davies at Highbury, near Newbury, Berks."

HALDANE, Brigadier-General George.

Three-quarter length, canvas 50¼ × 40 in.

Only son of Patrick Haldane, M.P. for St. Andrew's Burghs; Solicitor-General, and a Royal Commissioner for selling the forfeited estates, who died in 1769. He was M.P. for Dundee, and also for Forfar Burghs; was appointed Captain-General and Governor of Jamaica in 1757; sailed with the expedition to the West Indies in 1758; died at Jamaica, July 26, 1759.

Full face, standing, leaning left arm on a pedestal; right arm hanging down, wearing glove and holding the other; brown hair; in scarlet uniform, with blue facings and gold lace; coat open, showing cuirass, and the lapels of a buff waistcoat below it; crimson sash round waist; sea to the right, and a dark rock to the left.

Sat in April, 1755, and April, 1758, as Colonel Haldane.

Note to the 1757 sitting of *Mr.* Haldane: "George Haldane in August this year made Governor of Jamaica."—TOM TAYLOR, vol. i., p. 155.

The picture belongs to the Earl of Camperdown.

HALDANE, Captain Robert.

Three-quarter length, canvas 50 × 40 in.

Of the East India Company's service and of Gleneagles, Perthshire; M.P. for Stirlingshire, 1758; youngest son of John Haldane, M.P., and Helen, daughter of Sir Charles Erskine, of Alva, ninth son of John, Earl of Mar; married Miss Oglander, daughter of Sir John Oglander, of Ninewells, Isle of

Wight. He is said to have been the first Scotchman who ever commanded an East India Company's ship. He died in January, 1768.

Leaning on a staff; his left hand resting on a stick, wearing a glove and holding the other; the right arm extending across the body, and right hand pointing to the left; lace ruffles on both wrists; high rock to right; sea and sky to left.

Sat in June, 1762, and June, 1764. Paid for, August 8, 1764, Captain Haldane, given to Sir Lawrence Dundas, £52 10s.

EXHIBITED.

British Institution, 1845, No. 131, by the Earl of Zetland.

ENGRAVED.

G. Clint, A.R.A., 1805, 17¼ × 13¼ in.
S. W. Reynolds, 5 × 4 in.

The picture, which was given to his great friend, Sir Lawrence Dundas belongs to his descendant, the Marquess of Zetland, at 19, Arlington Street.

HALDANE, Captain Robert.

Three-quarter length, canvas 50 × 40 *in.*

His left hand resting on a stick; wearing a glove and holding the other; right arm extending across the body; ruffles on right wrist only; right hand pointing to the left; high rock extending over the head to right; sea and sky to left.

Sat in January, 1757, and March, 1759. Paid for before 1760, Captain Haldane, senior, £31 10s.; 2 frames, half length, £12 12s.

The picture, which was painted for Captain Haldane, descended to his sister's eldest son, Admiral Viscount Duncan, and now belongs to the Earl of Camperdown.

Note on the 1755 sitting: "M.P. for the Stirling Burghs, and highly distinguished for his services in the West Indies in 1759."—TOM TAYLOR, vol. i., p. 145.

Memo.: "October, 1759. Mr. Haldane's picture to be sent home."

HALDANE, Captain Robert, R.N.

Three-quarter length, canvas 50 × 40 *in.*

Of H.M.S. "Tryal," 20 guns, and, in 1760, of H.M.S. "America," 60 guns; cousin of the above; died at Madras, August 22, 1768, aged thirty-eight. On March 7, 1760, he sailed for the East Indies, and was favourably mentioned by Sir Eyre Coote, February 3, 1761.

Standing full face, looking to the right; right arm extended, resting on stick; left hand in belt; blue naval uniform with white waistcoat and gold facings; rock to left; sea and sky to right.

Sat in March, 1757, as "Capt. Tryal" (?). Paid for before 1760, Haldane, £30.

In 1746 Adam Duncan, afterwards Viscount, entered the Navy and served under his relative, Captain Haldane, on board H.M.S. "Tryal."

The picture belongs to the Earl of Camperdown.

HALDANE, Captain James, Junior.

Half length, canvas 30 × 25 *in.*

Of the East India Company's service. Died June 30, 1768.

Seated, in pink silk dress, with white cravat and lace frill; lace ruffle on right hand placed in waistcoat; left arm leaning over the back of a chair; brown background.

Paid for before 1760, Captain Haldane, jun., £21; 3 frames, ½, £12 12s.; 2 frames that went, Mr. Haldane's, one for the Capt.'s pictures, about July, 1762 (this entry is struck out).

Captain Haldane, sold at Greenwood's, April 14, 1796, Lot 20, as Captain Halden, for £7 17s. 6d., to Captain Walsh. Captain Haldane, unfinished, sold at Christie's, April 8, 1869 (H. W. Phillips, owner), Lot 230, for £2 10s., to Parker. Same picture, June 12, 1875, Lot 62 (Woolner, R.A., owner), for £34 13s.

The picture belongs to the Earl of Camperdown.

HALDEMAND, General, afterwards Sir Frederick, K.B.

Pocket-book for 1778 missing. Paid for, June, 1778, General Haldeman, £36 15s., and ditto copy, £26 5s. In December, 1779, General Haldeman, a copy, £26 5s.

"General Haldemund, just arrived from America, was introduced to His Majesty and graciously received, being sent for, as it is said, to give His Majesty *true* information."—*Gentleman's Magazine*, 1775, p. 404.
"Frederick Haldemand, Esq., Governor of Quebec, *vice* Sir Guy Carleton, K.B."—*Gentleman's Magazine*, 1777, p. 460.
"His Majesty's ship tbe 'Hussar' arrived at Portsmouth with General Holdemand on board, who was going out Governor of Quebec, but has since received counter orders."—*Gentleman's Magazine*, 1777, p. 506.
"October 7, 1785. This day Sir Frederick Haldemand took his final leave of the King previous to his going to Canada, of which he is appointed Governor."—*Gentleman's Magazine*, 1785, p. 831.
"July 30, 1787. General Sir Frederick Haldemand, Knt., appointed Governor-in-chief of Gibraltar *vice* Lord Heathfield."—*Gentleman's Magazine*, 1787, p. 746.
"Lately at Yeverdon in Switzerland, Sir Frederick Haldemand, K.B., Lieutenant-General of His Majesty's Forces, Colonel of the 60th Regiment of Foot, and late Governor of the Province of Canada."—*Gentleman's Magazine*, 1791, p. 586.

HALSEY, Mrs.

Sat in 1768. Paid for, February 21, 1768, Mrs. Halsey, £36 15s.

HALSEY, Miss.

Sat in 1767.

Memo. : "October, 1767, at Mendham Hall near Harlsden, Norfolk, 10 o'clock, by Waggon from the 'Saracen's Head,' Snow Hill."

HAMILTON, Captain the Hon. John.

Three-quarter length, canvas 50 × 40 in.

Second son of James, 7th Earl of Abercorn; was bred to the sea service, and was made lieutenant of the ship "Louisa," and in that station in December, 1736, attended His Majesty on his return from Hanover to England ; when a violent storm arising, wherein all the fleet narrowly escaped being lost, his ship was wrecked; and boats being sent to their relief, he bravely refused to go into them before the sailors, saying, "In that common calamity he would claim no precedency," and was the last that quitted the ship. Upon his going ashore he was presented to the king, who graciously received him, and his father was complimented by the queen on the gallant behaviour of his son. On February 12 following he was made lieutenant of "The Diamond," 40 guns, and October 14, 1741, first lieutenant of "The Russell," of 70 guns, whence he was appointed commander of "The Kingsale," and, February 10, 1742, to "The Augusta"; in April, 1748, to "The Van-guard," 60 guns, and, December 18, 1755, was unfortunately drowned, being overset in his boat as he was going from his ship to Portsmouth (Collins's "Peerage"). In November, 1749, he married Harriot, daughter of the Right Hon. James Craggs, and widow of Richard Eliot, by whom he had issue, John James, created 1st Marquess of Abercorn, October 2, 1790.

Standing ; full face ; in a large fur cloak ; left arm resting on his hip and right extended, leaning on a stick ; a hunting-knife in his girdle ; ship in stormy sea in background.

Sat in 1746.

EXHIBITED.

British Institution, 1813, first catalogue, No. 43, } by the Marquess of
Royal Academy, 1875, No. 114,   Abercorn.

ENGRAVED.

Richard Josey, 1876, 5¼ × 4¼ in.

The picture belongs to the Duke of Abercorn.

"In 1746 Reynolds painted the portrait of Captain Hamilton, father of the Marquis of Abercorn, which, it is said, was the first of his pictures at this period which brought him into notice. When, later in life, he again saw it, he was surprised to find it so well done, and comparing it with subsequent works, lamented that, in such a series of years, he should not have made a greater progress in his art. This portrait is now in the possession of the Marquis of Abercorn. Captain Hamilton is also introduced into a small family picture, painted by Reynolds about the same time, in the collection of the Earl of St. Germans at Port Eliot. It represents Richard, 1st Lord Eliot, his wife, and their children, together with Mrs. Goldsworthy. Captain Hamilton, who married Lady Eliot after Lord Eliot's death in 1748, is carrying one of the children on his back."—TOM TAYLOR, vol. i., p. 29.

"This Captain Hamilton was a very uncommon character: very obstinate, very whimsical, very pious, a rigid disciplinarian, yet very kind to his men. He lost his life as he was proceeding from his ship to land at Plymouth (TOM TAYLOR, vol. i., p. 29). The wind and sea were extremely high, and his officers remonstrated against the imprudence of venturing in a boat where the danger seemed imminent. But he was impatient to see his wife, and would not be persuaded. In a few minutes after he left the ship the boat was upset and turned keel upwards. The Captain being a good swimmer, trusted to his skill and would not accept a place on the keel, in order to make room for others, and then clung to the edge of the boat. Unluckily he had kept on his great coat. At length, seeming exhausted, those on the keel exhorted him to take a place beside them, and he attempted to throw off his coat; but finding his strength fail him, told the men he must yield to his fate, and soon afterwards sunk while singing a psalm."—PRIOR'S *Life of Malone*, p. 404.

HAMILTON, Captain the Hon. John, R.N.

Three-quarter length, canvas 50 × 40 *in.*

This picture belongs to the Earl of St. Germans, and is No. 221 in the Port Eliot catalogue.

HAMILTON, Captain.

Sat in 1757, 1758, and September, 1762, as Captain Hamilton, and April, 1762, as Major Hamilton. Paid for, 1762, Major Hamilton, £21. Frame paid.

From the sittings it appears there are two pictures of different persons.

HAMILTON, Douglas, 8th Duke, and his Duchess.

Douglas, 8th Duke of Hamilton, was born July 24, 1756, and succeeded to the dukedom, July 7, 1769. On November 25, 1777, he was appointed Keeper of the Palace of Linlithgow; he married, April 5, 1778, Elizabeth, daughter of Peter Burrell, which marriage was dissolved by the Scotch Commissary Court in 1794. He died, without issue, August 19, 1799. The Duchess married, secondly, August 19, 1800, Henry, 1st Marquess of Exeter.

On horseback ; in a red habit and hat ; the Duke standing beside her.

Sat in 1779.

Referring to Elizabeth Gunning Tom Taylor erroneously says : "He painted her again in a red habit and hat, on horseback, with the Duke standing near her ; in a fine picture, now at Hadzor, near Droitwich."—Vol. i., p. 102.

Sold at Greenwood's, April 16, 1796, Lot 62, the Duke of Hamilton with the Duchess on horseback, in a noble and rich landscape, for £105, to Colonel Hamilton.

Major Galton, of 36, Thurloe Square, writes on December 7, 1898 : "The picture used to hang in my dining-room at Hadzor House. Mr. Woods found a purchaser in 1889. The picture was bought by my great-grandfather, Mr. Joseph Strutt, at the sale of Sir Thomas Lawrence's pictures. It was in an unfinished condition, and was not considered good enough to be shown with the rest of the collection, but likely purchasers were taken to see it in another room. The tradition handed down with the picture was that after the divorce of the Duchess, the Duke gave the picture to a lady, who rolled it up and kept it out of sight. She subsequently wished to have her own portrait painted by Lawrence, and offered him this picture as part payment of his fee, an offer which he willingly accepted. It was a very large picture, and when it came to Hadzor the window had to be taken out to get it into the room, an operation I had to repeat to get it out."

Note from Mr. Strutt's catalogue : "Duke and Duchess of Hamilton (now Dowager Marchioness of Exeter). This picture the Duke gave to Mrs. Estings, the actress, who gave it to Sir T. Lawrence in exchange for her full-length portrait."

The picture does not appear in the catalogue of the Lawrence sale in 1830.

The picture belongs to Lord Iveagh.

HAMILTON, Alexander, 10th Duke of, and 7th Duke of Brandon, K.G., F.R.S., F.S.A.

Head size, canvas 26 x 20¼ *in.*

Son of Archibald, 9th Duke ; born October 3, 1767 ; educated at Christ Church ; M.P. for Lancaster, 1800 to 1806 ; Ambassador to St. Petersburg, 1807 ; created Baron Dutton in 1819 ; was Lord High Steward of England at the coronation of Queen Victoria ; married, April 24, 1810, Susan Euphemia, second daughter and co-heiress of William Beckford, of Fonthill Abbey ; succeeded as Duke, February 16, 1819 ; died August 18, 1852, and was interred in a splendid mausoleum, erected by himself, in the grounds at Hamilton Palace.

Three-quarter face, looking to the left ; long curly hair ; in crimson velvet coat and waistcoat, with white frilled shirt open at the neck.

Sat in 1782 as Mr. Hamilton. Paid for before 1783, Mr. Beckford, for Master Hamilton, £50, not carried out ; followed by, February 10, 1785, Mr. Wm. Beckford, bill paid, £50.

At the Royal Academy, 1783, No. 115, was the portrait of a young nobleman, that was at the time considered to be Lord Albemarle. As that picture is not to be found, possibly it was a mistake, and was really this picture. *See ante*, p. 11.

EXHIBITED.

British Institution, 1823, No. 33, by William Beckford.

"   "   1861, No. 198,
Grosvenor, 1884, No. 99,   } by the Duke of Hamilton.
Guelph, 1891, No. 107,   .

ENGRAVED.

Frederick Bromley, 1861, $4\frac{1}{4} \times 3\frac{1}{4}$ in.

The picture was probably bequeathed to the Duke by William Beckford in 1844, together with the picture of Mrs. Peter Beckford and his own portrait. It now belongs to the Duke of Hamilton.

HAMILTON, Elizabeth, Duchess of.

Whole length, canvas 94 × 58 in.

Second daughter of John Gunning, of Castle Coote, co. Roscommon ; married, first, February 14, 1752, James, 6th Duke of Hamilton, who died January 19, 1758, and secondly, March 3, 1759, General John Campbell, afterwards 5th Duke of Argyll. Her Grace was created a peeress of Great Britain as Baroness Hamilton of Hambledon, co. Leicestershire, in 1776 ; she was one of the ladies of the bedchamber to Queen Charlotte, and escorted Her Majesty to London when she came to be married to George III. ; died December 20, 1790.

Life size ; leaning on a sculptured pedestal ; white dress ; ermine mantle ; landscape background.

Sat in 1758, 1759, and 1764. Exhibited in the Society of Artists, 1760, No. 47. Paid for April 13, 1764, Duchess of Hamilton, £26 5s.

EXHIBITED.

Grosvenor, 1884, No 26,   }
Guelph, 1891, No. 130,   } by the Duke of Hamilton.

Walpole to Sir Horace Mann, February 27, 1752, writes : "About a fortnight since, at an assembly at my Lord Chesterfield's, Duke Hamilton made violent love at one end of the room while he was playing at pharaoh at the other end. I own I was so little a professor of love that I think all the parade looked ill for the poor girl. However, two nights afterwards, being left alone with her while her mother and sister were at Bedford House, he found himself so impatient that he sent for a parson. The doctor refused to perform the ceremony without licence or ring ; the Duke swore he would send for the archbishop. At last they were married with a ring from the bed-curtain at half an hour after twelve at night at Mayfair Chapel. When the Duchess was presented at court after her marriage, the noble mob clambered upon chairs to look at her."

Wraxall says that, "even in advanced life and with very decayed health she was remarkably beautiful, and seemed composed of a finer clay than the rest of her sex."

No public event of the time filled half so much space in the mouth, eye, and ear of London as those lovely Irish sisters, who had been married at the beginning of 1752. Walpole records how even the noble mob in the drawing-room clambered upon chairs and tables to look at them ; how their doors were mobbed by crowds eager to see them get into their chairs, and places taken early at the theatres when they were expected ; how seven hundred people sat up all night, in and about a Yorkshire inn, to see the Duchess of Hamilton get into her postchaise in the morning ; while a Worcester shoe-maker made money by showing the shoe he was making for the Countess of Coventry.

The picture belongs to the Duke of Hamilton.

HAMILTON, Lady Anne, afterwards Countess of Donegal.

Whole length, canvas 93 × 58 in.

Anne, daughter of James, 3rd Duke of Hamilton and 2nd Duke of Brandon ; born September 30, 1738 ; married, September 22, 1761, Arthur Chichester, 5th Earl of Donegal, afterwards, 1791, 1st Marquess of Donegal ; died November 11, 1780.

In a white dress and crimson robe lined with ermine ; pearl necklace and earrings ; standing on a terrace, her right hand resting on the pedestal of a column.

Sat in 1755 as Lady Ann Hamilton.

Sold at Christie's, June 28, 1890, Lot 26, Storer Collection, described as *Marchioness* of Donegal, for £38 17s., to Doyle, for National Gallery of Ireland. A fine and highly interesting portrait absolutely given away for want of biographical description.

"Lady Ann Hamilton, another of the royal bridesmaids Reynolds had painted some years before."—TOM TAYLOR, vol. i., p. 196.

HAMILTON, Lady Elizabeth, afterwards Countess of Derby.

Small whole length, canvas 46 × 31¼ in.

Lady Elizabeth Hamilton, only daughter of James, 6th Duke of Hamilton and Brandon, and Elizabeth Gunning ; born January 26, 1753 ;

married, June 12, 1774, Edward Smith Stanley, Lord Strange, afterwards 12th Earl of Derby; she died March 14, 1797.

When a child; seated on a bank, holding a bouquet of flowers in her lap; pink dress trimmed with lace; landscape background.

Sat in 1758 as Lady Betty Hamilton.

EXHIBITED.
Royal Academy, 1882, No. 33, by the Earl of Normanton.

Sold at Christie's, March 17, 1855, Lot 91 (Duke of Argyll, owner), for £840, to King, for the Earl of Normanton. Sold as Lady *Anne*, and described as one of the most fascinating and perfect works of the great English master. *See Illustration Vol 1, p 224*

"Another beauty whom he had known from the cradle, and painted as a bride this year (1774) or next, was Lady Betty Hamilton, who in the same June made a splendid match with Lord Stanley. All the town rang with the splendour of the *fête champêtre* given by the lover to his intended bride, a few days before the wedding, at The Oaks, Lord Stanley's villa near Epsom. 'It will cost £5,000,' says Walpole, writing the day before; 'everybody is going in masquerade but not in mask.' When the great people had enjoyed the fête, it was served up again to the public by Garrick, in General Burgoyne's 'Maid of the Oaks,' produced at Drury Lane in November."—TOM TAYLOR, vol. i., p. 82.

HAMILTON, Sir William.

Whole length, canvas 102 × 71 *in.*

Born 1730; died 1803; diplomatist and antiquary; son of Admiral Lord Archibald Hamilton. His mother, Jane, daughter of the 6th Earl of Abercorn, was Mistress of the Robes to the Princess of Wales and Governess to George III.; hence probably the position young Hamilton attained at so early an age. In 1758 he married the daughter of Hugh Barlow, and in 1764 was sent to Naples as Envoy Extraordinary, and while there made several ascents of Vesuvius and investigations at Pompeii, collecting many Etruscan and Grecian vases, which he sold to the British Museum. He wrote "Antiquités Etrusques" and "Campi Philegræi," and was elected Fellow of the Royal Society in 1766. He was created a Knight of the Bath in 1772. In 1784, when on leave in London, he met Emma Lyon, who returned with him to Naples, whom he married in 1791 as his second wife. In that year he became a Privy Councillor, and was a member of the Dilettanti Society, but remained at Naples till 1800, though obliged for a time to retire with the royal family to Palermo. Both Nelson and his wife were present at his death, which took place in London.

Sitting, looking to his left; in velvet dress, with the ribbon and star of the Order of the Bath; ruffles at the wrists; knee breeches, and buckles in his shoes; his left arm resting on a table on which stands the Etruscan vase; the famous Meidias vase stands at his feet; he holds a book, "Antiquités Etrusques," etc., with both his hands; in the distance a view of Vesuvius.

Sat in 1784. Paid for, September, 1784, Sir William Hamilton, Museum Picture, £105. Frame paid.

EXHIBITED.
British Institution, 1831, No. 114, by the Trustees of the British Museum.

ENGRAVED.
H. Hudson, 1787, 22¼ × 14⅞ in.
S. W. Reynolds, 6¼ × 4¼ in.

The picture was presented to the British Museum by Sir William Hamilton, and was deposited in the National Gallery in 1843 by the Trustees of the British Museum, and in 1883 deposited in the National Portrait Gallery, where it now hangs.

A fine sketch of this picture, 22 × 14½ in., was sold in 1898 by Messrs. Thomas Agnew and Sons to George Harland-Peek, of 9, Belgrave Square, the present owner.

HAMILTON, Sir William.

Half length, canvas.

Coat trimmed with fur; star of the Bath on coat; ribbon underneath; right hand on waistcoat; white neckcloth; looking to the left.

Sat in 1777. Paid for before 1775, Sir Wm. Hamilton, £12 12s.

A picture described as head of Sir W. Hamilton was sold at Christie's, April 8, 1843, Lot 633 (Andrew Geddes, A.R.A., owner), for £11 0s. 6d., to Norton, and a portrait of Sir Wm. Hamilton was sold, November 28, 1879, Lot 93 (Warner, owner), for £3 13s. 6d., to Durham.

ENGRAVED.
W. Sharp, 7¼ × 5¼ in.

HAMILTON, Sir William.

Paid for September, 1784, Sir Wm. Hamilton, Dilettanti picture, £36 15s. *See* DILETTANTI.

HAMILTON, Sir William.

Half length, canvas 29 × 24 in.

Profile; seated to right; his right hand holds the leaves of a book which lies on a table before him; in red coat, black collar and waistcoat; dark background.

"In January, 1785, Sir Joshua hearing from Miss Hamilton that her uncle had presented her with this picture, desired her to send it to him and he would 'renovate it with lasting colours.' This was done, and in February, 1785, Miss Hamilton saw the picture in Sir Joshua's studio, and described it as re-touched and made very beautiful indeed."—Royal Academy Catalogue, 1888.

EXHIBITED.

Royal Academy, 1888, No. 29, by Sir W. Anson, Bart.

The picture, which has been in the possession of her family since it was given back to Miss Hamilton after re-touching, is in the possession of Sir William R. Anson, Bart.

HAMILTON, Emma, Lady.

Half length.

As a Bacchante.

Emma Hart, wife of Sir William Hamilton, ambassador at Naples. Chiefly noted for her friendship with Lord Nelson. She was the daughter of a servant named Hart. After being reduced to great distress, was exhibited in London by a Doctor Graham, a notorious charlatan of the day, as the goddess Hygeia, covered with a transparent veil. Married Sir William Hamilton, 1791, who took her to Naples, where she became a friend of Caroline of Austria. It is said that by her advice Prince Caraccioli was put to death, but this she denied. She died near Calais in 1816. Smith, in his "Book for a Rainy Day," calls her Emma Lyon, and says : "This generous woman, better known under her lawful title of Lady Hamilton, when I shewed her my etching of the funeral procession of her husband's friend, the immortal Nelson, she fainted and fell into my arms, and believe me, reader, her mouth was equal to any production of Greek sculpture I have yet seen." Romney painted her under a variety of titles many times.

As a Bacchante ; moving to right ; with forefinger to her lips ; while laughing she looks over her shoulder at the spectator ; a long tress of chestnut hair is blown forward by the wind ; white dress.

Paid for September, 1784, Sir Wm. Hamilton, for a "Bacchante," £52 10s. Exhibited at the Royal Academy, 1784, No. 342, as a "Bacchante."

Morning Herald, 1784: "No. 342, 'A Boy Reading.' This portrait appears to the natural eye one of the nymphs in the train of Comus, and all the aid of Mr. Storer's optics will not transform it to a Boy reading ! The painter who wrote Bruin under his bear to prevent it being called a lion, well knew how necessary the aid of letters were to his science."

Tom Taylor, in vol. ii., p. 436, records it as a boy reading, with Walpole's note "Grand expression," and in a note says, "It was bought by Lord de Tabley, but was sold with his pictures."

It is difficult to explain this confusion. It is evident that in the first edition of the 1784 catalogue, No. 342 must have been printed as "A Boy Reading ;" but in the later editions, and in the copy owned by Mr. A. Graves, it is clearly printed " A Bacchante." The probable explanation is that Sir Joshua originally sent " A Boy Reading," and it must have been hung and catalogued, and then at the last moment substituted the " Bacchante." The critic of the " Morning Herald " must have had the first edition of the catalogue (probably on the Press day) after the pictures had been changed ; hence his remarks. Walpole's criticism might apply to either picture.

EXHIBITED.

British Institution, 1843, No. 34, by T. Chamberlayne.

Sold in Sir William Hamilton's sale, 1801, £131 5s., to Mr. Chamberlayne (Cotton, 1856).

HAMILTON, Emma, Lady.

As a Bacchante.

EXHIBITED.

British Institution, 1817, No. 37, as Lady Hamilton, by the Earl of Lauderdale.

Sold at Greenwood's, April 16, 1796, Lot 48, as a Bacchante, for £78 15s., to Lord Lauderdale.

ENGRAVED.

J. R. Smith, 1784, $9\frac{1}{8} \times 8$ in.
Unknown, $9\frac{1}{4} \times 7\frac{1}{4}$ in.
    " $7\frac{1}{4} \times 6$ in.
S. W. Reynolds, $3\frac{1}{4} \times 3\frac{1}{4}$ in.

A proof in the First State by Smith, Buccleuch Collection, was sold at Christie's, in 1887, for £43 1s.

The picture belongs to the Earl of Lauderdale.

HAMILTON, Emma, Lady.

As a Bacchante.

EXHIBITED.

Bı

Aı

Sc

toward

Tł

This portrait from the collection of the Earl of Durham was sold at Christie's July 6, 1934 for £31 10sh.

Purchaser, Ravin.

HAMILTON, Emma, Lady.

Half length, panel 29 × 24¼ *in.*

As a Bacchante.

The picture belongs to the Earl of Normanton, and is No. 166 in the Somerley catalogue.

HAMILTON, Emma, Lady.

Half length, canvas 30 × 25 *in.*

As a Bacchante.

This picture belonged to the Marquess of Lansdowne, and was sold by him to Messrs. T. Agnew and Sons, from whom it passed to Baron Ferdinand de Rothschild.

Fine copies of Lady Hamilton and Miss Palmer with a muff, both formerly in the Bowood collection, were made by the Hon. Sophia De Clifford, who died in 1795. They belong to the Hon. Maud Russell, at 13, Draycott Place.

HAMILTON, Emma, Lady.

Half length, canvas 29¼ × 24¼ *in.*

EXHIBITED.

Grosvenor, 1888, No. 195, by Sir Clare Ford, G.C.B.

The picture belonged to Mr. Benjamin Booth, whose daughter married Sir R. Ford ; it descended to her son, Richard Ford. It afterwards belonged to his son, Sir Clare Ford, G.C.B., and hung at 17, Park Street, London.

Sold at Foster's, June 28, 1899, Lot 114, and described as " Portrait of Lady Hamilton as a Bacchante, 30 × 25, the engraved and well-known work, an exceptionally fine example of the master,". for £4,515, to Davis.

A portrait of Lady Hamilton was bought in at Christie's, March 7, 1846, Lot 118, for £3 5s., by the owner, Colchester ; a sketch as a Bacchante was sold at Christie's, March 20, 1897, Lot 98 (Nuttall, owner), 8 × 6¼ in., to Boddington, for £18 18s.

HAMILTON, Mrs.

Sold at Christie's, February 16, 1810, Lot 60 (Boydell, owner), for £1 12s., to Stevens.

HAMMOND, Mr.

Sat in October, 1761. Paid for before 1760, Mr. Hammond, £10 10s., frame paid, and in 1761, Mr. Hammond, £10 10s. Frame paid.

"July 1, 1769, Ambrose Hammond at Barnet."—*Gentleman's Magazine*, 1769, p. 367.

HAMMOND, Mrs.

Half length, canvas 29 × 24 in.

Full face; in a white dress, with a cloak trimmed with ermine; a sash round the waist.

Sat in October, 1761. Paid for before 1761, Mrs. Hammond, £21.

Possibly Susan, sister of Sir Robert Walpole; married A. Hammond, of Wotton, Norfolk; she died January 20, 1763.

The picture was purchased from P. and D. Colnaghi and Co. in 1895 by Charles Sedelmeyer, of Paris, and was sold by him to Rodman Wanamaker, of Philadelphia, the present owner.

HANBURY, Mrs. William.

Three-quarter length, canvas 50 × 40 in.

Charlotte, younger daughter of Charles James Packe, of Prestwold Hall, Leicestershire; born June 19, 1755; married, October 24, 1775, William Hanbury, of Kelmarsh, co. Northampton; died December, 1815. Her eldest son, who inherited the estates of his cousin, John, 2nd Viscount Bateman, was created Lord Bateman in 1837.

Seated on a sofa, looking to the left, with right arm over the end, left arm resting in lap; white dress, with outer mantle lined with fur; column and sky to left; curtain to right.

Sat in March, 1777. Paid for September 8, 1783, Mrs. Hanbury, £73 10s.

EXHIBITED.

Royal Academy, 1881, No. 8, by Lord Bateman.

ENGRAVED.

G. S. Shury, 1866, 5¼ × 4¼ in.

The picture was sold some years ago by Lord Bateman to T. Agnew and Sons, from whom it passed to Lord Iveagh, the present owner.

HANBURY, Miss.

Sat in February, 1779.

HANCOCK, Mr.

Paid for August 12, 1765, Mr. Hancock, £50; August 27, 1767, Mr. Hancock, £75.

HANCOCK, Mrs.

Sat in August, 1765, and February, 1766. Paid for August 12, 1765, Mrs. Hancock, £30.

HANGER, Colonel William, afterwards 3rd Lord Coleraine.

Half length, canvas 23¼ × 19¼ *in.*

John Hanger, brother to Sir Francis Ainger, or Aungier, knight, Master of the Rolls, was created, 1621, Baron of Longford, which title became extinct 1704. He was an eminent Turkey merchant, acquiring a considerable fortune; purchased the estate and mansion of Driffield, co. Gloucester, in which estate he was succeeded by his descendant, George Hanger, many years a director of the Bank of England; father of Sir George Hanger, knight; married Anne, daughter and co-heiress of Sir John Beale, of Farningham, co. Kent, Bart., and by her had George, John, Gabriel, 1st Lord, and three daughters. Gabriel was, in 1762, created Baron Coleraine, of Coleraine, co. Londonderry; married Elizabeth, daughter and heiress of Richard Bond, of Clowbury, co. Hereford, and had issue, John, 2nd Lord, William, 3rd Lord, and George, 4th Lord, who wrote an amusing autobiography, and Anne, who married Col. Arthur Vansittart, M.P., of Shottesbrooke. The 3rd Lord, as Mr. Hanger, was conspicuous in the *mêlée* which took place when Mrs. Baddeley was refused admittance to the Pantheon. He was her first aristocratic lover, and paid Sir Joshua for the picture for which she sat in 1771 and 1772.

Three-quarter face, turned to the left; dark coat; white cravat.

Sat in June, 1771, as Mr. Hanger. Paid for in 1771, Mr. Hanger, £36 15s.; frame paid.

EXHIBITED.

Grosvenor, 1884, No. 108, by Wm. Agnew.

In the Grosvenor catalogue of 1884 the wrong descriptions were given to Nos. 108 and 148; they were transposed. *See* MALONE, page 610.

Sold at Christie's, May 26, 1851, Lot 173, Sir M. A. Shee's collection, for £15 4s. 6d., to Norton; May 5, 1883, Lot 24, General Hanger, "painted for Mrs. Geo. Bellamy" (Mrs. B. Gibbons, owner), for £90 6s., to Agnew.

"Mr. William Hanger, afterwards Lord Coleraine, Mrs. Baddeley's first aristocratic lover, brought her to Sir Joshua, to whom he was sitting himself while his mistress's portrait was in progress, and paid for the picture. The young bloods who associated with him vowed that, whoever was excluded from the Pantheon, Sophia Baddeley should be let in. Sir Joshua, as I find from the pocket-book, was present at the Pantheon on the opening night. He may have seen the triumphal entry of his beautiful sitter. Twenty gentlemen, headed by Mr. Hanger and Mr. Conway, son of the Earl of Hertford, met at Almack's and bound themselves to escort her and stand by her chair. 'When she was set down under the portico, her escort had swelled,' says Mrs. Steele, 'to nearly fifty gentlemen.' The constables allowed Mrs. Steele to pass, but when Mrs. Baddeley followed they crossed their staves and civilly, but resolutely, said their orders were to admit no players. On this the gallant escort drew, compelled the constables to give way at the sword's point, and protected Mrs. Baddeley as she passed proudly into the Rotunda."—LESLIE AND TAYLOR's *Life of Reynolds*, vol. i., p. 431.

HANMER, Sir Walden.

M.P. for Sudbury in 1768 as Mr. Walden Hanmer, and 1774 as Sir Walden; he was created a baronet on May 3, 1774; married Anne, youngest daughter and co-heiress of Henry Vere Graham, of Holbrook Hall; he died on October 20, 1783, at Sympson Place, Bucks, in his sixty-fifth year, and was succeeded by his son, Sir Thomas Hanmer, Bart.

Sat in June, 1784. Paid for, July 30, 1786, Sir Waldron Hanmer, £36 15s.

The picture belongs to Sir Wyndham Charles Hanmer, Bart., Bettisfield Park, Flintshire.

HANMER, Miss.

Anne Eleanor, only daughter of Sir Walden Hanmer, Bart.; married the Rev. George Turner.

Paid for, July 30, 1786, Miss Hanmer, £36 15s.; frames paid for same time, 6 guineas.

HARCOURT, Simon, 1st Earl.

Half length, canvas 34½ × 27½ *in.*

Grandson of the 1st Viscount; succeeded to the title in 1727; was present at Dettingen, and served in the Rebellion of 1745; created Viscount Harcourt of Nuneham Courtenay, and Earl Harcourt of Stanton Harcourt, December, 1749; Governor to George, Prince of Wales, in 1751; Ambassador-Extraordinary to Mecklenburgh-Strelitz to demand Princess Charlotte in marriage, 1761; Ambassador to France, 1768; Lord-Lieutenant of Ireland, 1772; died September 16, 1777, having lost his life by falling into a well in his own park at Nuneham.

In red dress; powdered hair; head to right; left hand in waistcoat.

Sat in April, 1755. In Lord Harcourt's accounts appears this entry: " Paid Mr. Reynolds, the painter, for picture of myself and the boy, £26 5s."

See note on the 2nd Earl's portrait.

EXHIBITED.

Royal Academy, 1880, No. 146, } by Edward William Harcourt.
Guelph, 1891, No. 145,

Note to the 1755 sitting : " Late Governor to the Prince of Wales, a marvel of pomposity and propriety. 'Sir, pray hold up your head! Sir, for God's sake turn out your toes!' Such, says Walpole, are Mentor's precepts to the Prince."—TOM TAYLOR, vol. i., p. 145.

"Nuneham was a favourite visiting place of Sir Joshua's. Not only was he intimate with Lord Harcourt, who had a fine and cultivated taste in the arts, but was an excellent etcher, a clever draughtsman, and a most accomplished landscape gardener. Mrs. Harcourt, the wife of the earl's brother and successor, was also an enthusiastic landscape painter. In September this year—perhaps while Sir Joshua was at Nuneham—Mason was giving her lessons in a new method of painting, uniting water-colours with oil. He seems to have communicated his discovery to Sir Joshua, who tried the method on some prints from his own pictures, colouring them first in water-colours, and then glazing them with transparent varnish.

"Mr. Boger, of Antony, has a print of the Duchess of Rutland coloured in this way, given to his family by the duke, with the information that the colouring was by Sir Joshua."
—TOM TAYLOR, vol. ii., pp. 417, 418.

HARCOURT, George Simon, Viscount Nuneham, afterwards 2nd Earl.

Half length, canvas 34¼ × 27¼ *in.*

Aged seventeen.

Lord Harcourt in his catalogue states this charming portrait cost £12 10s., adding that "the transparent colouring of the head cannot be surpassed."

To right; black dress; holds in his left hand a sketch.

Painted in 1753.

EXHIBITED.

Guelph, 1891, No. 169, by Edward William Harcourt.

HARCOURT, George Simon, 2nd Earl, with ELIZABETH, COUNTESS HARCOURT, and GENERAL THE HON. WILLIAM HARCOURT.

Half lengths, canvas 68 × 58 *in., oblong.*

The Right Hon. George Simon, 2nd Earl Harcourt, was born August 1, 1736. In 1761 M.P. for St. Albans, which he represented up to 1768; succeeded to the peerage, 1777; Master of the Horse to the Queen in 1790, which he held up to his death, April 20, 1809. He had a taste for the Fine Arts, and executed four etchings of the ruins of Stanton Court, published by the Society of Antiquaries. He was the author of "An Account of the Church and Remains of the Manor House of Stanton Harcourt in the County of Oxford," privately printed in 1808.

Elizabeth, Countess Harcourt, eldest daughter of George, 1st Lord Vernon, by his third wife, the Hon. Martha Harcourt, was born 1746; married, September 26, 1765, the above-mentioned Earl Harcourt; died 1826.

The Hon. William, 3rd Earl Harcourt, G.C.B., younger son of Simon, 1st Earl Harcourt, was born March 20, 1743; entered the army in 1759, and, as a reward for his distinguished services during the American war, was appointed Colonel of the 16th Light Dragoons in 1779, Major-General in 1782, Lieut.-General, 1793, and General, 1798. He commanded the

431

cavalry in the expedition to the Continent in 1793-94, and on the foundation of the Royal Military College of Sandhurst in 1799 was nominated
Governor ; next appointed Governor of Portsmouth, which he exchanged in
1827 for Plymouth. Upon the death of the 2nd Earl on April 20, 1809, he
became 3rd Earl. He received the Order of the Bath in 1820, and was made
Field-Marshal in 1821. Died June 18, 1830.

Standing figures ; the Earl in robes, holding a coronet in his right hand ;
Colonel Harcourt behind holding sword.

Sat in May, 1780, as Lord Harcourt; Lady Harcourt sat in May, 1781.
Paid for, March, 1781, Lord Harcourt, £73 10s.

EXHIBITED.
British Institution, 1823, No. 29, by Earl Harcourt.
National Portrait Exhibition, 1867, No. 495, by W. V. Harcourt.

ENGRAVED.
C. A. Tomkins, 1868, 6¼ × 5¼ in., ⎱
S. W. Reynolds (unfinished), ⎰ oblong.

HARCOURT, George Simon, 2nd Earl.

In his early days Lord Nuneham spent much time on foreign travels ; in
consequence, his entry into public life was marked by a decided preference for
French manners and fashions, and his appearance so adapted to it as almost
to disguise the exterior of an Englishman.

Paid for, December 27, 1777, Lord Harcourt, £36.

HARCOURT, Colonel William, afterwards 3rd Earl.

Born March 20, 1743 ; was Colonel of the 16th Regiment of Dragoons ;
served in America ; Groom of the Bedchamber to George III., with whom he
was a personal favourite ; succeeded as 3rd Earl in 1809, and died June 18,
1830, when all the honours became extinct.

Paid for, December 27, 1777, Colonel Harcourt, £36 15s.

HARCOURT, Mrs., afterwards Countess.

Half length, canvas 50 × 39 *in.*

Mary, relict of Thomas Lockhart, and daughter of the Rev. William
Danby, D.D., of Marhamshire, co. York ; married, September 3rd, 1778,
William Harcourt, who became 3rd Earl on April 20, 1809.

Lady and son and son

Seated to left; three-quarter face, looking up; hands clasped; white and yellow dress.

Sat in March, 1780, as Mrs. Harcourt. Paid for, March, 1781, Mrs. Harcourt, by Bill, £105.

British Institution, 1813, No. 10 (third catalogue), by Earl Harcourt.

S. W. Reynolds, 1824, $11\frac{1}{4} \times 8\frac{1}{4}$ in.
  „   „   1836, $4\frac{1}{4} \times 4$ in.

An amateur painter. *See* note on Simon, 1st Earl.

HARCOURT, Mrs., afterwards Countess.

Half length, canvas 30 × 25 *in.*

Seated to left; three-quarter face, looking up; hands clasped; white and yellow dress.

Royal Academy, 1893, No. 18, by Colonel F. A. Fane.

HARCOURT, Mrs., afterwards Countess.

Three-quarter length, canvas 50 × 40 *in.*

The picture was purchased from the Marquis d'Harcourt by Messrs. Laurie and Co., who sold it to Arthur Sanderson, of Edinburgh.

HARDINGE, Mr.

Paid for, February, 1778, Mr. Harding, £35; and in March, 1781, Mr. Harding, £31 10s. February, 1778, Mr. Harding for a Boy, £42; Do. for a Girl, £42.

The picture is at Boundes Park, Southborough, Kent.

HARDINGE, Mrs.

Three-quarter length, canvas 50 × 40 *in.*

Lucy, daughter of Richard Long, and widow of Mr. Stanley, married, October 20, 1777, George Hardinge, F.R.S., F.S.A., Wadham College, Oxon; M.P. for Old Sarum, and Justice of the Peace for Brecon, Radnor, and Glamorgan; died in 1820.

In a landscape, with trees ; headdress of ribbon and pearls ; a loose scarf over her shoulder ; she is patting a dog.

Paid for, February, 1778, Mrs. G. Harding, £73 10s.

EXHIBITED.

Royal Academy, 1873, No. 112, as Mrs. Stanley, afterwards married to Mr. Justice Hardinge, by the Marquess of Clanricarde.

ENGRAVED.

Thomas Watson, 16¼ × 12¼ in.

S. W. Reynolds (S. Cousins, R.A.), 5¼ × 4 in.

A Second State (Buccleuch Collection) sold at Christie's in 1887 for £37 16s.

The picture belongs to the Marquess of Clanricarde.

The picture was painted for Georgiana, Lady Peachey, afterwards, in 1794, Lady Selsey, and on the death of her granddaughter, the Hon. Mrs. Leveson-Vernon, as part of the estate of Lord Selsey, her brother, it was inherited by her cousin, the late Marquess of Clanricarde.

HARDWICKE, Philip Yorke, 2nd Earl.

Three-quarter length, canvas 50 × 40 in.

Eldest son of Philip, Lord Chancellor Hardwicke ; born December 9, 1720 ; married, May 22, 1740, Lady Jemima Campbell, who on the death of her maternal grandfather became Baroness Lucas and Marchioness de Grey ; she was the only daughter of John, 3rd Earl of Breadalbane, editor of the "Hardwicke State Papers." He succeeded to the earldom, March 6, 1764 ; died May 16, 1796.

Standing ; peer's robes ; the right hand raised in front, holding the border of his robe ; left resting on a book, which lies on a table by his side.

Sat in 1765, 1766, and 1769. Paid for before 1765, Lord Hardwick, £30 ; November 24, 1766, Lord Hardwick, £40.

EXHIBITED.

British Institution, 1813, No. 114,
National Portrait, 1867, No. 788, } by the Earl of Hardwicke.

Lord Hardwicke paid in 1783 £52 10s. for a copy of Lord Rockingham.

HARDWICKE CHILDREN. *See* YORKE.

HARE, Francis.

Half length, canvas 30 × 25 *in.*

"The Hare and many friends," the associate of Charles James Fox.

In a fur coat ; full neckcloth ; looking to the right.

Sat in 1774. Paid for, April 22, 1775, Mr. Hare (paid by Mr. Storer), £36 15*s.*

"Anthony Storer, the son of a wealthy West Indian proprietor, and himself eminent for his taste in art and letters, his pleasant manners and elegant breeding. Storer was the friend of Fox, Hare, Fitzpatrick, William Eden, and Lord Carlisle. He had brought from Eton and Oxford the dangerous reputation of an 'admirable Crichton,' but had taken the wrong twist in politics, and died an unsuccessful man."—TOM TAYLOR, vol. ii., p. 124.

ENGRAVED.
S. W. Reynolds, 1804, 13¼ × 11 in.

      "   "   1¼ × 1¼ in.

The picture belonged in 1886 to Major Storer, Purley Park, Reading.

"Mr. Hare, August 15, 1774. Biacca, nero, ultramarine, verm ; sed principalmente minio / red lead—won't stand—becomes green. Beechy senza / giallo l'ultima volta, oiled out and painted over. Except glazed with varnish and all giallo di Napoli, finito quasi con asphaltum, minio verm ; poi un poco di ultramarine qua e la senza giallo."

HARE, Doctor.

The name appears in Sir Joshua's private notes. *See* Haydon's " Life," Appendix.

HARE, Master Francis George.

Three-quarter length, canvas 29 × 24 *in.*

" Infancy." Son of Francis Hare.

A child in a white frock and black sash ; in a landscape ; right hand and arm raised and pointing.

Sat in 1788 and 1789.

EXHIBITED.
British Institution, 1845, No. 65, by Sir J. Dean Paul.

Royal Academy, 1872, No. 62, Francis John Hare, known as " Infancy," by Augustus J. C. Hare.

Bought in at Christie's, May 11, 1816 (J. G. Hare, owner), as Portrait of a little Boy, for £52 10*s.* Sold at Christie's, June 8, 1872, Lot 63 (W. H. Milligan named as owner), for £2,415, to the New York Museum.

ENGRAVED.
R. Thew, 1790, 5¼ × 4¼ in., as Francis George Hare, afterwards altered to " Infancy."

S. W. Reynolds, 4¼ × 3¼ in.

Painted for Lady Jones, wife of Sir William Jones—his aunt—in 1789;
left by her to her only surviving sister, Miss Shipley, who left it by will to
Marcus Theodore Hare, and from him it passed to Julius Charles Hare, next
to his widow, and finally to Augustus J. C. Hare. When Sir J. D. Paul
exhibited the portrait he was only the custodian of it for Miss Shipley. In
1869 the picture was the subject of a lawsuit at Westminster Hall as to its
ownership.

HARE, Mrs.

Paid for, November, 1785, Mrs. Hare, £52 10s.

HARE, Miss.

Paid for before 1760, Miss Hare, £5 5s.

HARENC, Mr.

Sat in 1762.

HAREWOOD, Edwin, 1st Lord. *See* LASCELLES.

HAREWOOD, Edward, 1st Earl of. *See* LASCELLES.

HAREWOOD, Jane, Lady. *See* MRS. FLEMING, *in Addenda*.

HAREWOOD, Anne, Countess of. *See* MRS. LASCELLES.

HARGRAVE, Francis.

Head size, canvas 30 × 25 *in.*

Recorder of Liverpool; born 1741; published "State Trials" and "Law
Trials"; died August 16, 1821.

Black coat; crimson background.

Sat in 1787. Paid for, November, 1787, Mr. Councillor Hargrave,
£52 10s.

EXHIBITED.

National Portrait Exhibition, 1867, No. 718, by the Society of Lincoln's
Inn.

ENGRAVED.

John Jones, 1793, 10¼ × 7¼ in.
S. W. Reynolds, 1¼ × 1¼ in.

Mr. Whitbread moved a resolution in the House of Commons to purchase Mr. Hargrave's library; a sum of £8,000 was voted, and it now forms part of the library of Lincoln's Inn.

The picture belongs to the Society of Lincoln's Inn.

HARLAND, Mrs.

Sat in 1761, 1762, and 1764. Paid for, February 14, 1765, Mrs. Harland, £40.

HARRINGTON, Charles, 3rd Earl of.

Whole length, canvas 93 × 57 *in.*

Born March 17, 1753; married, May 23, 1779, Jane, daughter and co-heiress of Sir John Fleming, Bart.; succeeded to the earldom, April 1, 1779; General Officer in the Army; Colonel, 1st Regiment of Life Guards; Captain, Governor, and Constable of Windsor Castle, and Knight Grand Cross of the Bath; died September 5, 1829.

In armour; attended by a black boy; battle going on in the distance.

Sat in June, 1782. Exhibited in the Royal Academy, 1783, No. 193.

Morning Herald, 1783: "No. 193. Lord Harrington is represented in armour, evidently with the view of expressing his military character, at the same time that it has the advantage of not being liable to the awkward appearance which a soldier in his proper uniform always makes upon canvas after a lapse of a few years; the likeness is good; there is a firmness in the attitude; the objects in the background, and the sky, have effect, but the painting is very coarse."

Morning Chronicle: "No. 193, Sir Joshua's whole length of Lord Harrington, is to be commended for the display of accomplishments much more arduous to be attained, and when attained, much more estimable; and in addition to the most faithful preservation of countenance likeness, discovers great show of mind and character, the most graceful dispositions, and in the background a most affluent imagination."

London Courant, 1783: "His portrait, No. 193, of Lord Harrington (as we hear), is the worst production we have seen of Sir Joshua's; the head is a frightful dirty daubing; the figure is badly drawn—on the whole it looks like a devil hunted, escaping from the infernal regions, which appear too hot to hold him."

A constant reader "was both surprised and shocked at a paragraph in the 'London Courant' on Friday—a criticism on one of the finest productions of Sir Joshua Reynolds! who has long shone the brightest luminary of the heaven-born art of painting. Who is this mighty critic? some artist we know! and must the greatest ornament of the present Exhibition, the portrait of Lord Harrington, be fixed on as a proper object on which to vent all his 'proud spite and burning envy'? but let him take care, nor attempt again a task, which to a mind unbiassed by hatred would be impracticable, by vainly endeavouring to blast the well-deserved fame of one who will ever rise superior to such little arts, and to whose exalted excellence he must never dare to aspire!"

Another critic says: "No. 193, a noble, striking, and capital whole length of Lord Harrington in armour, in which the dignity of the hero is agreeably softened by the elegance of the gentleman. The attitude is bold, animated, and natural; but a sort of brown tinge pervades the armour, which gives an unfinished appearance to the whole."

British Institution, 1813, No. 103, by the Earl of Harrington.

The picture belongs to the Earl of Harrington at Elvaston Castle, Derby.

There is a copy from a portion of this picture by P. E. Stroëhling (29 × 24 in.), belonging to the Duke of Bedford, No. 271 in the Woburn catalogue.

HARRINGTON, Charles, 3rd Earl of.

Whole length, canvas, small study.

The finished study for the large picture was sold at Christie's, June 25, 1859, Lot 85 (Hon. C. Phipps, owner), for £123 18s., to Lord Stanhope.

The picture belongs to Earl Stanhope at Chevening.

HARRINGTON, Jane, Countess of, when Miss Jane Fleming.

Whole length, canvas 93 × 57 in.

Jane, daughter of Sir John Fleming, Bart., of Brompton Park ; born 1755 ; married, May 23, 1779, Charles, 3rd Earl of Harrington ; died February 3, 1824.

Standing to left, in a landscape ; profile to left ; white dress ; figured gauze scarf ; feather headdress ; holds a garland of flowers in left hand.

Paid for, November 25, 1775, Miss Fleming, £157 10s.

This picture should have been entered as Miss Fleming. According to the Royal Academy Catalogue of 1886 the picture was painted in 1778. *See ante*, p. 319.

EXHIBITED.

British Institution, 1851, No. 132, } by the Earl of Harewood.
Royal Academy, 1886, No. 154,   }

ENGRAVED.

Val Green, 1780, 23¼ × 15 in.   } as Jane, Countess of
S. W. Reynolds (S. Cousins, R.A.), 6 × 3¾ in.}   Harrington.

A First State by Green, in the Barlow Collection, sold at Christie's in 1894 for £130 4s.

The picture was painted for her mother, Mrs. Lascelles, formerly Jane, Lady Fleming, who became afterwards Lady Harewood ; from her it passed to Henry, 2nd Earl of Harewood. It now belongs to the Earl of Harewood.

A finished study, small whole length, of this picture belongs to Mr. Dexter, printseller, 10, Great Russell Street, London.

There is a small copy of this picture by J. R. Powell, 1852 (37 × 24 in.), belonging to the Duke of Bedford, No. 272 in the Woburn catalogue.

HARRINGTON, Jane, Countess of, when Miss Jane Fleming.

Whole length, canvas 93 × 57 in.

Standing, with one hand extended, leaning against a low balustrade on which stands a *large stone vase ;* beyond is a landscape ; she is dressed in a long flowing pink dress.

Paid for, March, 1779, Miss Fleming, with an urn, £157 10s.

EXHIBITED.

British Institution, 1813, No. 92 (fourth catalogue), by the Countess of Harrington.   *See   ...   ?'c ...   III. b. 026*

The picture belongs to the Earl of Harrington at Elvaston Castle, Derby.

HARRINGTON, Jane, Countess of.

Three-quarter length, canvas.

With her sons : Charles, Viscount Petersham, born April 8, 1780, and Hon. Lincoln Edwin Robert Stanhope, born November 26, 1781.

Sitting, looking up to her son, Lord Petersham, who is standing by her side on a stone balustrade ; she holds him with her right hand ; the other child is seen behind her ; a column, with drapery and landscape.

Sat in 1786 and 1787.

ENGRAVED.

F. Bartolozzi, 1789, 11¼ × 8⅞ in.

A. N. Sanders, 1878, 5¼ × 4¼ in.

The Bartolozzi print sold at Sotheby's in 1896, an impression in brown, for £13 10s.; and an impression beautifully printed in colours, with margins, together with one of Lady Smyth and Children, same state and same time, February 13, 1896, one Lot, for £142, to Vaughan.

"He had in hand at the same time (1784) his three important groups of the Countess of Harrington, Lady Dashwood, and Lady Honywood, with their children."—TOM TAYLOR, vol. ii., p. 431.

"Here Sir Joshua had nature before him in the form he loved best, of air women and beautiful children ; and he had only to use his observation and taste to make exquisite pictures."—TOM TAYLOR, vol. ii., p. 500.

The picture belongs to Elizabeth, Countess of Harrington, at Harrington House, Charing Cross, London. *See also* STANHOPE.

HARRINGTON, Jane, Countess of.

Sat in 1782 and 1784.

These sittings indicate the painting of another earlier portrait of her after she became Countess.

HARRIS, James, M.P.

Three-quarter length, canvas 50 × 40 in.

Was the elder son of James Harris, of the Close, Salisbury; born July 25, 1709; educated at the Grammar School at Salisbury, and at Wadham College, Oxford, in 1726, from whence he removed to Lincoln's Inn; married, July 8, 1745, Elizabeth, daughter of John Clarke, of Sandford, Somerset. He was M.P. for Christchurch in 1762, and retained that seat until his death. He was appointed a Lord of the Admiralty in 1763, and in the same year was removed to the Treasury Board, where he remained until 1765. He was Secretary and Comptroller to Queen Charlotte from 1774 until his death. His first appearance as an author was in 1744, when he published his three treatises on art, and in 1751 he wrote his celebrated work, "Hermes." He died December 22, 1780.

Seated in an armchair studded with nails; profile, looking to the left; dark coat, with white necktie and lace frill; in a wig tied with black ribbon at the back; arms resting on the arms of the chair; curtain background, with books on a table to the left.

ENGRAVED.

G. H. Every, 1866, 5 × 4 in.

The picture is at Wadham College, Oxford.

HARRIS, James, M.P.

Half length, canvas 24 × 20 in.

Painted in 1775.

Sold at Greenwood's, April 14, 1796, Lot 66, for 10s. 6d., to Seguier.

The picture now belongs to the Earl of Malmesbury.

HARRIS, Mrs.

Sat in 1755.

Probably Elizabeth, daughter of John Clarke, of Sandford, who married James Harris, author of "Hermes." She died in 1757.

HARRIS, Misses Catherine Gertrude and Louisa Margaret.

Canvas 40 × 33 in.

Miss Catherine Gertrude Harris, eldest surviving daughter of James Harris, M.P.; born April 18, 1750; married the Hon. Frederick Robinson, second son of Thomas, 1st Lord Grantham, who died December 28, 1792.

Miss Louisa Margaret Harris, the youngest daughter, was born January 11, 1753, and was living unmarried in 1797.

The picture belongs to the Earl of Malmesbury.

HARRIS, Master James, afterwards 1st Earl of Malmesbury.

Half length, oval, canvas 33 × 28 *in.*

Full face; walking in a garden; coat buttoned up with cloak over left shoulder; right hand resting on the stump of a tree; left hand held in front of breast; landscape background.

ENGRAVED.

R. Josey, 1874, 5 × 4 in. (oval).

The picture belongs to the Earl of Malmesbury.

HARRIS, Sir James, K.B., afterwards 1st Earl of Malmesbury.

Three-quarter length, canvas 50 × 40 *in.*

Eldest son of James Harris; born at Salisbury, April 9, 1746; M.P. for the Borough of Christchurch, 1772; appointed, in 1767, Secretary of Embassy at Madrid; Minister at the Courts of Madrid, 1768; Berlin, 1772; St. Petersburg, 1776; and Paris, 1796; His Majesty's Envoy-Extraordinary and Minister Plenipotentiary at the States General, 1784. He was invested with the Order of the Bath, 1779; created Baron Malmesbury, September 19, 1788; and Viscount Fitzharris and Earl of Malmesbury, December 29, 1800. Married, July 28, 1777, Harriet Mary, youngest daughter of Sir George Amyand, Bart. Died 1820.

Sitting, holding a letter in his right hand; looking to the left; ribbon and star of the Bath; left hand and arm on table.

Paid for January, 1788, Sir James Harris, £105; July, 1789, Lord Malmsbury, £105.

ENGRAVED.

Caroline Watson, 1786, 12¼ × 9¼ in.
S. W. Reynolds, 5 × 4 in.

The picture belongs to the Earl of Malmesbury.

From the payments there seem to have been two pictures painted.

HARRIS, Lady Harriet Mary, afterwards Countess of Malmesbury.

Three-quarter length, canvas 50 × 40 in.

Harriet Mary, youngest daughter of Sir George Amyand, Bart.; married, July 28, 1777, Sir James Harris, afterwards 1st Earl of Malmesbury. She died 1830.

Walking towards the right; hands crossed, holding a glove; white dress, with muslin cape; black cloak hanging down the back, and supported by the arms; powdered hair in curls; landscape background, river in distance to the right.

Sat in February, 1788. Exhibited in the Royal Academy, 1788, No. 84.

ENGRAVED.

James Scott, 1888, 5¼ × 4¼ in.

The picture was sold by the Earl of Malmesbury to Charles J. Wertheimer in 1898.

HARRIS, The Hon. Miss Frances, afterwards Lady Frances Cole.

Whole length, canvas 55¼ × 44 in.

Second daughter of Sir James Harris, K.B., afterwards 1st Earl of Malmesbury; born August 22, 1784; married the Hon. Lieutenant-General Sir Galbraith Lowry Cole, G.C.B., Governor of the Mauritius and the Cape. She died in 1842.

A girl in a white dress over a green skirt; her right hand resting on the head of a dog; landscape background.

Sat in 1789 as Miss Harris. Paid for, May, 1789, Miss Harris, for Lord Darnly, £105.

London Chronicle, 1790: "No. 243, portrait of a young lady, is amongst the best of Sir Joshua's works, and inferior to none that has been produced in this line of painting."

St. James's Chronicle: "No. 243. Portrait of the daughter of Lord Malmesbury. This is one of those beautiful and elegant productions which captivate all beholders. The figure is easy, natural, and interesting. The dog is finely painted, and the background, viewed at a certain distance, is nature itself. The freedom of touch is truly astonishing."

Another critic says: "The daughter of Lord Malmesbury, No. 243, is a charming picture; the background contains a sweet bit of landscape, and the dog is painted with Sir Joshua's usual success in animals."

EXHIBITED.

British Institution, 1813, No. 9 (third catalogue),
Manchester Art Treasures, 1857, No. 63, } by the Earl of Darnley
Royal Academy, 1876, No. 249,
Grosvenor, 1884, No. 75,

J. Grozer, 1791, 17¼ × 14 in.
S. W. Reynolds, 1836, 5⅞ × 4¼ in.
J. Scott, 1875, 18¼ × 14 in.

First State by Grozer, Buccleuch Collection, sold at Christie's, 1887, for £40 19s.

The picture belongs to the Earl of Darnley.

HARRISON, Mr.

Sat in 1768.   Paid for 1767, Mr. Harrison, £18 17s.

HARRISON, Mrs.

Sat in 1768.   Paid for 1767, Mrs. Harrison, £18 17s.

HARRISON, Sir Thomas.

Three-quarter length, canvas 48 × 39 in.

Chamberlain of London and Receiver-General of the Land Tax; knighted, 1752, with the Lord Mayor, Recorder, and Sheriffs, on presenting an address to the King on his return from visiting his German dominions; died, 1765, in his sixty-fifth year.

Full face; sitting, in his official robes and wig; velvet coat; white cravat; knee breeches; hands on the arms of his chair; column and curtain.

Sat in 1758.   The following is a copy of the receipt in the possession of Archdeacon Harrison :

"Received, July 18, 1759, of Sir Thomas Harrison, for his and Lady Harrison's portraits, the sum of sixty guineas in full of all demands by me, £63.

"J. REYNOLDS."

EXHIBITED.
Royal Academy, 1871, No. 69, by Archdeacon Harrison.

ENGRAVED.
E. Fisher, 1765, 13¾ × 11 in.
S. W. Reynolds, 3¼ × 2¼ in.

Note to the sitting : "Chamberlain of London ; one of his finest and most characteristic pictures."—TOM TAYLOR, vol. i., p. 162.

HARRISON, Lady.

Three-quarter length, canvas 49 × 39 in.

Daughter of Richard Snow; wife of Sir Thomas.

Sat in 1758.

EXHIBITED.

Royal Academy, 1871, No. 60, by Archdeacon Harrison.

HARRISON, Commodore.

Half length, canvas.

Full face; in naval uniform; white waistcoat; coat with broad white lapels; white neckcloth; own hair; dark background.

Paid for 1765, Commodore Harrison, £25; not carried out.

"Died February 1, 1768, John Harrison, late Commodore of His Majesty's squadron in the Mediterranean."—*Gentleman's Magazine*, 1768, p. 94.

ENGRAVED.

S. W. Reynolds, 1822, 4¼ × 3¼ in.

The picture belongs to the Earl of Morley.

HARTLEY, Mrs., and Child.

Three-quarter length, canvas 35 × 27 in.

Born 1751; died at Woolwich, 1824. She made her appearance on the stage in Edinburgh at an early age, and her beauty and ability gained her at once a prominent position. She performed in Bath about 1777, and subsequently had a permanent engagement at Drury Lane, where she was highly appreciated in tragedy until Mrs. Siddons appeared there, in 1783, and became the heroine of the stage. Mrs. Hartley retired in 1789. Along with the Reynolds portraits, she was painted by H. D. Hamilton, engraved by R. Houston (profile, looking to right), a tinted print, showing dark brown hair and in a red dress; by J. K. Sherwin, as Andromache in the "Distrest Mother," act iv., last scene (oval; looking to left; pearls and feathers in her hair, which is dressed high, with a veil falling from the back; white dress; holding a dagger in her right hand), also engraved by him; and by J. Nixon, A.R.A., engraved by W. Dickinson, as Elfrida, in Mason's play (oval; face nearly in profile, looking to the right; hands crossed on her bosom; a building to the right, umbrageous trees to the left); six small whole-length drawings by James Roberts, Amayda, in "Don Sebastian, King of Portugal,"

444

Jane Shore, Mary Queen of Scots, Elvira, Imoinda, and Jane Shore, in a second scene; and in the following engravings—book size illustrations—Andromache, by Sherwin, a later date than the painting; Hermione, published by Fielding and Walker, 1780; Imoinda, in "Oroonoka," by Thornwaite; Elfrida, Liney; another, no name given; Mercia, in "Cato," Dodd, Walker; Hermione, "Winter's Tale," Grignion; Jane Shore, for "Bell's British Theatre;" in another scene, by Thornwaite; Amayda, "Don Sebastian," Reading; Cleopatra, "All for Love," Page; another scene, no name; "Lady Jane Grey," three scenes, first published by Wenman, second, by Page, third, Sherwin; Albion's Queens, "Bell's British Theatre," Thornwaite; Elvira, also by him; Elfrida, with Mrs. Matthews as one of the chorus, and Mr. Hill in the character of Edwin relating the downfall of Athelwold; "Rosamonde," or "Henry II.," Fall of Rosamond, Pegg; Andromache, in a circle, published by Wenman, 1777; in a circle, no name; in a square, a bust similar to the engraving by Marchi; underneath a draped monument, inscribed Mrs. Hartley (with a cup and dagger, round which a snake is twined), by Hopwood, 1807.

With her child, as a youthful Bacchanal; in a landscape; the child sits on her right arm, which is supported at her hip; her left hand holds the child's right wrist.

Sat in 1771. Paid for June 8, 1774, Lord Carysfort, for Mrs. Hartley and Bacchus, £52 10s. Exhibited in the Royal Academy, 1773, No. 241, as a Nymph with a young Bacchus.

EXHIBITED.

British Institution, 1813, No. 59 (fourth catalogue), by Lord Carysfort.

"   "   1849, No. 119, ⎫
International, 1862, No. 135, ⎬ by J. Bentley.

Grosvenor, 1884, No. 139, ⎫
Grafton, 1894, No. 127, ⎬ by Lord Northbrook.

Sold at Christie's, June 24, 1828, Lot 63 (Lord Carysfort, owner), for £105, to Bentley; June 27, 1863, Lot 116, bought in by the owner (Bentley), for £1,942 10s.

"Mr. Bentley, the owner of Mrs. Hartley, has been offered £2,000 for the picture. When he bought it at Lord Carysfort's sale, a strange gentleman accosted him, congratulated him on his purchase, and after making excuses for the liberty he was taking, cautioned him never to allow a cleaner to touch the picture. He afterwards came up again and repeated this caution. Then, as if to justify himself for advising so authoritatively, he said, 'You may believe me I speak with some knowledge, when I tell you my name is Thomas Lawrence.' Mr. Bentley has followed his advice, and the picture is in the very finest preservation. It is painted in a glowing golden tone, that breathes of the south and vintage sunshine, and being thoughout finished by glazing on varnish, would, of course, be destroyed by any application of the cleaner's solvents."—TOM TAYLOR, vol. ii., p. 20, note 2.

G. Marchi, 1773, 18¼ × 14 in.
G. Nutter, 1800, 19 × 15¼ in.
Hopwood, bust in a square, without the boy, 1807, 4 × 3 in.
S. W. Reynolds, 5 × 3¾ in.

First State by Marchi, Palmerston Collection, sold at Christie's in 1890 for £31 10*s.*

This picture was bought from the artist by the Earl of Carysfort in 1774, and was sold at his sale in 1828 to John Bentley, of Birch House, Lancashire. After being bought in at his sale in 1874, it passed to John Naylor, from whom it was purchased by Messrs. T. Agnew and Sons, who sold it to Alfred de Rothschild, from whom it passed to the Earl of Northbrook. It was afterwards purchased from him by Sir William Agnew, Bart., the present owner.

There is a previous " Nymph and Bacchus," exhibited in the Royal Academy, 1771, No. 157, mentioned in Sir Joshua's private notes, 1770. *See* " INO AND INFANT BACCHUS," under FANCY SUBJECTS.

HARTLEY, Mrs., and Child.

Half length, canvas 30 × 25 in.

Standing in a landscape, carrying her child on her shoulder.

EXHIBITED.

British Institution, 1813, No. 53 (second catalogue), as Nymph and young Bacchus (Mrs. Hartley and child), by the Marchioness of Thomond.
British Institution, 1844, No. 159, as Mrs. Hartley, the actress, by the Hon. Fulke Greville Howard.
National Portrait Exhibition, 1868, No. 810, by Hon. Mrs. Greville Howard.

Bought in at Greenwood's, April 14, 1796, Lot 58, a Bacchante and Child, for £19 19*s.*, by Captain Walsh ; sold at Christie's, May 18, 1821, Lot 67, Thomond sale, for £304 10*s.*, to Colonel Fulke Howard ; July 4, 1874, Lot 80 (Hon. Mrs. Howard, owner), for £2,520, to Agnew.

This picture was bought at Lady Thomond's sale by Hon. Fulke G. Howard and was sold at his widow's sale, in 1874, to Messrs. T. Agnew and Sons, who sold it to the late Richard Johnson, whose family are probably the present owners of the picture.

HARTLEY, Mrs., and Child.

Sold at Christie's (Marchioness of Thomond, owner), May 18, 1821, Lot 24, a Bacchante with a young Satyr on her back, for £24 3s., to Lord Dunstanville; July 11, 1835, Lot 57, bought in by the owner (Lady Basset), for £79 16s.; June 6, 1842, Lot 106 (same owner), sold for £32 11s., to Rutley.

Frances, Baroness Basset, of Stratton, co. Cornwall; born 1781; inherited the peerage at the decease of her father, Francis, Lord de Dunstanville and Basset, February 5, 1835. She died 1855, when the title became extinct.

HARTLEY, Mrs., and Child.

Half length, canvas 30 × 25 in.

Sold in the Shandon Collection, Christie's sales, Robert Napier, April 13, 1877, Lot 546, for £69 6s., to Toovey.

Messrs. Henry Graves and Co. sold, in 1877, a copy of Mrs. Hartley and child, by Wood, for £21 to Viscount Hardinge.

HARTLEY, Mrs.

Bust, canvas 21 × 18 in.

As a Madonna.

Red dress; brown scarf over head and shoulders.

EXHIBITED.

British Institution, 1813, No. 117, as Mrs. Hartley as a Madonna, by Earl Grosvenor.

British Institution, 1833, No. 26,
" " 1834, No. 122, } by the Marquess of Westminster.
" " 1855, No. 133,
Manchester, 1857, No. 66,
Guelph, 1891, No. 246, by the Duke of Westminster.

Cotton notes: "The Westminster picture, as a Madonna, painted for Mr. Burke." In Edmund Burke's sale, June 5, 1812, No. 77, was a picture of a female head, purchased by Earl Grosvenor for £32 11s.

This picture is not now in the collection of the Duke of Westminster.

HARTLEY, Mrs.

As Jane Shore.

Sat in August, 1773.

Note to the sitting : "Her picture as a Nymph with an infant Bacchus had been exhibited in May, and he was now painting another study from her as Jane Shore."

Bought in at Greenwood's, April 16, 1796, Lot 17, half length, for £36 15s., by Captain Walsh ; May 18, 1821, Lot 12, Thomond sale, for £18 7s. 6d., to Ellison. Put up by Robins, Piazza, Covent Garden, July 12, 1819 (property of T. Harris), Lot 49, Mrs. Hartley as Hermione in the statue scene, withdrawn.

"In 1773 Sir Joshua painted an admirable portrait of Mrs. Hartley as a gipsy with a child at her back, and began another in the character of Jane Shore."—NORTHCOTE.

HARTOPP, Miss Catherine. *See* MRS. HEYWOOD.

. .

HARTWELL, Captain.

Sat in 1765.

HARVEY, Master.

Sat in March, 1789.

HARVEY, Miss.

Three-quarter length, canvas 21 × 16 *in.*

Afterwards Mrs. Payne.

A child, about three years old, seated, and facing to the left; head turned three-quarters to the front ; auburn hair, curls across the forehead ; white muslin frock, with blue sash ; a bunch of pink honeysuckle in right hand ; left clasps another to her breast ; foliage and sky background.

Sat in May, 1789, as Miss Hervey. Paid for, May, 1789, Mr. Hervey, for his daughter, £52 10s.

EXHIBITED.

Grosvenor, 1889, No. 83, by Sir Robert Harvey, Bart.

The picture belongs to Sir Robert Grenville Harvey, Bart., of Langley Park, Slough. A copy of this picture belongs to Lady Kinloss at Stowe

Mrs. Baldwin

House, Bucks. The late Duke of Buckingham, who married Miss Caroline Harvey, the daughter of Robert Harvey, of Langley Park, was the father of Lady Kinloss.

A portrait of Mr. Harvey was bought in by the owner, Howard, at Christie's, July 4, 1874, No. 83, for £26 5s.

HASTINGS, Francis, 1st Marquess of. *See* LORD RAWDON.

HASTINGS, Lady Selina.

Half length, canvas 29 × 24 *in.*

Younger daughter of the 9th Earl of Huntingdon and Selina, his wife, noted for her patronage of Whitfield and other Nonconformists.

Leaning on her folded arms ; pearls in hair ; a plait of hair falling over her right shoulder ; a bouquet of roses in her bosom.

Sat in 1759. Paid for 1763, Lady Selina Hastings ; no price given.

EXHIBITED.
Grosvenor, 1884, No. 169, by Lord Donington.

The picture was once the property of the Marquess of Hastings, and on the death of the 4th Marquess it descended to his sister, Edith, Countess of Loudoun, who married Charles Abney Hastings, created Lord Donington in 1880 ; it now belongs to the Earl of Loudoun.

ENGRAVED.
R. Houston, 11 × 8¼ in.
C. Spooner, 5¼ × 4¼ in.
R. B. Parkes, 1874, 5 × 4¼ in.

Lady Selina Hastings, one of the Earls' daughters who bore Her Majesty's train at the coronation ; she died in 1763, on the eve of her marriage with Captain George Hastings, at the age of twenty-two. Another portrait, according to a statement in the Grosvenor Catalogue, 1884, belongs to Colonel Clifford.

HASTINGS, The Right Hon. Warren.

Three-quarter length, canvas 49 × 39¼ *in.*

Born 1732 ; English administrator in India ; went to Bengal as a writer in 1750, and seven years later was appointed agent of the East India

449   3 M

Company at the court of the Nabob of Bengal. In 1764 he returned to England, and remained four years studying Eastern literature. On his return to India he became a member of the Council of Madras, and in 1772 Governor of Bengal, a position which, in 1774, became that of Governor-General of India. He involved himself in quarrels with his council, which the Supreme Court decided in his favour. His most important step was the measures taken against the Rajah of Benares and the Nabob of Oude, which became the foundation of the impeachment against him before the House of Lords, 1787, which proceeded at intervals for seven years, and, in spite of the eloquence of Burke and Sheridan, ended in his acquittal in 1795. The expense ruined him, but the Court of Directors granted him an annuity. He died August 22, 1818.

Seated in a chair covered with crimson velvet; his right hand resting upon a table strewn with papers, his left hand upon the arm of the chair; blue coat; flowered white waistcoat; red velvet curtain draped behind the head.

Sat in 1766 and 1768. Paid for October 9, 1768, Mr. Hastings, £73 10s.

EXHIBITED.

British Institution, 1823, No. 36, by G. W. Taylor.
        "   "   1854, No. 149, } by Lord Northwick.
Grosvenor, 1884, No. 102,

Sold by Robins in 1832 (Watson Taylor, owner), for £57 15s., to Newton, who sold it to Lord Northwick.

ENGRAVED.

T. Watson, 1777, 16 × 12¾ in.
M. Zell, 1786 (in border), 7¼ × 5¼ in.
Herbert Davis, 1862, 5¼ × 4¼ in.

First State by Watson, Buccleuch Collection, sold at Christie's, 1887, for £10 10s.

Messrs. Henry Graves and Co. bought a portrait of Warren Hastings from Holmes of Birmingham in 1868, which they sold to Edward Akroyd, Esq.

HASTINGS, The Right Hon. Warren.

Sold at Christie's, June 9, 1888, No. 349 (Hastings, owner), described as "Equestrian portrait of Warren Hastings by Sir J. Reynolds and Stubbs, R.A.," for £273, to Agnew.

HASTINGS, The Right Hon. Warren.

ENGRAVED.
H. Robinson, 1832, 4¼ × 3¼ in.

Sir Joshua is given as the painter on this plate; it is evidently the Lawrence portrait that is engraved.

HASWELL, Captain.

Sat in October, 1773.

HATTON, Mr.

Sat in May, 1789.

HATTON, Mrs.

Sat in April, 1777.

HAWKESWORTH, Doctor John, LL.D.

Half length, canvas 28 × 24 in.

Essayist and novelist; editor of the " Adventurer," " Voyages of Captain Cook," and other works. In 1772 he was engaged in preparing for the press the account of Cook's voyage, with the earlier voyages of Byron, Wallis, and Carteret, at the price of £6,000, then considered startling, and which is still larger, probably, than any ever paid to a literary hack, however respectable. He was so elated with his good fortune that he is said to have died of it, though others attribute his death to some disparaging criticisms on his heavy quartos. His death took place in 1773.

Writing, sitting at a table, pen in right hand; coat trimmed with fur; left arm bent, hand in waistcoat; curtain draped; bookshelves with books.

Sat in 1769, 1770, 1772, and 1773. Paid for 1775, Mr. Fitzmaurice, for Dr. Hawkesworth, £10 10s.

EXHIBITED.
British Institution, 1860, No. 180, by the Earl of Orkney.

Sold at Christie's, June 15, 1861, Lot 109 (Lord Orkney, owner), for £170 2s., to Munro. Same rooms, April 6, 1878, Lot 46 (Munro, owner), for £173 5s., to Mievelle.

J. Watson, 1773, 12¼ × 11 in.
J. Hall, 1775 (in border), 4¾ × 2⅞ in.
N. Schiavonetti, 1806, 3 × 2¼ in.
S. W. Reynolds, 2¼ × 2 in.
Unknown (head only), 3 × 2¼ in.
Unknown, 2⅞ × 2¼ in.
E. W. (oval), 3 × 2¼ in.
Halpin (vignette), 4¼ × 4 in.

HAWKESWORTH, Doctor John, LL.D.

Half length, canvas 30 × 25 *in.*

Sold at Christie's, June 22, 1872, Lot 157 (Agnew, owner), for £30 9s., to Solomon, who sold it to Henry Graves and Co. Bought in at Christie's, May 27, 1882, Lot 163, for £23 12s. 6d.; sold by Henry Graves and Co., in 1889, to Howard and Co.

A replica belongs to Mr. Dexter, 10, Great Russell Street, London.

HAY, Sir George, D.C.L.

Half length, canvas 30 × 25 *in.*

Judge of the High Court of Admiralty; educated at St. John's College, Oxford, where he graduated B.C.L. in 1737; D.C.L., 1741; M.P. for Stockbridge, 1755; Vicar-General of the diocese of Canterbury and King's Advocate up to 1764; M.P. for Newcastle under Lyne, November 28, 1768, and October 11, 1774; Lord of the Admiralty, 1753-63; Dean of Arches in the following year; Judge of the Prerogative Court, and Judge of the Consistory Court, London; knighted in 1763, and made Judge of the High Court of Admiralty, which office he held until his death in 1778.

Full face in wig; in black gown and white lapels; holding in his right hand a letter and a pair of spectacles; dark background.

Sat in 1761 and 1764. Paid for 1762, Doctor Hay of the Admiralty, £21.

British Institution, 1863, No. 100, by Rev. V. Edwards.

Bought in at Christie's, June 23, 1866, Lot 174, by the owner, Boore, for £5 5s.

R. B. Parkes, 1863, 5 × 4 in.

The original portrait was painted in 1761, and was bequeathed in 1859 by Mrs. Edwards, wife of George Hay Edwards, of Southampton, to the Rev. Samuel Valentine Edwards, B.A., of Hanwell.

HAY, Colonel.

Sat in May, 1784. Paid for May, 1784, Col. Hay, £26 5s.; May, 1786, Col. Hay, £26 5s. Mr. Hay's dog sat in June, 1784.

HAY, Mr.

Sat in 1762. Paid for July 5, 1762, Mr. Hay, £21. Frame paid.

HAYES, Dr. Philip.

Head size, canvas 30 × 25 *in.*

Born 1740; died March 19, 1797; Musical Doctor, Oxford, 1777.

In robes, with a cap.

Paid for before 1765, Mr. Hayes, two pictures, £95.

"On March 19, 1797, Philip Hayes, professor of music in the University of Oxford. He had just come to town to preside at the ensuing festival for the new Musical Fund. He ressed himself in the morning to attend the Chapel Royal, St. James's, but suddenly showed symptoms of approaching dissolution and expired a short time afterwards. He was supposed to be the largest man in England, and nearly equal in weight to the late celebrated Mr. Bright the miller."—*Gentleman's Magazine*, vol. lxvii., p. 354.

Sold at Christie's, as a portrait of a gentleman by Hoppner, in 1872, to Messrs. Henry Graves and Co., who disposed of it in 1872 to J. C. Robinson, for 80 guineas.

The picture belongs to Sir J. C. Robinson, F.S.A.

On the examination of the portrait by Mr. Henry Graves he was certain it was by Reynolds. The picture has a wart on the cheek, and there is an impression of a private plate by J. K. Sherwin, after a picture by J. Cornish, in the British Museum, which has a similar wart, and is inscribed "Dr. Hayes." This established the identity of the above portrait as that of Dr. Hayes.

HAYES, Mrs.

Head size, oval, 30 × 25 *in.*

In a white and gold dress; three-quarter face, looking to right; scarf over right shoulder; light ribbon in hair.

S. W. Reynolds (S. Cousins, R.A.), 1823, 4⅛ × 3⅛ in.

HAYES, Mrs.

White and gold dress; purple scarf; seated in a landscape, holding a book.

Sat in June, 1759, as Mrs. Hays.

Bought in at Christie's, June 15, 1861, Lot 105, by the owner, Gray, for £80 17s.

HAYMAN, Francis, R.A.

Head size, canvas 30 × 25 in.

Born at Exeter, 1708; scholar of Robert Brown; designed much for the booksellers; illustrations to Sir Thomas Hanmer's "Shakespeare," Pope's works, Milton, etc.; librarian to the Royal Academy on its foundation; died 1776.

Profile to left; seated; reddish brown dress; open collar; dark background.

EXHIBITED.

British Institution, 1854, No. 157,
Manchester, 1857, No. 28,
National Portrait Exhibition, 1867, No. 340,
Royal Academy, 1884, No. 204,
} by the Royal Academy.

ENGRAVED.

G. H. Every, 1864, 4¼ × 4 in.

Also a plate by Gimber cancelled.

"Hayman, the chairman of the Artists' Committee, had one special claim on Reynolds's regard which was always honoured by him. He was a Devonshire man; of no great note as an historical or portrait painter, but more famous for the conversation pieces in the manner of Hogarth, with which he ornamented the alcoves and supper boxes of Vauxhall. He was the master of Gainsborough and the intimate friend and associate of Hogarth and Quin, had often made one with the former at the Cockpit or Southwark Fair, and 'beaten the rounds' of Covent Garden in his company. It was at Moll King's 'Finish' that Hogarth, in company with Hayman, saw the incident he has introduced into the bagnio scene of the 'Rake's Progress,' of the woman squirting a mouthful of wine into the face of the sister drab she is quarrelling with. Hayman was a straightforward John Bull, rough in his manners, blunt in speech, more at home over his bottle and pipe at the Artists' Club at Slaughter's than in more refined haunts and more highly bred company. Smith tells a story of him rolling drunk in a Covent Garden kennel with Quin. Hayman kicked. 'What are you at now?' asked Quin. 'Trying to get up,' stuttered Hayman. 'Pooh!' was Quin's rejoinder, 'lie still; the watch will be round shortly, they'll take us both up.'"—LESLIE AND TAYLOR'S *Life of Sir Joshua*, vol. i., pp. 136-137.

The picture belongs to the Royal Academy.

HAYWARD, Mr.

Sat in March, 1757.

HAYWOOD, Mr.

Sat in January, 1755.

HEAD, Lady.

Mary, daughter of Sir William Boys, Knt., M.D.; married the Rev. Sir Francis Head, Bart.

Sat in 1758.

Mrs. Head, seated in a landscape, holding a guitar, 36 × 29 in., sold at Christie's, June 20, 1896, Lot 94 (Biscoe, owner), for £84, to Benjamin.

HEATHFIELD, Lord.

Three-quarter length, canvas 56 × 44 in.

George Augustus Elliott, Lord Heathfield, K.B.; born December 25,. 1717; youngest son of Sir Gilbert Elliott; studied at Leyden, and at the military school of La Fère in Picardy; served in Germany, and was wounded at Dettingen; appointed in 1759 to raise the 15th Regiment of Light Horse, called Elliott's Light Horse, with which he served on the Continent with great reputation; and in 1775 was Commander-in-Chief in Ireland. From thence he was made Governor of Gibraltar; that fortress he defended from 1779 to 1783, and on his return to England he was raised to the peerage under the title of Lord Heathfield, Baron Gibraltar, July 6, 1787, and made a K.B. He married, June 10, 1748, Anne Pollexfen Drake, daughter of Sir Francis Drake, Bart., by whom he had Francis Augustus, 2nd Lord Heathfield, who died in 1813, when the title expired. Died July 6, 1790, at his Château Kalcofen, near Aix-la-Chapelle.

With the key of Gibraltar in his hand. The background is a view of the rock, with the smoke of artillery.

Sat in August, 1787, as Lord Heathfield. Paid for, October, 1787, Lord Heathfield, paid by Aldm. Boydell, £105. Painted for Alderman Boydell in 1787. Exhibited in the Royal Academy, 1788, No. 115, as a portrait of a nobleman, half length. "St. James's Chronicle" says, "No. 115, Lord Heathfield." It was afterwards in the Angerstein Collection, and was purchased by Parliament in 1824 with the remainder of the collection to found the National Gallery.

Copy in enamel by H. Bone, R.A., sold in his sale at Christie's, July 20, 1832, Lot 17, $6\frac{1}{2} \times 5$ in., for £6 15*s*., to Money.

ENGRAVED.

Earlom, 1788, $16\frac{1}{4} \times 13\frac{1}{4}$ in.

Unknown, 1823 (etching), $6\frac{3}{8} \times 5\frac{1}{4}$ in., for Angerstein Gallery.

A. Roffe, 1830 (in part), $3\frac{1}{8} \times 2\frac{1}{2}$ in.

H. Robinson, 1832, 5×4 in., for "Lodge's Portraits."

G. T. Doo, R.A., 1836, $9\frac{1}{4} \times 7\frac{1}{4}$ in.

F. Bromley, 1862, $5\frac{1}{4} \times 4\frac{1}{8}$ in.

R. Page and Son, $5\frac{1}{2} \times 4\frac{1}{2}$ in., for Jones's "National Gallery."

Unknown (stipple), $7\frac{3}{4} \times 5\frac{7}{8}$ in.

J. Cochran, $4\frac{1}{2} \times 3\frac{5}{8}$ in.

J. Rogers, $4\frac{3}{4} \times 3\frac{7}{8}$ in.

"This picture," says Mr. Ottley, "is in all respects one of the finest and most strikingly characteristic portraits Sir Joshua ever painted. The intrepid veteran firmly grasping in his hand the key of the fortress, stands like the rock of which he was the defender." Barry spoke in the highest terms of the introduction of the key of the fortress into the general's hand, "than which," he says, "imagination cannot conceive anything more ingenious and heroically characteristic."

"Haydon affirmed that he would rather be the painter of this picture than of Vandyke's 'Gavartius.' 'There is more' (he said) 'of what is understood by the word genius in it than in the other, and it is astonishing how its breadth and tone comes upon you as you enter the room. It affected me like the explosion of a bomb.'"—COTTON, 1856, p. 172.

HEATHFIELD, George Augustus Elliott, Lord.

Three-quarter length, canvas 56×45 *in.*

Facing head to left; in naval uniform and star of the Bath; in right hand key, which rests on left; on left sextant, on right mortar.

Called a copy in the catalogue of the works of art of the Corporation of London, 1886, but it is more likely to be a replica.

EXHIBITED.

Guelph, 1891, No. 175, by the Corporation of London.

ENGRAVED.

W. Bond, 1813, $10\frac{1}{2} \times 8\frac{1}{2}$ in.

Copy of the National Gallery picture, presented to the Corporation of London by Alderman John Boydell in 1793.

HEILIGER, Master.

Sat in 1757.

Miss Peggy Porter

HENDERSON, Mr.

Probably John Henderson, the actor.

Quin's only successor in Falstaff; born 1747; died 1785; made his first appearance at Bath, 1772, in Hamlet under the name of Courtenay, followed by a representation of nine other characters, Richard III., Macbeth, Don Felix, etc., etc. He is found next at the Haymarket under Foote, opening with Shylock, which was such a success that the theatre was filled every night he performed; at Drury Lane under the Sheridan management, and finally at Covent Garden, where his last appearance was Horatius in the "Roman Father." He excelled in public readings from the best English writers.

Exhibited.

British Institution, 1817, No. 64, by Mrs. Henderson.

There are no sittings or payments to confirm the authenticity of this picture. Sir Joshua dined with Lord Shelburne on September 15, 1773, and went to the play, in which Henderson acted.

HENNESSY, Hon. Mrs.

Bust, panel 29 × 24¼ *in.*

Three-quarter face to right; powdered hair falling in ringlets on her right shoulder; dress, a low-cut dark robe; white muslin kerchief; a rose to the front of the bodice.

No record in pocket-book or ledger.

In the collection of C. P. Huntington, of New York, purchased from M. Charles Sedelmeyer, Paris.

HENNIKER, Sir John, Bart, M.P.

Married, February 24, 1747, Anne, eldest daughter of John Major, who was created a baronet, July 8, 1765, with remainder to his son-in-law, who succeeded to the baronetcy in January, 1781; elevated to the peerage of Ireland as Baron Henniker of Stratford-upon-Slaney, July 30, 1800; died April 18, 1803.

Sat in November, 1781. Paid for, November, 1781, Sir John Henniker, £52 10s.

HERBERT, George Augustus, Lord.

Son of Henry, 10th Earl of Pembroke (for the picture of him standing with his book at his mother's knee), afterwards 11th Earl; born 1759; married, first, in 1787, Elizabeth, second daughter of Topham Beauclerc; secondly, January 23, 1808, Catherine, only daughter of Simon, Count Woronzow; died October 26, 1827. *See* PEMBROKE.

Sat in 1765, 1766, and 1767.

HERBERT, Lady Elizabeth, and Son.

Whole length, canvas 55 × 44¼ *in.*

Elizabeth Alicia Maria, daughter of Charles, 1st Earl of Egremont; born 1752; married, July 15, 1771, Henry Herbert, created October 17, 1780, Lord Porchester, and Earl of Carnarvon, July 3, 1793; died February 10, 1826.

In a landscape; Lady Elizabeth is seated in white dress, open in front, with a brown scarf over her shoulders; on a low seat, resting her right arm on the back of it. The child also seated, undraped, is looking up in her face, and holding her chin in his left hand. Trees on each side, through which is seen the sky.

EXHIBITED.

British Institution, 1813, No. 36, ⎫
     „   „   1844, No. 166, ⎬ by the Earl of Carnarvon.
Royal Academy, 1881, No. 180, ⎭ .

Lady Elizabeth Herbert sat in February, 1777. Paid for, November 13, 1775, Lady Elizabeth and Mr. Herbert, £54 12s. 6d. Exhibited in the Royal Academy, 1777, No. 289, as a lady and child.

ENGRAVED.

J. Dean, 1779, 17¼ × 13⅞ in.
S. W. Reynolds (S. Cousins, R.A.), 5¼ × 4¼ in.

Proof by Dean, Johnson Collection, was sold at Christie's in 1873 for £96 12s.

This picture was sent to Mr. Henry Graves in 1862 for repairs, as the paint was dropping off in blisters; he, without consulting the owner, who acknowledged he would have been afraid to sanction it, had the picture laid on a bed of paste, and when thoroughly dry the unprimed canvas on which it was painted was removed from the paint. The first sketch was then visible, showing that it was Sir Joshua's habit to sketch in the figures nude before adding the drapery. Mr. A. Graves was sent for to see the back of the paint before the new canvas was added. The process of transferring a picture from panel to canvas had often been carried out, but this was the first instance in which a canvas picture had been transferred. The work was successfully carried out by Mr. W. Morrill.

The picture belongs to the Earl of Carnarvon.

458

HERBERT, Lady Elizabeth, and Son.

Whole length, canvas 60 × 48 in.

Seated, in white dress; the child on her knee with his hand under his mother's chin.

The picture belongs to the Earl of Ducie at Tortworth, Falfield.

Lady Frances Herbert, the only daughter of the Earl of Carnarvon, married, in 1797, Thomas, Lord Ducie.

HERBERT, Lady Elizabeth, afterwards Countess of Carnarvon.

Half length, canvas 28 × 24 in.

Seated, in a white dress; hands down.

The picture belongs to the Earl of Ducie at Tortworth, Falfield.

HERBERT, Lady Elizabeth, afterwards Countess of Carnarvon.

Canvas 22¼ × 19¼ in.

The picture was the property of T. McLean, who sold it to Charles Sedelmeyer, of Paris; from him it went to R. Mortimer, of New York, the present owner.

A portrait of Lady Carnarvon seated in a landscape was sold at Christie's, May 13, 1837, Lot 67 (Pringle, owner), for £43 1s., to Gritten; June 28, 1875, Lot 139 (Sharpe, owner), Countess of Carnarvon, to Dodd, for £5 5s.; November 30, 1890, Lot 449, Lady Elizabeth Herbert and child (Howell, owner), for £38 17s., to Renton. The original sketch was sold in these rooms, May 12, 1838, Lot 10 (Lord Northwick, owner), for £4 4s., to Darby.

HERBERT, Master Henry George.

Whole length, canvas 50 × 40 in.

As the " Infant Bacchus."

Born June 3, 1772; afterwards (1793) Lord Porchester; succeeded as 2nd Earl Carnarvon on June 3, 1811; married, April 26, 1796, Elizabeth Kitty, daughter and sole heir of Colonel Dyke Acland, of Pixton, co. Somerset; died, April 16, 1833.

Hands on a basket of grapes; two panthers by his side; thyrsus on the ground.

Sat in 1776. Paid for, November 13, 1775, Master Herbert, £36 15s.;

February 10, 1777, Master Herbert, £36 15*s*. Exhibited in the Royal Academy, 1776, No. 242, as a portrait of a child in the character of Bacchus.

EXHIBITED.

British Institution, 1813, No. 124 (third catalogue), as ⎫
    Master Henry Herbert, as " Infant Bacchus," ⎬ by the Earl of
British Institution, 1844, No. 162, as Lord Porchester ⎪ Carnarvon.
    as Bacchus with Tigers, ⎭

ENGRAVED.

J. R. Smith, 1776, 18¼ × 13¼ in.
S. W. Reynolds, 1834, 5¼ × 4¼ in.

This picture was engraved with leopards, but when cleaned lions appeared.

HERBERT, Lady Henrietta, afterwards Henrietta Antonia, Lady Clive, and Countess of Powis.

Three-quarter length, canvas 56 × 45 *in.*

Daughter of Henry Arthur Herbert, Earl Powis, the last of the Herbert family ; born 1758 ; married, May 7, 1784, Edward, 2nd Lord Powis, created Baron Clive in 1794, Baron Herbert of Cherbury, Viscount Clive of Ludlow, and Earl Powis in 1804. She died, June 3, 1830.

In a white dress, looking over her left shoulder; spotted scarf; she is pulling on a long glove over the left hand and arm ; landscape, with trees and water.

Sat in September, 1777, as Lady Herbert, and in 1786 as Lady Clive. Paid for, June, 1786, Lady Clive ; no money entered. There is a leaf torn out in the second ledger that probably contained the payment by Lord Powis in 1777.

This picture was painted in 1777, before she was married, and was altered by Reynolds in 1786, a large hat being added. This explains the absence of a price to the 1786 entry in the ledger.

EXHIBITED.

British Institution, 1844, ⎫
Leeds, 1868, No. 1051, ⎬ by the Earl of Powis.
National Portrait Exhibition, 1867, No. 697, ⎭

ENGRAVED.

Valentine Green, 1778, 16¼ × 12¾ in., as Right Hon. Lady Harriot Herbert
    (without a hat).
James Scott, 1875, 5¼ × 4¼ in. (with a hat).

A First State of the Green plate sold at Christie's, Palmerston Collection, 1890, for £118 13*s*.

The picture belongs to the Earl of Powis.

HERBERT, Mr.

There is an entry in the first ledger in 1762, Mr. Herbert ("I think' erased), with no price.

HERBERT, Mrs.

Sat in 1761.

HERTFORD, Francis, Earl of, afterwards 1st Marquess of.

Half length, 29½ × 24½ in.

Francis, 2nd Baron Conway; born 1719; succeeded to the title, February 3, 1732; created Viscount Beauchamp and Earl of Hertford, August 3, 1750; Viscount Yarmouth and Marquess of Hertford, June 29, 1793; Lord-Lieutenant of County of Warwick in 1757; K.G., August 30, 1757; married, May 29, 1741, Isabella, youngest daughter of Charles, 2nd Duke of Grafton; died June 14, 1794.

In his peer's robes; star on coat, which is trimmed with fur; the coat has a lappet, which reaches to the shoulder; powdered hair.

Sat in 1781. Paid for, January, 1786, Lord Hertford, given to Captain Conway, £52 10s.; 1784, Lord Hertford, for Lady Lincoln and Lady Elizabeth Conway, £110; 1766, Earl of Hertford, for a picture of Charles II., £26 5s.

EXHIBITED.

Royal Academy, 1873, No. 22, } by the Marquess of Hertford.
Grosvenor, 1884, No. 187,

ENGRAVED.

J. Watts, 1786, 12⅞ × 10⅞ in.

HERTFORD, Francis, 2nd Marquess of.

Half length, canvas 24½ × 20½ in.

As a boy. *See* LORD BEAUCHAMP, *ante*, p. 67, second portrait.

Francis Ingram Seymour Conway, better known as Lord Beauchamp, was the eldest son of Francis, Earl of Hertford, afterwards (1793) 1st Marquess; born February 12, 1743; educated at Eton and Christ Church College, Oxford. At the coronation of George III. he was one of the eldest sons of peers who supported the sovereign's train. In 1766 he was M.P. for Lostwithiel in Cornwall, and from 1768 for Oxford. On June 14, 1794, he succeeded as 2nd Marquess, he having the previous year exchanged his courtesy title of Viscount Beauchamp to that of Earl of Yarmouth. In 1804 he was Master of the Horse, and in 1807 K.G. He married, first, February 1, 1768, the Hon. Alicia Elizabeth Windsor; she died February 11, 1772; and he married, secondly, May 19, 1776, the Hon. Isabella Anne Ingram Shepherd, daughter of Charles, 9th Viscount Irvine; he assumed the name of Ingram on the latter's death in 1807. He died June 17, 1822.

Three-quarter face, turned to the right; loose robe, showing vest; Vandyke white collar; left arm resting on a column, on which is inscribed "Viscount Beauchamp, son of the Earl of Hertford," and the hand, white-cuffed, grasping a two-edged sword; pillar for a background; a glimpse of sky to the right.

EXHIBITED.
Grosvenor, 1884, No. 37, by the Marquess of Hertford (*ante*, p. 67, first portrait).

Sold at Christie's, May 10, 1890 (Wells, owner), for £94 10*s*., to McLean, 24¼ × 20¼ in.

HERTFORD, Isabella, Marchioness of. *See* LADY BEAUCHAMP, *ante*, p. 67.

HERTFORD, Frances, Countess of, afterwards Duchess of Somerset. *See* SOMERSET.

HERVEY, Captain The Hon. Augustus John, R.N.
Three-quarter length, canvas 50 × 40 *in.*

Born May 19, 1724; M.P. for Bury St. Edmunds from 1757 to 1775; became 3rd Earl of Bristol, March 18, 1775; privately married, August 5, 1744, to Miss Chudleigh, known afterwards as the Duchess of Kingston; died December 22, 1779.

In naval uniform; coat open; left arm resting on a cannon, with plan of fortification in his hand; right hand holding a sword; ships in the distance attacking a fortress. On the plan are the names of the ships engaged— "Marlborough," "Dragon," "Cambridge," etc.

Sat in 1762, as Captain Hervey. Paid for, May 20, 1763, Capt. Augustus Hervey, £42.

ENGRAVED.
Edward Fisher, 12¼ × 9⅞ in.
S. W. Reynolds, 3¼ × 2¼ in.

The sitting is in October, within a fortnight of his return with the despatches announcing the capture of Moro Castle at Havannah.

The picture, which was probably presented to the town by Captain Hervey, is in the Guildhall, Bury St. Edmunds.

HERVEY, Captain The Hon. Augustus John, R.N.

Half length, canvas, oval, in square, 30 × 25 in.

Full face; blue naval uniform; white and gold facings; coat buttoned up; white cravat and lace frills; sky background.

Paid for, April 5, 1763, Capt. Hervey, given to Lord Pembroke, £21.

The picture is in the possession of the Earl of Pembroke.

HERVEY, Master. *See* HARVEY.

HERVEY, Miss. *See* HARVEY.

HESKITH, Mrs.

Sat in 1757.

HEWGILL, Rev. Mr.

Head size, canvas 24 × 18 in.

He belonged to a family that emigrated to Canada.

In black gown and white bands.

Sat in 1758.

The picture was purchased some years ago by Albert G. Sandeman, of Presdales, Ware, the present owner.

HEWGILL, General.

Head size, canvas 22 × 16 in.

In uniform, with cocked hat.

The picture was purchased some years ago by Albert G. Sandeman, the present owner.

HEWGILL, Mrs.

Sat in 1758, 1759, and 1760. Paid for, 1762, Mrs. Hewgill, £15 15s.

HEWS, Mrs.

Sat in 1764. Paid for, January 16, 1764, Mrs. Hews, £13 2s. 6d. February 27, 1764, Mrs. Hews, £13 2s. 6d.

HEWITT, Mrs.

Sat in 1759 and 1760.

HEYWOOD, Mrs.

Half length, canvas 29¼ × 24¼ *in.*

Mrs. Heywood, formerly Miss Catherine Hartopp.

To left; full face; low dress; pink cloak trimmed with ermine; cap tied with pink ribbon; both hands in a large muff; dark background.

James Modyford Heywood, of Mariston, Devon, born 1732, married in 1755 Catherine Hartopp, who, with her sister, Mary, who married Richard, 4th Viscount Howe, were heiresses, daughters of Chiverton Hartopp, of Welby, Notts, High Sheriff of the County Devon, Commissioner of the Admiralty, 1784. Mr. Heywood died March 22, 1798. His eldest daughter, Sophia Catherine, married, in 1766, John Musters, of Colwick Hall, near Nottingham.

EXHIBITED.
Royal Academy, 1885, No. 66, by J. C. Musters.

Another portrait of Mrs. Heywood belonged to Lady Geo. Gordon, of 9, Curzon Street, who also had a second portrait of her, painted about 1775.

The picture was recently at Annesley Park, Nottingham.

HICKEY, Joseph.

Sat in 1771 and 1773. Paid for, January 10, 1771, Mr. Hicky, £36 15s. Painted for Burke. Exhibited in the Royal Academy, 1772, No. 208.

EXHIBITED.
British Institution, 1833, No. 34, by T. H. Burke.

Counsellor Hickey, small, Ely Collection, was sold at Christie's, April 14, 1864, No. 15, for £7 10s. to Waters.

"Hickey, the 'special attorney' of 'Retaliation,' is another figure of Goldsmith's particular circle who turns up in this year's pocket-book. Reynolds dined with him on Saturday, the 6th of August. Hickey was Sir Joshua's legal adviser as well as Burke's, for whom his portrait was painted. He appears to have been a plain, hearty, jovial man, of no great polish or pretension to culture."—TOM TAYLOR, vol. i., p. 264.

Burke, writing to his wife, November 8, 1774, from Bristol, says: "I embrace my father, Jack and Mrs. Nugent, Joe Hickey, our Knight (Reynolds), and every other friend that wishes us well."

HICKEY, Miss.

Half length, canvas 31 × 24 *in.*

Daughter of Burke's lawyer.

Sat in February, 1769, and August, 1773. Paid for, December, 1773, Miss Hicky, £36 15s.

EXHIBITED.

British Institution, 1833, No. 11, by T. H. Burke.
Royal Academy, 1872, No. 105, by John Heugh.
Grosvenor, 1884, No. 147, by Sir Charles Mills, Bart.

Full face, with grey eyes and reflected light from a large white round hat; with a black mantle and long grey gloves, and a very narrow ribbon round her neck; left arm on a pedestal; hands clasped.

The picture, which was painted for Edmund Burke, was purchased by Sir Charles Mills, Bart., in 1877, and belongs to Lord Hillingdon at Camelford House, Hereford Gardens, Park Lane.

HILL, Mr. and Mrs.

Sat in December, 1757.

Mrs. Hill, head only, copy by Rising, bought in at his sale at Christie's, May 2, 1818, No. 87, for £1 11s. 6d.

HILL, Miss.

Sat in August, 1770, February, 1771, and March and October, 1773.

HILLISON, Mrs., or ELLISON.

Sat in December, 1757.

HILLSBOROUGH, Wills, Earl of.

Created Earl of Hillsborough, October 3, 1751, and Marquess of Downshire, August 19, 1789. He held several important offices, and became one of the leaders of the administration which had to bear the unpopularity of the American War. He married, first, in 1747, Margaretta, daughter of Robert, Earl of Kildare, and, secondly, Mary, Baroness Stawell, and widow of the Right Hon. Henry Legge. He died October 7, 1792.

Sat in March, 1755, as Lord Hillsborough.

On the 9th of July, 1762, Sir Joshua, like all the rest of the town, pays his respects to the "King of the Cherokees and his ministers," who came to make a lasting peace between the Red Indians of South Carolina and this country. They had an audience with the king, and were much fêted. The rage passed away and they fell among thieves, were plundered and reduced to starvation, from which they were rescued by the benevolence of Lord Hillsborough, who had them taken back to Carolina.

HILDYARD, Sir Robert, Bart.

Of Winestead, near Patrington, East Riding, Yorkshire; represented the borough of Great Bedwin in Wiltshire in the time of George II.; married, 1738, Maria Catherina, only child of Henry D'Arcy, of Sedbury, Yorkshire; died 1781.

Sat in January, 1761, as Mr. Hillyard. Paid for in 1760, Mr. Hillyard, £10 10s.; 1762, Mr. Hillyard, £10 10s.

EXHIBITED.

British Institution, 1855, No. 126, by T. B. T. Hildyard.

Died "March 13, 1764, Mrs. Hildiard, mother of Sir Rob. Hildiard."—*Gentleman's Magazine*, 1764, p. 147. *

"September 21, 1747, at Bishop Burton, in the county of York, the lady Hildyard, whose distinguished good qualities render her an irreparable loss to her family."—*Gentleman's Magazine*, 1747, p. 448.

HINCHCLIFFE, Doctor John.

His father kept a livery stable in Swallow Street; born 1731, at Westminster; admitted on the foundation there; elected then to Trinity College, Cambridge, 1750; Fellow, 1755; Head Master of Westminster School in succession to Dr. Markham; was companion to the Duke of Grafton on his tour of Europe, and afterwards to the Duke of Devonshire and Mr. Crewe; he was installed as Master of Trinity College, Cambridge, March 3, 1768; consecrated Bishop of Peterborough, 1769. He died January 11, 1794.

Sat in November, 1766, as Mr. Hinchcliffe.

HOARE, Hester, Lady.

Half length, canvas 30 × 25 *in.*

Daughter of William Henry, Lord Lyttelton; born in Jamaica, March 17, 1762; married, August 20, 1783, Sir Richard Colt Hoare, Bart.; she died in 1785.

In a white dress, embroidered with gold; pearl and diamond brooch, and diamond bracelet on right wrist, the hand being raised to the left breast; diamond necklace and earrings; lace frill round the top of the dress; a gauze scarf with gold lines; background, two rows of books, lettered "Spectator" and Gray's poems.

Sold at Christie's, June 20, 1896, Lot 97 (Biscowe, owner), for £26 5s., to Donald; December 19, 1896, Lot 73, for £48 6s., to Wigzell, who sold it to Messrs. Duveen, of Bond Street, the present owners.

It is said that the jewels are still in the possession of a member of the family.

HOARE, Mrs.

Paid for, September 12, 1765, Mrs. Hoare, £73 10s.

HOARE, Mrs. Richard, and Child.

Whole length, canvas 52¼ × 43 in.

Miss Susanna Cecilia Dingley, of Lamb Abbey, near Eltham, Kent; born 1743; married, June 24, 1762, Richard Hoare, of Boreham House, co. Essex (a partner with Messrs. Hoare, bankers), who died May 26, 1778. She died May 20, 1795. The child was Henry Richard Hoare; born April 7, 1766; died March 9, 1768.

In a white and gold dress; seated in a landscape, with the infant on her lap. *See plate vol. 11 - p 631*

EXHIBITED.

British Institution, 1813, No. 105, as a lady and child, by the Hon. W. Bucknall.

Bethnal Green, 1872, No. 17, } by Sir Richard Wallace, Bart.
Royal Academy, 1872, No. 7, }

Sold at Christie's, March 26, 1859, Lot 70 (Colonel F. Paget, executor of the Hon. Mrs. B. Paget), for £2,677 10s., to Holmes, for the Marquess of Hertford, who bequeathed it to Sir Richard Wallace, Bart. It was left to the nation by Lady Wallace in 1878, with the Hertford House Collection. For particulars as to how it descended to Col. Paget, *see* MISS HOARE.

Miss Frances A. Hoare writes, December 26, 1898: "I can affirm that Mrs. Hoare and child, of Hertford House, hung in the house of Colonel and Mrs. Webb, at Hall Place, Harbledown, near Canterbury, where I made a pencil sketch of it in 1837, and that Mrs. Webb was her daughter and sister of Mrs. Bucknall. . . . On the death of Mrs. Webb the picture passed into the possession of the Hon. Mrs. Berkeley Paget, of Hampton Court Palace. By her will (to which her eldest son, Col. Paget, was executor) she directed that the picture should be sold and the proceeds equally divided between her two grandchildren, the Hon. Sophia O'Grady (since married to Edw. Wilmot Williams, of Herrington, Dorset), and Berkeley, eldest son of her second son, Catesby Paget.

HOARE, Miss.

Half length, canvas 36 × 27 in.

Sophia, daughter and co-heiress of Richard Hoare, of Boreham (who died May 26, 1778), grandson of Sir Richard Hoare, Lord Mayor of London in 1713; married, February 3, 1783, Hon. William Grimston, brother of James, the 3rd Viscount, born June 23, 1750, who assumed the name of Bucknall in 1797, in compliance with the will of his maternal uncle, John Askell Bucknall, and died April 25, 1814. She died March 4, 1826 (Burke says, 1836), leaving an only daughter, Sophia Askell, who married, November 22, 1804, the Hon. Berkeley Paget (brother of Henry, 1st Marquess of Anglesey), who died October 26, 1842. The Hon. Mrs. Paget died February 18, 1859. *See* BUCKNELL, *ante*, p. 122.

Seated, fronting the spectator; nearly full face; hands clasped in front holding a book; white fur-lined cloak over her shoulders; dark grey background.

Sat in October, 1782. Paid for, January 4, 1783, Miss Hoare, paid by Mr. Grimpston, £78 15s.

Royal Academy, 1884, No. 199, by Mrs. Frederick Paget.

This picture, which was purchased at Christie's, March 26, 1859, Lot 71, by Mr. Grenfell for £378, was evidently bought by him for Mrs. Paget.

HOARE, Miss.

Sat in 1759.

Probably Ellen, sister of Richard Hoare, of Boreham; married May 8, 1765, Robert Hazelwood.

HOARE, Master Henry.

Whole length.

Son of Sir Richard Colt Hoare, Bart., F.R.S.; great-grandson of Sir Richard Hoare, Lord Mayor; born September 17, 1784; married, February 20, 1808, Charlotte, only daughter of Sir Edward Dering, Bart.; died September 18, 1836, in the lifetime of his father, who died in 1838.

In a white frock; holding a spade; a barrowful of flowers on his left, a dog on his right; his straw hat on the ground; landscape.

Sat in May, 1788. Paid for June, 1788, Master Hoare, £105.

A newspaper critic, October 8, 1788, says: "Master Hoare, son of Mr. Hoare, of St. James's Square, is painted digging, with his foot on a spade. But a picture we more admire is the *boy* with the *drum*."

C. Wilkin, 1789, 9¼ × 7¼ in.
S. W. Reynolds, 5¼ × 4¼ in.

The picture was sold privately to the father of Asher Wertheimer, of Bond Street, in 1883, together with Gainsborough's "Hobbinol;" he sold it to Baron S. Albert de Rothschild, of Vienna, the present owner.

HOBART, Miss.

Sat in 1760.

HODGES, Sir James.

Town Clerk of the City of London ; died at Bath in 1774.

Sat in 1765. Paid for June 21, 1765, Sir James Hodges, £31 10s.

HODGES, Lady.

Sat in 1765. Paid for June 21, 1765, Lady Hodges, £31 10s.

HODGES, Mrs.

Sat in 1761.

"Mrs. Hodges, a charming example," was sold at Christie's, May 25, 1867, Lot 133 (Wiltshire, owner), for £43 1s., to Cox.

HODGSON, Miss.

Probably the following lady :

"Married, March 27, 1788, at Stonehouse, near Plymouth, Mr. Edmund Squire to Miss Hodgson, daughter of William Hodgson of Clapham, Surrey."—*Gentleman's Magazine,* 1788, p. 365.

Sat in 1787. Paid for November, 1787, Miss Hodgson, £26 5s.; June, 1788, Miss Hodgson, £26 5s.

HODGKINSON, Mr.

Had an engagement with Reynolds for January 1, 1780, but there is no record of a portrait.

HOGARTH, William.

Portrait of Hogarth, bought in at Christie's, February 16, 1810 (Josiah Boydell, owner), for £1 1s.

There is no record of Hogarth having sat to Reynolds; but as the Boydells were well known to Reynolds, they must have had some reason for knowing it was by him.

HOGGETT, Mr., or HAGGETT.

Sat in February, 1765. Paid for, 1765, Mr. Haget, two pictures, £95, frame not paid.

HOLBURNE, Admiral Francis, and his Son.

Three-quarter length, canvas 50 × 40 in.

The admiral was third son of Sir James Holburne, Bart., of Menstrie, in the county of Edinburgh ; born about 1704 ; entered the navy, and having served some time as lieutenant, was promoted to be captain of the "Dolphin" frigate, in 1748, under Hawke, for the Bay of Biscay ; in 1750 was sent to St. Louis, Martinique, St. Vincent, and Tobago; in 1755 he was advanced to the rank of rear-admiral, and soon after appointed to command a squadron, ordered to America, to reinforce Admiral Boscawen; in 1756 at Brest, and in 1757 commander-in-chief of the expedition against Louisburg, but nothing came of it. On his return to England he was nominated port-admiral at Portsmouth, which he gave up in 1761. He became M.P. for Stirling Burghs, April 20, 1761, and afterwards, March 15, 1768, for Plymouth, which he continued to represent up to his death on July 15, 1771 ; in 1767 promoted to the rank of admiral ; in 1770 a lord of the admiralty ; a few months later to be rear-admiral of Great Britain, and early in 1771 was made Governor of Greenwich Hospital. The admiral married Frances, daughter of Guy Ball, of Barbadoes, widow of Edward Lascelles (who died, October 31, 1747), collector of customs at Barbadoes, father of the 1st Earl of Harewood. She died May 18, 1761, and Admiral Holburne, July 15, 1771.

Sir Francis Holburne, Bart., only son of the above, succeeded to the baronetcy upon the decease of his cousin, Captain Sir Alexander Holburne, R.N., 3rd Baronet, January 22, 1772. He married, June 12, 1786, Alicia, daughter of Thomas Brayne ; died September 13, 1820.

Standing, full face, in naval uniform, and wig; his right hand on the shoulder of his son ; left hand on hilt of sword ; the boy is standing to his right, leaning his right arm on an anchor, holding a glove in his right hand, and wearing a cocked hat ; rock to the left ; background and ship at sea to the right.

Master Holburne sat in 1757 for this picture.

ENGRAVED.

G. H. Every, 1864, 5¼ × 4 in.

The picture in 1864 belonged to Sir Thomas William Holburne, Bart., of Cavendish Crescent, Bath.

HOLDERNESS, Robert D'Arcy, 4th Earl of.

Half length, canvas 30 × 25 in.

Robert D'Arcy, 4th Earl of Holderness, Lord-Lieutenant of the North Riding of Yorkshire in 1740; in the following year, a gentleman of His Majesty's bedchamber; in 1744, ambassador to the republic of Venice; 1749, minister plenipotentiary to the States-General of the United Provinces; in 1751 one of the principal secretaries of state; in 1752 one of the lords justices during the king's absence at Hanover; admiral and warden of the Cinque Ports. His lordship married at the Hague in November, 1742 (*Burke*), Mary, daughter of Francis Doublet, member of the States of Holland; died March 16, 1778, when the earldom became extinct.

Looking to his right; in a crimson velvet coat; right arm showing; white cravat and frill; powdered wig.

Sat in February, 1755.

ENGRAVED.

R. Cooper, 1811, 3¼ × 2¾ in., from a picture in the possession of the Rev. C. Alderson.

"It was upon seeing this picture—Lord Huntingdon's—that Lord Holderness was induced to sit for his portrait, which he was afterwards pleased to make me a present of, on which occasion he employed me to go to the painter, and fix with him his lordship's time of sitting. Here our acquaintance commenced, and, as he permitted me to attend every sitting, I shall here set down the observations I made upon his manner of painting at this early time, which, to the best of my remembrance, was 1754—Cotton says 1755, but the first sitting may have been 1754. On his light-coloured canvas he had already laid a ground of white, where he meant to place the head, and which was still wet. He had nothing upon his palette but flake white, lake, and black, and, without making any previous sketch or outline, he began with much celerity to scumble these pigments together, till he had produced, in less than an hour, a likeness sufficiently intelligible, yet withal, as might be expected, cold and pallid to the last degree. At the second sitting he added, I believe, to the other three colours a little Naples yellow, but I do not remember that he used any vermilion, neither then nor at the third trial; but it is to be noted that his lordship's countenance was much heightened by scorbutic eruption. Lake alone might produce the carnation required. However this be, the portrait turned out a striking likeness, and the attitude, so far as three-quarters canvas would admit, perfectly natural and peculiar to his person, which at all times bespoke a fashioned gentleman. His drapery was crimson velvet, copied from a coat he then wore, and apparently not only painted, but glazed with lake, which has stood to this hour perfectly well, though the face, which, as well as the whole picture, was highly varnished before he sent it home, *very soon faded,* and soon after the forehead particularly cracked, almost to peeling off, which it would have done long since had not his pupil, Doughty, repaired it."—MASON, pp. 51, 53.

The picture belongs to the Earl of Chichester at Stanmer, Lewes. The granddaughter of Lord Holderness married Thomas, 2nd Earl of Chichester.

HOLDERNESS, Mary, Countess of.

Head size, canvas 25 × 20 in.

Mary, daughter of Francis Doublet, member of the States of Holland; born 1721; married, at the Hague in November, 1742 (*Burke*), the 4th Earl of Holderness, then minister plenipotentiary; she died in Hertford Street, Park Lane, October 13, 1801.

Seated, in pink dress, with a quilted body; arms crossed in lap; powdered hair, with two oblong curls; white lace cap.

Sat in April, 1786.

"She was the daughter of Sieur Doublet, one of the nobles of Holland, and niece to the Gressier Fagel, and married Robert D'Arcy, Earl of Holderness, at the Hague, 1745, who was secretary of state in 1761, but resigned the seals to Lord Bute, and died March 16, 1778, by whom she had two sons who both died young, and a daughter, Amelia, married to the Marquis of Carmarthen, and divorced 1779."—*Gentleman's Magazine*, 1801, p. 966.

The picture belongs to the Earl of Chichester.

This picture, which was painted after she became a widow, was probably left to her daughter, Lady Chichester.

There is at Hornby Castle a crayon drawing which is an exact counterpart of this picture, signed J. Russell, R.A., 1790. Did Russell copy Reynolds's picture?

HOLDITCH, Mr.

Sat in January, 1761.

HOLDITCH, Miss.

Sat in December, 1760.

HOLLAND, Henry Fox, 1st Lord Holland.

Three-quarter length, canvas 50 × 40 in.

Henry Fox, born 1705, who filled several high offices in the reign of George II., from 1735, when he was first returned to Parliament for Hendon, until the accession of George III., at which period he was a member of the Privy Council and Paymaster-General of the Forces, which he retained until 1765; elected member for Hendon, February 28, 1735; New Windsor, May 2, 1741, June 26, 1747, April 13, 1754; member for Dunwich, March 27, 1761. During his tenure of this office he accumulated so much wealth that he was loudly accused of appropriating the public money, and his executor was compelled to reimburse the large sum of £200,000. He was created a peer on

April 16, 1763, by the title of Baron Holland of Foxley, and shortly after retired from public life, but not before he secured for himself and for the lives of two of his sons the office of Clerk of the Pells in Ireland. His lordship strengthened his political influence by a runaway marriage, in 1744, with Lady Georgina Carolina Lennox, eldest daughter of Charles, 2nd Duke of Richmond, for whom he obtained, May 6, 1762, a peerage in her own right as Baroness Holland of Holland. His lordship died at Holland House, July 1, 1774.

Seated, in wig, with light coat and waistcoat, and dark velvet overcoat; right hand on table, pointing to paper; left arm resting on the arm of a damask chair studded with nails; curtain background.

Sat in 1762 as Henry Fox, and in 1764 as Lord Holland. Paid for, 1763, Lord Holland, £50, given to Mr. Nichols (partly erased).

EXHIBITED.

British Institution, 1820, No. 46, by Lord Holland.

ENGRAVED.

S. Gimber, 1864, 5¼ × 4¼ in., and by H. Robinson, 5 × 4 in., for " Lodge's Portraits."

" It is said that Lord Holland, when he received his portrait, could not help remarking that it had been hastily executed, and, making some demur about the price, asked Reynolds how long he had been painting it. The offended artist replied, ' All my life, my lord ! ' "— *Northcote MS. in the Plymouth Library.*

The picture belongs to the Earl of Ilchester at Holland House.

HOLLAND, Henry, 1st Lord.

Three-quarter length, canvas 50 × 40 *in.*

Full face, seated; blue coat, trimmed with gold lace; red waistcoat, also trimmed with gold lace; right elbow on table, holding paper in right hand; left hand on hilt of sword; landscape background, with view of Holland House painted three years later.

" This picture belonged to Miss Fox, sister of the 3rd Lord Holland, and is supposed to have been stolen from her house in London, when she was removing into Little Holland House. It eventually found its way into Colnaghi's shop; and after a separation of nearly thirty years, Miss Fox was able to buy back her property."—PRINCESS MARIE LIECHTENSTEIN, *Holland House*, p. 38.

Sold at Greenwood's, April 15, 1796, Lot 44, Lord Holland, for £42 2s., to the Earl of Upper Ossory, who probably gave it to Miss Fox, who in turn may have left it to the 4th Lord Holland, her nephew, in 1845.

The picture belongs to the Earl of Ilchester at Holland House.

473

HOLLAND, Henry, 1st Lord.

Three-quarter length, canvas 50 × 40 in.

Seated ; in blue coat, trimmed with gold lace ; red waistcoat, also trimmed with gold lace ; left hand on hip ; no landscape in background.

Paid for, 1765, Lord Holland, for the Gallery, £50.

The picture belongs to the Earl of Ilchester at Holland House.

HOLLAND, Henry, 1st Lord.

Paid for, 1765, Lord Holland, for Mr. Selwin, £50.

HOLLAND, Henry, 1st Lord.

Paid for, July 29, 1765, Lord Holland, for Mr. Powel, £52 10s.

HOLLAND, Henry, 1st Lord.

Paid for, 1765, Lord Holland, given to Lord Hillsborough, £25. The latter part erased.

Other portraits of Lord Holland sold by auction :

At Greenwood's.			£	s.	d.	
April 15, 1796.	Lot 1.	A copy, three-quarter length	1	2	0	Bayley.
„ „	„ 17.	Half length, a copy . .	3	13	6	Lord Ossory.
At Christie's.						
June 27, 1812.	„ 44.	Bute, owner, Lord Holland, and a fruit-piece . .	0	14	0	Fulwood.
Dec. 15, 1848.	„ 196.	Same picture . . .	1	11	6	Bought in.
Feb. 17, 1849.	„ 51.	. . . . . .	1	10	0	Rodd.

The Rev. J. Parry mentions that there were, in 1827, portraits of Lord Holland and Lady Caroline Holland, by Sir Joshua Reynolds, at Ampthill.

HOLLAND, Stephen, 2nd Lord. *See* HON. STEPHEN FOX, *ante*, p. 336.

HOLLAND, Caroline, Lady. *See* LADY CAROLINE FOX, *ante*, p. 336.

EXHIBITED.

Grosvenor, 1884, No. 74, as Caroline, Lady Holland, by Lady Holland.

HOLLAND, Mary, Lady. *See* LADY MARY FOX, *ante*, p. 337.

Guelph, 1891, No. 153, by the Earl of Ilchester.

Her character is thus described by her brother, Lord Ossory : "Lady Holland was the most amiable person that ever lived. She possessed the most perfect sweetness of manners, joined to an excellent understanding ; the most elegant person, but alas ! too delicate a frame. Her temper was the sweetest I was ever acquainted with, her heart the tenderest and most sincere. She was the best wife that ever lived, and in the most trying situation that can be conceived, nothing could exceed her tenderness of attention to her children."

HOME, Mr.

Sat in November, 1767.

"Died, 1768, Andrew Home, Accomptant General of Excise in Scotland."—*Gentleman's Magazine*, 1768, p. 302.

HOME, Mr. Sal.

Sat in 1787 and 1789. Paid, July, 1789, for Mr. Sal. Home, £52 10s. ; May, 1790, a copy of Mr. Home for a Mr. Home, £26 5s., and under same date, Mr. Home, the original, I believe, paid for, £50 10s.

The 1789 entry is placed under G. ; therefore the last does not count as a payment. Sir Joshua evidently believed it had been paid for, but could not find it under H.

Tom Taylor considered that this name might be Hume, but there is no possibility of a mistake in the ledgers ; in the 1790 entry it was Hume, and it was altered into Home by Reynolds.

HONE, Miss.

Bought in at Christie's, March 23, 1868, Lot 41, by Wright (owner), for £16 16s.

HONEYCOMB, Dr., and MISS GAYER.

Sold at Christie's, July 14, 1883, Lot 81 (Rev. C. Gregory, owner), for £28 17s. 6d., to Smith.

HONYWOOD, Colonel.

Sat in February, 1757, as Colonel Honywood. Before 1760, General Honeywood, £12 12s. (erased); 1762, General Honeywood, £12 12s.

"July 19, 1766. To appoint Lieut.-General Philip Honeywood, Esq., Governor of, and Captain of the town of Kingston-upon-Hull, in the room of General Pulteney."—*Gentleman's Magazine*, 1766, p. 343.

"February 20, 1785. In Charles Street, Berkeley Square, Philip Honeywood, Esq., of Markes Hall, Essex. A general in the army, colonel of the 4th Regiment of Horse and Governor of Kingston-upon-Hull; he was nephew of the late Sir Philip Honywood, K.B., and represented Appleby in several parliaments. General Honywood rose gradually to the highest rank in his profession with great reputation acquired by painful service; at the battle of Dettingen in 1743 he was desperately wounded, as he was also at the skirmish of Clifton in 1745. He married Miss Wastall, by whom he left no issue."—*Gentleman's Magazine*, 1785, p. 159.

"At Marks Hall, Essex, Mrs. Honeywood, the very respectable relict of the late General Honeywood. By his will his large estate now devolves to Filmer Honeywood, Esq., M.P. for Kent."—*Gentleman's Magazine*, 1785, p. 667.

Gainsborough also painted an equestrian portrait of General Honywood, which the king was anxious to buy, marked in Walpole's catalogue, 1765, as "very good."

HONYWOOD, Sir John, Bart.

Three-quarter length, canvas 55 × 44 in.

Succeeded as 4th Baronet in 1781; died in 1806.

Standing, three-quarter face to left; left hand in waistcoat pocket, right caressing a large dog, head and neck only seen; dark coat and waistcoat; foliage background.

Sat in 1784. Paid for, 1786, Sir John Honeywood, £100. Exhibited in the Royal Academy, 1784, No. 138.

Morning Chronicle: "No. 138. Portrait of Mr. Honeywood, wants ease."
Morning Herald: "No. 138. The colouring of this picture is firm and even."

EXHIBITED.
Royal Academy, 1880, No. 39, by Sir C. Honywood, Bart.

ENGRAVED.
C. A. Tomkins, 1879, 5¾ × 4¼ in.

This picture has since been sold.

HONYWOOD, Frances, Lady, and Child.

Three-quarter length, canvas 55 × 44 in.

Frances, daughter of William, 2nd Viscount Courtenay; born January, 1763; married, December, 1778, John Honywood, afterwards Sir John, the 4th Baronet.

Seated, with a child standing on her lap.

Sat in February, 1784, as Mrs. Honywood. Paid for, 1786, Lady Honeywood and child, £150. Exhibited in the Royal Academy, 1784, No. 58.

> Miss Honywood sat in April, 1784. Tom Taylor says: " A child of six."
> " Bad, in the style of Rubens."—WALPOLE.
> *Morning Chronicle*, 1784 : "That the portrait of lady and child, No. 58, is an admirable proof of the President's superior talent."
> *Morning Herald :* " No. 58. Lady and child. There is great beauty in this performance."

The picture belongs to the Rev. the Earl of Devon at Powderham Rectory, Exeter.

HONYWOOD, Master.

Probably Filmer Honywood, son of John Honywood, 3rd Bart., by his second wife, Dorothy, daughter of Sir Edward Filmer, Bart.; born in 1744. He was M.P. for Kent for many years, and succeeded to the estates of General Honywood in 1785. He died June 2, 1809.

Sat in December, 1757, as Master Honeywood. Paid for before 1760, Master Honeywood, £12 12s.

Sold at Christie's, May 30, 1840, Lot 27 (Marsland, owner), Master Honeywood, in a pink dress, for £9 9s., to Bryant.

HOOD, Admiral Samuel, Lord.

Three-quarter length.

Born 1724. After service under Rodney and Saunders, became commander of the West Indian Squadron, and received a peerage for his participation in Rodney's victory over Count de Grasse. He had previously opposed Fox for Westminster. As Commander of the Mediterranean Fleet he captured Toulon and drove the French from Corsica. Created a baronet as a reward for his achievement, May 19, 1778, and elevated to the peerage of Ireland, September 12, 1782, as Baron Hood. Created a viscount in the peerage of Great Britain, June 1, 1796, and appointed Governor of Greenwich

Hospital, 1796. He married in 1749 Susannah, daughter of Edward Lindzee of Portsmouth, and she was created Baroness Hood in her own right, March 27, 1795. She died May 25, 1806, and he died at Bath, June 27, 1816.

In naval uniform; leaning on a rock; hand holding a paper; two ships engaged in the distance; clouds and smoke; rocks to the right.

Paid for July, 1783, Lord Hood, £105.

ENGRAVED.

J. Jones, 1785, 18 × 14 in.
H. Robinson, 1831, 5¼ × 4 in.
S. W. Reynolds, 3¼ × 2¼ in.

Sold at Christie's, July 13, 1895 (Lord Bridport, owner), as Admiral Samuel, Viscount Hood, for £546, to Agnew, and sold by them to the Corporation Art Gallery, Manchester, where it now hangs.

A portrait of Admiral Lord Hood, in uniform, half length, was sold at Christie's, June 11, 1842, Lot 72 (Miller of Liverpool, owner), for £13 13s., to Winstanley.

HOOD, Captain Alexander, afterwards Viscount Bridport, K.B.

Half length, 50 × 40 *in.*

Second son of the Rev. Samuel Hood, vicar of Thorncombe, Devonshire, and the younger brother of Lord Hood; born 1727; entered the Navy; captured two French vessels, 1757; retook the "Warwick," 1761; from 1761 to 1763 he served in the Mediterranean under Admiral Sir Charles Saunders, and in 1778 under Admiral Keppel; Rear-Admiral under Lord Howe at the relief of Gibraltar, 1782. Rear-Admiral Hood was M.P. for Bridgewater from 1784 to 1790, and for Buckingham until 1796; K.B., 1788; second in command in Lord Howe's victory, June 1, 1794, and afterwards was presented with a gold chain and created Baron Bridport, Ireland; defeated the French fleet close to L'Orient, and took three ships of the line in 1795; created Baron Bridport, in the peerage of Great Britain, June 13, 1796; died at Bath, May 3, 1814.

Standing; full face; naval uniform; cocked hat in hand; leaning on an anchor.

Sat in October, 1758, as Captain Hood. Paid for October 9, 1760, Captain Hood, £21.

EXHIBITED.

British Institution, 1866, No. 46,
National Portrait Exhibition, 1867, No. 731, } by Viscount Hood.

HOOD, Captain Alexander, afterwards Viscount Bridport, K.B.

Three-quarter length, canvas 50 × 40 in.

Standing, looking to left; right hand on sword; left elbow leaning on a rock; two ships in background.

Sat in 1761 as Captain Hood. 1764, Captain Hood, no price; August 2, 1765, Captain Hood, £21 10s.

EXHIBITED.

International, 1862, No. 26, by Greenwich Hospital.

ENGRAVED.

H. Robinson, 1831, 5 × 4 in., for " Lodge's Portraits," as Alexander, Viscount Bridport, K.B.
J. R. Jackson, 1867, 5¼ × 4 in.,

Presented to Greenwich Hospital by the Viscountess Bridport in 1825.

HOOLE, John.

Born 1727; English scholar in the service of the East India Company; translated Tasso's " Gerusalemme Liberata," Ariosto's " Orlando Furioso," and some pieces of Metastasio; died 1803.

Sat in 1777.

"In 1768 Miss Frances Reynolds established herself as a lodger in the house of Dr. Hoole, the translator of Ariosto, whose portrait, prefixed to the first edition of his translation, she painted."—TOM TAYLOR, vol. i., p. 92.

HOPE, Charles, Lord.

Eldest son of John, 2nd Earl of Hopetoun; died in the lifetime of his father, in June, 1767. His next brother, James, born in 1741, succeeded as 3rd Earl.

Sat in January, 1758, as Baron Hope.

HOPE, Henry.

Three-quarter length, canvas 50 × 40 in.

Of Amsterdam; founder of the collection of pictures known as the Hope Collection; born 1736.

"February 25, 1811. Died in Harley Street, Henry Hope, the most eminent merchant of his time. He descended from a branch of the noble family of the same name in Scotland, and was born at Boston in New England in 1736. At the age of thirteen he came to

479

England to complete his education, and in 1754 entered into the house of Gurnell, Hoare and Co. There he remained until 1760, when, making a visit to his uncles, who were great merchants in Holland, they were so pleased with his amiable manners and disposition, as well as with his talents, that they engaged him to quit the house in London and become a partner with them in Amsterdam. On the death of his uncle Adrian in 1780, the whole business of the house devolved upon him; and he managed it in so high a style of good conduct and liberality as to draw the attention and raise the admiration of all Europe. Though he constantly refused to take any office, yet he was always held in the highest consideration by the Government. He was visited by all distinguished travellers, even by crowned heads. His acquaintance was courted by all ranks of people; at the Exchange he was the chief object of attention. . . . From Holland he made occasional visits to this country, partly for health, and partly to keep up his connection with many friends and eminent persons here; and, particularly, he employed the summer of 1786 in a general tour round this island, accompanied by two of his nieces, the daughters of his sister, Mrs. Goddard, the eldest of whom married Mr. John Williams Hope, son of the Rev. Mr. Williams, of Cornwall; who, during the latter part of his residence in Holland, assisted, and now succeeds him in his important commercial concerns. The second daughter was married to John Langston, of Sanden House, Oxfordshire, and the youngest to Admiral Sir Charles Pole, Bart.

"When Holland was invaded by the French in 1794, he determined finally to quit that country and settle in England. Not long after he purchased from the Earl of Hopetoun the large house in Harley Street, where he deposited his noble collection of pictures, and resided to the day of his death. . . . He devoted himself entirely to the encouragement of the arts, of which he was a munificent patron. . . . Notwithstanding his advanced age he remained in tolerable health, always cheerful and good-humoured. . . . His remains were interred at Woodford in Essex, March 4. Property to the amount of more than a million sterling has by his death devolved to his relations, which, it is said, he has thus demised by will:

"To his three nieces, the daughters of the late Mrs. Goddard, his sister, viz., Mrs. Williams Hope, Lady Pole, and Mrs. Langston, each £110,000 . . . . £330,000
"To the three children of Mrs. W. Hope, £40,000 each . . . 120,000
"To the four children of the other sisters ditto . . . 160,000
"To Mr. Williams Hope his houses at Sheen and Cavendish Square, with the fine collection of pictures in each, rich furniture, etc., and all his other residuary property, together estimated at . . . 550,000
_____
£1,160,000."

Gentleman's Magazine, 1811, pp. 292, 293.

One uncle, "Thomas Hope of Amsterdam, died December 26th, 1780, in the seventy-fifth year of his age."—*Gentleman's Magazine*, 1780, p. 50.

Sitting; right hand holds a pen; left arm leaning on a table, over which is a rich cloth, with paper and writing materials; from a window is seen a landscape with trees to right; a curtain draped.

Sat in February, 1787, Mr. and Mrs. Hope. Paid for February, 1787, Mr. Hope, £105.

ENGRAVED.

C. H. Hodges, 1788, 11¼ × 11¼ in., as Henry Hope of Amsterdam.
S. W. Reynolds, 5¼ × 4 in.

Lady "Countess of Bute"

HOPE, Mrs. Williams.

Three-quarter length, canvas 50 × 40 in.

Anne, eldest daughter of William Goddard, of Woodford Hall, Essex, her mother being the sister of Henry Hope, of Amsterdam, the great capitalist, money merchant, and banker; she married John Williams, of Trevonick, Cornwall, who took the name of Hope by royal licence.

"April 8, 1782, at Woodford, Essex, John Williams Hope, of Amsterdam, to Miss Goddard, eldest daughter of John Goddard, of Woodford Hall."—*Gentleman's Magazine,* 1782, p. 205.

Seated in a garden; her right elbow resting on a pedestal on which is a large vase; hands clasped in lap; white dress with white muslin kerchief and black shawl dropped over her arms; looking to the left three-quarter face; in large white muslin mob-cap tied with black ribbon; black velvet round neck; sky background.

Sat in February, 1787, as Mr. and Mrs. Hope. Paid February, 1787, Mrs. Hope, £105. Exhibited in the Royal Academy, 1787, No. 200, as a lady, half length. A newspaper of 1787 calls it Mrs. Hope of Amsterdam.

ENGRAVED.

C. H. Hodges, 1788, 11¼ × 11¼ in., as Mrs. William Hope.

S. W. Reynolds (S. Cousins, R.A.), 5¼ × 4 in., as Mrs. Ann Hope.

HOPE, John.

Half length, canvas 29¼ × 24¼ in.

Born April 7, 1739. He was the second son of the Hon. Charles Hope Vere, son of the 1st Earl of Hopetoun; married, May 29, 1762, Mary, only daughter of Elial Breton, of Norton, Northamptonshire, by whom he had three sons, the Right Hon. Charles Hope, Lieut.-General Sir John Hope, and Sir William Johnstone Hope (Annandale). Died May 21, 1785.

In profile, turned to the left; a pen in his right hand, which he holds to his breast; the left arm hangs by his side; he wears a black cloak and a white neckcloth; books lie on a table in the lower corner; crimson curtain and landscape background.

Sat in March, 1769. Paid, April 12, 1769, Mr. Hope, £36·15s.

The picture belongs to Henry Cook, at 21, Eglinton Crescent, Edinburgh, whose mother was Margaret Sophia, third daughter of General Sir John Hope. The picture came to Henry Cook from his uncle, Henry Philip Hope.

HOPE, John.

Half length, canvas 30 × 25 in.

Replica.

The Right Hon. Charles Hope left in his will what are described as pictures by Sir Joshua Reynolds, to his son, the Right Hon. John Hope, from whom they passed to his son, Colonel William Hope, V.C., the present owner. It hangs at More House, 34, Tite Street, Chelsea.

HOPE, Mrs. John.

Half length, canvas 29½ × 24½ *in.*

Mary, daughter of Elial Breton, of Norton, Northamptonshire; married, May 29, 1762, John Hope, of London; died June 25, 1767, aged twenty-five. There is a monument to her in Poets' Corner, Westminster Abbey.

Sitting at a table; on her head a turban, tied under her chin; brocaded dress; left elbow rests on a book, hand raised to her neck; a string of pearls hangs from her finger and is looped to a pink rose on her bosom; right hand on book; landscape to right.

Sat in August, 1764, as Mrs. Hope. Paid for, August 8, 1764, Mrs. Hope, £31 10s.; frame, 3 guineas, paid.

ENGRAVED.

E. Fisher, 12¼ × 10 in.

S. W. Reynolds, 3¼ × 3¼ in.

Note by Tom Taylor to the 1764 sitting: "First wife of the great capitalist, money merchant, and banker."

The picture belongs to Henry Cook, of 21, Eglinton Crescent, Edinburgh, to whom it descended with her husband's portrait.

HOPE, Mrs. John.

Half length, canvas 30 × 25 *in.*

Replica.

The picture descended to Colonel William Hope, V.C., with her husband's portrait, and now hangs in the house of his son, Adrian F. Hope, at More House, 34, Tite Street, Chelsea.

HOPE, Mrs.

Sat in November, 1755, as Mrs. Hope.

HOPE, Mr.

Sat in December, 1757, as Mr. Hope.

These portraits were probably those of Mr. and Mrs. John Hope of Amsterdam.

HOPE, Lady Sophia, afterwards Countess of Haddington.

Three-quarter length, canvas 50 × 40 *in.*

Sophia, daughter of John, 2nd Earl of Hopetoun; born February 2, 1759; married, April 30, 1779, Charles, Lord Binning, afterwards 8th Earl of Haddington, who succeeded May 19, 1794. She died March 18, 1813

Seated, with right elbow on a stone pedestal; hands clasped; white dress and white turban with brooch in centre; plaits of hair over each shoulder; landscape background; moonlight in distance to the left.

Suffolk Street, 1834, No. 168, as Lady Sophia Hope, Lady Haddington, by the Earl of Egremont.

The picture is described in the Petworth catalogue as a "Lady in white with a turban." Sir Leonard Lyell, of Kinnordy, Forfarshire, has a very good copy of it by Phillips, and it is called "The White Lady." Mr. A. Graves, in view of the exhibit in 1834, is of opinion that this is the picture that was then called Lady Sophia Hope; he has examined carefully all the pictures at Petworth, and cannot find any other that could possibly represent her.

A copy by Thomas Phillips, R.A., was bought in at Christie's, May 9, 1846, Lot 40, as a copy of a lady from a picture at Petworth, for £22 1s.

The picture belongs to Lord Leconfield, No. 104 in the Petworth catalogue. *See* BINNING, *ante*, p. 85.

HOPKINS, Mr.

Sat in October, 1755, and October, 1765. Paid in full, September 27, 1766, Mr. Hopkins, £36 15s.

Memo.: "Mr. Hopkins' picture to be sent to Rev. Dr. Plumtree, Queen's College, Cambridge."

HOPKINS, Mr., Junior.

Sat in October, 1755.

HORNECK, Captain Kane William.

Sat in August, 1766, as Mr. Horneck.

British Institution, 1861, No. 155, as Captain Kane Horneck, by Sir C. J. F. Bunbury, Bart.

S. W. Reynolds, 1822, 4¼ × 3¼ in.

HORNECK, Mrs.

Half length, canvas 30 × 25 *in.*

Hannah, wife of Kane William Horneck, captain Royal Engineers; died March 12, 1803.

Left hand to her face; leaning on left hand, her left elbow on a book; right hand in lap; headdress ornamented with pearls; a lawn veil hangs from her head over her right shoulder; a large buckle on waistbelt, and sleeves looped up with pearls.

"At General Gwyn's, in the King's Mews, Mrs. Horneck, mother of General Horneck and Mrs. Gwyn."—*Gentleman's Magazine*, 1803, p. 292.

Her son, Captain Charles Horneck, married, May 31, 1773.

"Captain Horneck, of the 3rd Regiment of Footguards, to Miss Keppel, daughter of the late Earl of Albemarle."—*Gentleman's Magazine*, 1773, p. 303.

His wife eloped with Captain Scawen, in 1774, whilst Captain and Mrs. Horneck were staying in his house.

"The Plymouth beauty and mother of the 'Jessamy Bride' and 'Little Comedy,' Goldsmith's favourites. The portrait is at Barton, Sir Charles Bunbury's. It is a very pretty picture of a very pretty woman. She wears a lawn veil, from under which her hair flows down on one side; her arm, which supports her head, rests on a book. The likeness to her charming daughters is apparent."—TOM TAYLOR, vol. i., p. 162.

Sat in September, 1758.

ENGRAVED.

J. McArdell, 10⅞ × 9 in., as "Plimouth Beauty."

R. Purcell, 12¼ × 10 in., as "Plymouth Beauty."

S. W. Reynolds, left unfinished, 4⅛ × 3¼ in., published by Henry Graves and Co., Limited, 1898, as No. 18, anonymous.

The picture belongs to Sir Henry Bunbury, Bart, at Barton.

HORNECK, The Misses.

Half length, canvas 30 × 25 *in.*

Catherine and Mary, the beautiful Devonshire sisters. *See* MRS. BUNBURY, *ante*, page 126.

The elder sister in profile, standing erect, and the younger leaning against her, looking down, with her left hand on her sister's shoulder; the picture is unfinished.

Sat in March, 1764, December, 1765, and January, 1766. Notes by Tom Taylor, "1764, Miss Horneck, Goldsmith's 'Little Comedy,' afterwards Mrs. Bunbury;" "1765, The Miss Hornecks;" "1766, Miss Hornecks, two in one picture."

EXHIBITED.

British Institution, 1852, No. 151, as the two Miss Hornecks, by Sir H. E. Bunbury, Bart.

ENGRAVED.

S. W. Reynolds (S. Cousins, R.A.), 7 × 5¼ in.

From vol. i., p. 264, Taylor's "Life of Reynolds": "The original unfinished study of these charming sisters is at Barton. It is exquisitely refined in drawing, and delicate in pearly grey half tones. A finished replica is in Lord Normanton's gallery."

A sketch, probably of these sisters, was sold at Christie's, April 26, 1844,

Lot 547, described as two young ladies (Briggs, R.A., owner), for £13 13s., to Waters.

The picture belongs to Sir Henry Bunbury, Bart, at Barton.

HORNECK, The Misses.

Half length, canvas, 26 × 23 *in.*

Painted in 1766.

The picture was purchased from Sir H. Bunbury by the Earl of Normanton, and is No. 32 in the Somerley catalogue.

HORNECK, Miss Mary, afterwards Mrs. Gwyn.

Whole length, canvas 50 × 39¼ *in.*

Mary, youngest daughter of Captain Kane Horneck and Hannah, his wife; born 1754; married, 1779, General Francis Gwyn, equerry to George III. She was Lady of the Bedchamber to Queen Charlotte, and died January 14, 1840. She was known as the " Jessamy Bride " from verses written upon her by Goldsmith, with whom the Horneck family were very friendly.

Sat in January, 1767, as Miss Horneck. Exhibited at the Royal Academy in 1775, No. 230.

A critic, 1775, says: " That of *Mrs.* Horneck is also extremely beautiful, but is hung too near the skylight, which throws such a *glare* upon it as hurts the effect of the picture; surely this might have been altered."

Another critic, 1775, says : " No. 230 is Miss Horneck sitting as if in a Turkish mosque."

EXHIBITED.

British Institution, 1823, No. 9, by Mrs. Gwyn.

" " 1855, No. 121, by Sir Henry Edward Bunbury, Bart.

National Portrait Exhibition, 1867, No. 561, ⎫ by Sir Charles James Fox
Royal Academy, 1872, No. 15, ⎭ Bunbury, Bart.

ENGRAVED.

Richard Dunkarton, 1778, 18 × 14 in.

Charles A. Tomkins, 1866, 5¼ × 4¼ in.

An impression by Dunkarton sold in Paris in May, 1898, for 1,600 francs.

The picture was sold by Sir Henry Bunbury, Bart., to William Waldorf Astor, the present owner.

" Before the body (Goldsmith's) was buried, the Jessamy Bride and her sister turned from their family sorrows and scandals to pay a last tribute of affection to the poet. She had his coffin reopened and a lock cut from his head, which Mrs. Gwyn kept till she died, nearly seventy years after."—TOM TAYLOR, vol. ii., p. 71.

" Sir Joshua's bequest : ' To Mrs. Gwyn ; her own portrait, with a turban.' "—LESLIE AND TAYLOR's *Life of Reynolds*, vol. ii., p. 636.

Hoppner also painted a portrait of Mrs. Gwyn, now in the possession of Sir Charles Tennant, Bart.

A picture was sold at Christie's, June 15, 1810, Lot 35 (Caleb Whitefoord, owner), Miss Horneck, to Symmons, for £1 16s. Another picture was bought in at Christie's, February 26, 1880, Lot 102 (Fenton, owner), for £94 10s., described, Mrs. Gwyn in a turban and white dress trimmed with ermine.

HORTON, Mrs.

Formerly Nancy Parsons; married, in 1776, Charles, 6th Lord Maynard.

Sat in February, 1767, as Mrs. Horton (?), and January, 1769.

Note to the 1767 sitting: "This may be either Nancy Parsons or the handsome widow that married the Duke of Cumberland."—TOM TAYLOR, vol. i., p. 282.

"1769, Mrs. Horton, con copaiba senza giallo, giallo quando era finito de pingere, con lacca e giallo quasi solo, e poi glaze with ultramarine. Here successive glazings had been employed, first with yellow alone, then with lake, then yellow again, then ultramarine."

HORTOUN, Miss.

Paid for, January 19, 1767, Miss Hortoun, £26 5s.; 1767, Miss Hortoun, £26 5s.

HOUGHTON, Mr.

This was probably Henry Hoghton, of Hoghton Tower, co. Lancaster; born October 22, 1728; succeeded his uncle as 6th Baronet, February 23, 1768. He was for many years M.P. for Preston. Died March 9, 1795.

Sir James De Hoghton, Bart., writes, March 9, 1899: "I am sorry to say that all our family portraits were destroyed by fire in 1874 or 1875—the Pantechnicon fire."

In a grey coat.

Sold at Christie's, June 20, 1858, Lot 345 (Miss Colyear Dawkins, owner), for £5 10s., to Ripp.

HOUGHTON, Mrs.

This was probably Margaret, daughter of Edward Rigby, of Middleton. She was the second wife of Philip Hoghton, the father of the 6th Baronet of that name. She died February, 1795.

Paid for, December, 1773, by Mrs. Houghton, £52 10s.

HOUGHTON, Miss.

Probably Elizabeth, the only daughter of Henry Hoghton, by his first wife, Elizabeth Ashurst, of Hedingham Castle, Essex, who died in 1762. Her daughter married, July 15, 1783, Louis Majendie.

Sat in January, 1767.

HOWARD, The Hon. Edward.

Whole length, canvas.

Edward Howard was the only surviving son of Thomas Howard, the younger brother of Edward, 9th Duke of Norfolk, by Henrietta, daughter of Edward Blount, sister to the Duchess. He was born January 22, 1744, and died February 7, 1767.

The compilers must explain that the remark on page 693 about the son of the Earl of Effingham, applied to what was on this page before it was reprinted.

Paid for before 1760, Duke of Norfolk, for a whole length of Lord Howard, £50 8s.

He was evidently described as Lord Howard by Sir Joshua Reynolds in error.

HOWARD, General Sir George, K.B.

Half length, oval.

Colonel of the 1st Dragoon Guards, and Governor of Chelsea Hospital in 1768, and of Jersey until 1796; M.P. for Lostwithiel, March 31, 1761; Governor of Minorca, 1766; M.P. for Stamford, 1768 to 1796; Knight of the Bath, 1774; General in 1777; Field-Marshal, October 12, 1793; Privy Councillor, July 29, 1795. He married Elizabeth, daughter of Peter Beckford the elder, and widow of Thomas, 2nd Earl of Effingham; she died in 1774. He died July 16, 1796.

In uniform; breastplate appearing under the coat.

Sat in April, 1758, January, 1759, and March, 1762. Paid for, February 22, 1763, General Howard, £21.

ENGRAVED.

James Watson, 12 × 9¾ in., as George Howard, Esq., Lieut.-General of His Majesty's Forces, etc.

The picture has probably not got the star and ribbon of the Bath, as they are not in the first state of the engraving; they were added after 1774, together with the new title, Sir George Howard, LL.D., Knight of the Most Honourable Order of the Bath, etc.

HOWARD, Lady Caroline Isabella.

Whole length, canvas 55¼ × 44 in.

Daughter of Frederick, 5th Earl of Carlisle; born September 3, 1771; married, July 27, 1789, John, 1st Earl of Cawdor, and died in 1848.

When young; sitting in a landscape; cap and black mantilla; right arm extended to a vase of flowers, from which she is plucking a rose; landscape background.

Paid for, July, 1783, Lord Carlile, for Lady Caroline Howard, £73 10s.

That the portrait of Lady Caroline Howard was in the Royal Academy, 1779, No. 252, as a young lady, whole length, is confirmed by the critique of the "St. James's Chronicle," May 4, 1779:

"No. 252. A young lady; she is plucking a rose, but in what attitude we cannot conceive. She seems to be curtseying to the rose-bush, or to be deprived of the lower part of her limbs, and is a most unpleasing figure."

Her name does not appear among the sitters for 1779, but the diary for 1778 is missing. She would have been seven years of age then.

EXHIBITED.

British Institution, 1824, No. 162, as Lady Cawdor, ⎫
                             when a child,   ⎬ by the Earl of

  „   „   1851, No. 118, as Lady Caroline ⎪ Carlisle.
                             Howard,   ⎪
Irish Institution, Dublin, 1856, No. 20, as Lady ⎪
     Caroline Howard, afterwards Lady Cawdor, ⎭

ENGRAVED.

Val Green, 1778, 16⅞ × 13 in.

S. W. Reynolds, 5⅞ × 4⅛ in.

First State by Val Green sold at Christie's, Palmerston Collection, 1890, for £60 18s.

The picture belongs to the Earl of Carlisle, at Castle Howard.

HOWE, Admiral Lord, K.G.

Called by his men, "Black Dick;" took part in the Seven Years', the American, and the Revolutionary wars, winning a great victory over the French at Ushant in 1794. He was created Viscount Howe, April 20, 1782, and Earl of Howe, August 19, 1788 ; K.G., 1797; married, 1758, Mary, daughter of Chiverton Hartopp, of Welby, Notts ; died August 5, 1799.

Lord Fitzhardinge writes, June 24, 1898 : "There is also at Berkeley Castle a large portrait of Admiral 1st Lord Howe, which I bought at the sale of the late Admiral Sir W. P. P. Wallis at Funtington, about six years ago ; it is supposed to have been purchased by Sir W. Wallis at Devonport about 1856. I am told it is by Sir Joshua Reynolds in his early days."

The picture belongs to Lord Fitzhardinge.

HUDDESFORD, Rev. George, and JOHN CODRINGTON BAMFYLDE.

Three-quarter length, canvas 49 × 40 in.

The Rev. George Huddesford was the youngest son of the Rev. George Huddesford, President of Trinity College, Oxford ; he was educated at Winchester School, and at New College, Oxford, where he obtained a fellowship ; in 1804 he was presented to the vicarage of Loxley, Warwickshire. Mr. Huddesford was a pupil of Sir Joshua's ; in 1775 he sent three portraits to the Royal Academy, but his contributions from 1786 to 1810 were chiefly fruit-pieces. He died in London, October 7, 1809, in his fifty-ninth year.

"He published 'The Elements of General Knowledge,' called at Oxford 'The Elements of General Ignorance ;' and his last work, 'Emily,' procured him the name of 'Emily Kett.' The witty poems, 'Salmagundi,' were by him ; also 'The Barber's Nuptials,' and many fugitive pieces. He studied under Sir Joshua Reynolds, and had copied many of the President's pictures with some ability, having an intention of pursuing the arts ; but his talent was conspicuous in compositions of fruit, in which his representations of ripe peaches and rich grapes were inimitable. Sir George Beaumont had a fine specimen of this work he frequently allowed to be copied. Mr. Huddesford's appearance was peculiar, and his supposed resemblance to a horse was the occasion of much academical waggery—the letter-box was often filled with oats, and when he wished to have his portrait taken, he was sent to the famous Stubbs, the horse painter, who, on receiving him, and expecting to hear whether his commission was to be for a filly or a colt, was much surprised to find 'Kett' pompously announce that he expected the likeness to be in full canonicals."—*Book for a Rainy Day*, by JOHN THOMAS SMITH, pp. 80, 81.

John Codrington Warwick Bamfylde, third son of Sir Richard Warwick Bamfylde, Bart. ; born August 24, 1754 ; educated at the University of Cambridge ; in 1778 published his " Sonnets," which are described by Southey as " some of the most original in our language." The acquirements and intellectual powers of Bamfylde were of a high order, and his disposition most amiable. He became insane, and died in a lunatic asylum about the year 1796.

On the spectator's left is the Rev. George Huddesford, in a Vandyke dress ; the other is Mr. J. C. W. Bamfylde ; they are looking at a print of the Rev. Joseph Warton, who was Master of Winchester College, published in 1777 ; the latter gentleman holds a violin in his hand.

Sat in 1777. Paid for, October, 1778, Mr. Huddisford, for a picture of himself and Mr. Banfield, £105.

EXHIBITED.

British Institution, 1824, No. 172, as Mr. W. Bamfylde and Mr. Utterson, owner's name not given.

ENGRAVED.

A. N. Sanders, 1866, 6¼ × 4¾ in.

The picture was presented in 1866 to the National Gallery by Mrs. Plenge, in the name of her mother, Mrs. Martha Beaumont.

HUDDESFORD, Mrs.

Half length.

Wife of the Rev. George Huddesford, jun., author of " Salmagundi," " Topsey-Turvey," " Bubble and Squeak," etc.

Cloak trimmed with fur ; hands in a muff ; the face half turned to the spectator ; a black dog (head only) looking up at her.

Paid for, December 27, 1777, Mrs. Huddisfield, £20 ; 1778, Mrs. Huddesford, £17 7s.

Cotton says that the picture was in Mr. Yates's gallery in 1855.

Sold at Christie's, February 24, 1798, Lot 12 (Huddesford, owner), as a lady with a dog, for £4, purchaser's name not given ; and at Christie's, June 1, 1849, Lot 23 (Thomas Purvis, Q.C., owner), for £4 15s., to Anderson.

A Shedips 1853 property I Carman. Lot 17 point £14

ENGRAVED.

H. Meyer, 1850, 10¼ × 8¼ in., a private plate.

The picture belongs to F. Fleischmann.

HUDSON, Mr.

Paid for, 1766, Mr. Hudson, for prints and cleaning a picture, £9 19s. ; 1771, Mr. Hudson, of Yorkshire, for drapery, £10 10s.

HUDSON, Mrs.

Paid for, March 8, 1776, Mrs. Hudson, for draperies, £31 10s.

These receipts for draperies occur frequently in the ledgers, and it is difficult to understand to what they refer. They cannot be for payments to pupils, as the entries in these books refer exclusively to money received, and contain no entries of money expended. Probably they are extra receipts for additions to pictures.

HUGH, Mrs.

Sat in 1759.

HUGHES, Admiral Sir Edward, K.B.

Sat in January, 1758.

HUGHES, Admiral Sir Edward, K.B.

Whole length.

Son of Edward Hughes, of Hartingfordbury, Herts ; born 1717 ; Admiral, 1778 ; Knight of the Bath, December 9, 1778 ; died January 17, 1794.

"At his seat at Luxborough, full of years and honour, Sir Edward Hughes, K.B., Admiral of the Blue Squadron of His Majesty's Fleet. He had served in the Navy for more than half a century ; was made a lieutenant for his services at the taking of Porto Bello under Admiral Vernon, and served as captain under Admiral Boscawen at the taking of Louisbourg, and with Sir Charles Saunders at the taking of Quebec. As an admiral he commanded in chief in the East Indies during the late war, and supported the honour of his country in several actions with an active enemy, to whom he was always inferior in number of ships. In private life the goodness of his heart led him to acts of benevolence which remain recorded in the memory of many."—*Gentleman's Magazine*, 1794, p. 181.

In uniform, with star and ribbon of the Bath; right hand holding a staff and letter "On His Majesty's Service"; a fort and two ships in the distance.

Sat in 1786 and 1787.

Paid for, July 30, 1786, Sir Edward Hughs, whole length and a head,

Mr. Sharp,
Mr. Cuthbert,   £577 10s.
Capt. Gill,

ENGRAVED.

John Jones, 1786, 23 × 15 in.
Ridley, 1803, oval (in part), 3¼ × 3 in.

The picture was bequeathed by the admiral to Greenwich Hospital.

HUGHES, Admiral Sir Edward, K.B.

Sat in 1786 and 1787. Paid for, March, 1787, Sir Edward Hughes, given to the Imperial Ambassador, £52 10s.

The picture is now in the Picture Gallery at Buda Pesth; it came from the Esterhazy family.

HUGHES, Admiral Sir Edward, K.B.

Paid for, September 1, 1785, Mr. Robins for Sir Edward Hughs' picture, £52 10s.

HUME, Mr.

Paid for, April, 1788 [Sir Abraham Hume], for a copy of Mr. Hume, £26 5s.

This payment is evidently made by Sir Abraham, as it follows the entry for the picture of his daughter, but it cannot be for his own portrait, as Sir Joshua was familiar with his title; it might be for a copy of his father's portrait, who was only Mr. Abraham Hume when he married in 1746.

HUME, Hannah, Lady.

Hannah, youngest daughter of Sir Thomas Frederick, Bart.; married, October 8, 1746, Abraham Hume, Commissary-General of the Forces, afterwards Sir Abraham Hume, Bart., of Wormley Bury, Herts; he died October 10, 1772; she died January 23, 1771.

Paid for, October 11, 1760, Lady Hume, £42.

HUME, Sir Abraham, Bart., F.R.S.

Half length, oval, canvas 29¼ × 24¼ in.

The son of Abraham Hume, M.P. for Steyning in 1747, and for Tregony in 1761; born February 20, 1749; entered the Navy and served against the Dutch and French; succeeded his father, Sir Abraham Hume, of Wormley Bury, Herts, October 10, 1772; he was M.P. for Petersfield in 1774, and for Hastings, 1807 and 1812; F.R.S. 1775; was eminent as a patron of art and learning; an amateur painter; one of the founders of the British Institution in 1805; acquainted with all the dilettanti of the day, and an intimate friend of Sir Joshua's; died March 24, 1838.

Looking to the left; powdered hair; white cravat; white waistcoat; crimson coat, half open.

Sat in February, 1786, and January, 1789. Pocket-book of 1783 missing. Paid for, April 10, 1783, Sir Abraham Hume, £26 5s.; February, 1784, Sir Abraham Hume, £26 5s.

Exhibited at the Royal Academy in 1783, No. 160.

Morning Herald, 1783: "Sir Abraham Hume, who himself is a disciple of the pallet, has not received from the hand of painting the most grateful return for his liberality in her cause."

Morning Chronicle: "No. 160. Sir A. Hume is one of the best portraits in the room; when the attention of the spectator can be taken away from the more important parts of the picture, the drapery will well repay his regard. Velvet was never represented with more precise individual similitude."

Another authority calls No. 160, "Mr. Strahan."

EXHIBITED.

British Institution, 1813, No. 112, } by Sir Abraham Hume.
  „   „   1833, No. 28, }

  „   „   1838, No. 124, } by Viscount Alford.
  „   „   1843, No. 45, }

National Portrait Exhibition, 1868, No. 893, } by Earl Brownlow.
Grosvenor, 1884, No. 130, }

John, 2nd Earl Brownlow, married Sophia, second daughter of Sir Abraham Hume.

ENGRAVED.

J. Jones, 1783, 13¼ × 11 in.

C. H. Hodges, 1791, 11¼ × 9¼ in.

J. Lupton, 1814, 11¼ × 9¼ in.

G. Stodart, 8¼ × 6¼ in.

S. W. Reynolds, 5¼ × 4¼ in.

W. Sharp.

Unknown, 7¼ × 7 in.

The picture belongs to Earl Brownlow at Ashridge, Berkhampstead.

Sir Joshua in his will left "to Sir Abraham Hume the choice of any of my Claude Lorraines."

HUME, Sir Abraham, Bart.

Half length, canvas 27¼ × 21¼ in.

Replica.

Bequeathed to the National Gallery by Robert Vernon, No. 305 in the Catalogue.

The following portraits of Sir A. Hume have been sold at Christie's :

	Lot.		£	s.	d.	
1831, July 16.	76.	John Jackson, owner ; copy by Jackson	. 7	7	0	Hall.
1844, April 26.	465.	Briggs, owner ; copy by Briggs . .	. 1	8	0	Waters.
1847, April 24.	65.	Sharpe, owner ; the late Sir A. Hume .	. 15	4	6	Bought in.
1869, April 8.	190.	Phillips, owner ; Sir A. Hume . .	. 22	0	0	Colnaghi.

A small sketch is in the possession of Mrs. Thwaites.

HUME, Lady Amelia.

Half length, canvas 29 × 23 in.

Amelia, daughter of John Egerton, Bishop of Durham ; married, April 25, 1774, Sir Abraham Hume, Bart. On June 22, 1808, the King was graciously pleased to ordain and declare that . . . Dame Amelia Hume, wife of Sir Abraham Hume, Bart., only sister of the Earl of Bridgewater, shall enjoy the title and precedence as if her father, John, late Lord Bishop of Durham, had survived his cousin, Francis, late Duke of Bridgewater.

Sitting ; three-quarter face ; spaniel in her lap ; black mantilla ; white fichu ; hair curled.

Sat in March, 1760. 1760, Lady Hume, £42, first picture. A second picture, 1785, paid for, December, 1785, by Sir Abraham Hume, for Lady Hume, £52 10s. Exhibited in the Royal Academy, 1785, No. 23.

Morning Herald, 1785 : "No. 23, 'Portrait of a Lady,' is a good likeness of Lady Hume, but, from her fine figure, she should have sat for a full length."

EXHIBITED.

British Institution, 1813, No. 113,} by Sir Abraham Hume, Bart.
     "   "   1833, No. 32, }

     "   "   1843, No. 46, by Viscount Alford, M.P.

Grosvenor, 1884, No. 173, by Earl Brownlow.

ENGRAVED.

R. Edwards, 1795, 11¼ × 9¼ in.

The picture belongs to Earl Brownlow at Ashridge, Berkhampstead.

HUME, Sir Abraham and Lady.

Two small figures.

Bought in at Christie's, July 22, 1893, Lot 61, by the owner, Nutting, for £67 4s.

HUME, Miss Amelia, afterwards Lady Farnborough.

Amelia, daughter of Sir Abraham Hume; married, May 28, 1793, the Right Hon. Sir Charles Long, G.C.B., P.C., F.R.S., F.S.A., of Bromley Hill Place, co. Kent, who held several important public offices, and was raised to the peerage as Baron Farnborough in 1826. His lordship died January 17, 1838, left no issue, and the title became extinct.

Sat as Miss Hume in 1787, 1788, and 1789. Paid for, January, 1788, Sir Abraham Hume, for Miss Hume, £52 10s.

EXHIBITED.

British Institution, 1813, No. 61, as Mrs. Long, by the Right Hon. C. Long.

British Institution, 1850, No. 89, as Lady Farnborough, by Samuel Long.

Her younger sister married, July 24, 1810, Richard, 2nd Lord Brownlow.

A copy by Rising was put up at his sale at Christie's, as Mrs. Charles Long, after Sir Joshua Reynolds, May 2, 1818, Lot 84, and bought in for £5 5s.

HUME, David.

Scottish philosopher and historian; born 1711; died August 25, 1776, at Edinburgh.

Sold at Christie's, March 19, 1859, Lot 103 (Captain Davis, owner), for £4 15s., to B. B.

As there are no records of either sittings or payments, the picture must be considered as of doubtful authenticity.

HUMPHREY, Mr.

Sat in 1767 and 1771.

HUNT, Mr.

This is probably Vere Hunt, of Curragh, co. Limerick, eldest son of the Rev. Vere Hunt and Constantia, grand-daughter of William Fitzmaurice, Lord Kerry. He was born about 1712, and his son was created a baronet in 1784. The family in 1832 assumed by letters patent the surname and arms of De Vere only.

Sat in 1757.

HUNT, Mrs.

Probably Anne, daughter of Edmund Browne, who married, May 29, 1760, Vere Hunt, as his second wife.

Sat in April, 1761, and January, 1762. Paid for, April 27, 1761, Mrs. Hunt, £10 10s.; February, 1762, Mrs. Hunt, £10 10s.

Sir Stephen Edward de Vere writes, January 15, 1899: "There are at Curragh Chase portraits of Mr. Vere Hunt and his wife, but they have no pretension to be by Sir Joshua Reynolds."

HUNT, Mrs.

Sat in April, 1761, and January, 1762. Paid for, June 21, 1761, Mrs. Hunt with a vail, £10 10s.; 1762, Mrs. Hunt with a vail, £10 10s.

HUNTER, John.

Half length, canvas 50 × 45 in.

Born 1728; died 1793. Eminent surgeon, brought up a turner; came to London, 1748; was with the expedition to Belleisle in 1761; Surgeon-Extraordinary to George III., 1776; author of several works relating to his profession; his collection was bought for the nation for £15,000.

Seated, leaning on left hand; a table with a work on comparative anatomy open beside him; pen in right hand.

Sat in 1786, 1788, and 1789. Paid for, November, 1785, John Hunter, £52 10s.; June, 1786, John Hunter, £52 10s. Exhibited in the Royal Academy, 1786, No. 223, as "Portrait of a Gentleman," half length. "September, 1786, at work on Mr. Hunter after its return from the Exhibition."

Public Advertiser, 1786: "John Hunter strikes us as one of the greatest prodigies of perfection."

Morning Herald: "No. 223, a characteristic portrait of the scientific Dr. Hunter. This performance has considerable merit."

Public Advertiser: "Hunter, we hope, will be engraved."

"Both are very full half lengths—Joshua Sharpe's and John Hunter's. The lawyer's a calm, bland, sagacious face, the figure set in its square chair, with one hand resting on the thigh, the other supported by the table, as if collectedly listening to the statement of a case in consultation; the anatomist's, with the head raised, and abstracted eyes, as if following out some train of thought, closely linked and reaching far, till it can be fixed by the pen held in the relaxed hand. The mood of keen, close, connecting induction has never been so perfectly personified as in this figure. It looks as if the painter had been allowed to watch Hunter at work, himself unseen. In the careless custody of the College of Surgeons, the picture, a few months ago, appeared so irretrievably ruined by darkening and cracking, that the knowledge of what it had been seemed likely to be preserved to us only by Jackson's copy— acquired from Lady Bell by the trustees of the National Portrait Gallery—and Sharpe's admirable engraving. Thanks, however, to the intelligent and reverent pains of Mr. H. Farrer, the picture has been thoroughly cleaned, repaired, and relined, and now looks as it might have looked when fresh from the painter's easel. The dress is of dark crimson velvet; the picture is one of the most vigorous of the painter's best time. I have little doubt the whole is from his own hand down to the lower limbs of the skeleton and the anatomical preparations and drawings on the table. The story goes that, after the painter had made several ineffectual attempts of securing a pose, Hunter, fatigued, fell into a train of thought, and that Sir Joshua at once fixed him while thus absorbed in his own reflections."—LESLIE AND TAYLOR's *Life of Sir Joshua*, vol. ii., pp. 474, 475.

It seems probable that when John Hunter fell into deep thought Sir Joshua turned his canvas upside down and recommenced the picture. This is somewhat confirmed by the picture, which shows a thick cake of paint in a large patch between the legs, indicating where the first commenced head was painted out.

EXHIBITED.

British Institution, 1813, No. 38 (third catalogue), by Mrs. Hunter.

```
    „        „       1846, No. 14,                    ⎫
National Portrait Exhibition, 1867, No. 832,    ⎬  by the Royal College of
Royal Academy, 1873, No. 158,                   ⎭          Surgeons.
```

ENGRAVED.

William Sharp, 1788, $16\frac{1}{4} \times 13\frac{1}{4}$ in.

W. Sharp (head only), 1788, $5\frac{1}{4} \times 4\frac{1}{4}$ in.

J. Egan, $6 \times 4\frac{1}{4}$ in.

R. Cooper, 1814, $9 \times 7\frac{1}{4}$ in.

S. W. Reynolds (S. Cousins, R.A.), 5×4 in.

W. C. Collier.

R. Page, $5 \times 3\frac{1}{4}$ in.

S. Cousins, R.A., 1831.

W. O. Geller.

A First State by Sharp sold at Christie's, Buccleuch Collection, 1887, for £15 4s. 6d.

HUNTER, Doctor William.

Three-quarter length, canvas 50×40 *in.*

Scotch physician and surgeon; founder of the Hunterian Museum in Glasgow; born 1718; died 1783.

Standing, leaning with both hands on a table; pen in hand.

Paid for, November, 1789, Dr. Hunter, for Glascow, £105.

Public Advertiser, June 12, 1787 : " The Glasgow people begin to grow impatient for the head of Dr. Hunter to be painted for them by Sir Joshua."

The picture is now the property of the Hunterian Museum, and is No. 152 in the catalogue of the University of Glasgow.

There is a replica in the possession of the Faculty of Physicians at Glasgow.

Miss Murray

In a letter from James Connell and Sons, Glasgow, they say: "The Hunterian Museum was founded in 1812, and is located at the Glasgow University, Gilmore Hill. John Hunter was assistant to his distinguished brother, Dr. William Hunter. There is a portrait of the latter by Sir Joshua Reynolds, P.R.A., hanging in the museum. It is a half length of the three-quarter figure, standing, and painted about 1780. There is another portrait of Dr. William Hunter, aged about forty, by Robert Edge Pine, 1742, also in the museum."

HUNTER, Dr. William.

EXHIBITED.
British Institution, 1847, No. 140, by the Rev. R. F. Elwin.

"Doctor Hunter," sold at Christie's, May 2, 1865, Lot 58 (Lord Arran, owner), for £7, to Hawkins.

ENGRAVED.
Freeman (from the picture in the Hunterian Museum, Glasgow).
J. Smith, Edinburgh, for Dibdin's "Bibliographic (Northern) Tour."

HUNTER, Thomas Orby, M.P., and Lord of the Admiralty.

M.P. for Winchelsea; died October 20, 1769.

Sat in July, 1760. Paid for, 1760, Mr. and Mrs. and Miss Hunter, £100.

None of the Orby Hunter portraits have been exhibited.

HUNTER, Mrs.

Sat in April, 1758. Appears to be paid for, 1760, by Mr. Hunter. *See* previous name. This was his first wife.

HUNTER, Mrs. Orby.

Half length, canvas 30 × 25 *in.*

Jacomina Bellenden, daughter of Colonel Bellenden, second wife of Thomas Orby Hunter.

Sold at Christie's, June 6, 1856, Lot 540, as Mrs. Orby Hunter, very elegant (Rutley, owner), for £105, to Pennell. May 28, 1892, Lot 91, described as above (Egremont Collection, Wyndham), for £105, to Williams. Picture described as from the Goodricke Collection, 1842.

The Right Hon. James Fortescue married Henrietta, eldest daughter of T. Orby Hunter, and their second daughter, Charlotte, married Sir Harry Goodricke, Bart.

Memo.: "Mrs. Hunter's picture to be sent to Waverley Abbey, Farnham, Surrey."

HUNTER, Mrs. Orby, and her Son.

Sold at Greenwood's, April 16, 1796, Lot 29, Mrs. Orby Hunter and son, for £32 11s., to Huddesford. Christie's, February 24, 1798, Lot 80 (Huddesford, owner), for £10 10s., purchaser's name not given.

HUNTER, Miss Mary Henrietta Orby.

Eldest daughter of Thomas Orby Hunter. *See* MRS. FORTESCUE, *ante*, p. 327.

HUNTER, Miss Georgiana Orby.

Second daughter of Thomas Orby Hunter.

Sat in February, 1760, and March, 1761, as Miss Hunter.

Sold in Paris, 1872, Persigny Sale, for 2,300 francs.

HUNTER, Miss B.

Daughter of Thomas Orby Hunter.

Sat in July, 1760.

HUNTER, Miss Charlotte.

Daughter of Thomas Orby Hunter.

Sat in July, 1760, as Miss Charlotte Hunter.

HUNTER, Miss Kitty, afterwards Mrs. Clarke.

This lady, the "Kitty Hunter" of Horace Walpole's letters, was a younger daughter of Thomas Orby Hunter, of Croyland Abbey, Lincolnshire, one of the Lords of the Admiralty. She was maid of honour to Queen Charlotte, and acquired considerable notoriety through her elopement with Lord Pembroke, from a masked ball at Lord Middleton's in February, 1762. By him she became the mother of Colonel Montgomery, who was shot in a duel with Captain Macnamara in 1803. She subsequently married Captain Clarke, afterwards Field-Marshal Sir Alured Clarke, G.C.B., who died in 1832.

Sat in April, 1757, and February, 1758. Paid for, 1762, Miss Hunter, £15 15s.

EXHIBITED.

Suffolk Street, 1833, No. 187, by T. Orby Hunter, as Mrs. Clarke.

British Institution, 1856, No. 160, by Robert Crawfurd, as Miss Hunter.

R. B. Parkes, 1865, 4¼ × 4 in.

It is surmised that the picture was painted after the elopement, and that the mask was an allusion to the masked ball at Lord Middleton's on the day preceding the event referred to. She gave the picture to Gibbs Crawfurd, of Saint Hill, Sussex, from whom it passed to his grandson, Robert Crawfurd, of Colchester, the present owner.

"I find an entry in the pocket-book for Thursday, just a week after the elopement : 'Send Miss Hunter packed up to the Admiralty.' The picture was going home to her father, who, if he gave house-room to the picture, refused it to his daughter when the runaways were captured on their way to France. This may have been the fine picture in Mr. Crawfurd's possession."—TOM TAYLOR, vol. i., p. 207.

"On the 18th February, 1762, Miss Charlotte (sic) Hunter, daughter of Mr. Orby Hunter, M.P. for Winchelsea and a Lord of the Admiralty, a frequent sitter in 1761, had eloped with my Lord Pembroke, another of the painter's sitters and acquaintances. Miss Hunter was already in the mouth of the town, and Walpole calls her 'a miss' and speaks of her as 'Kitty Fisher.' This elopement created what Walpole calls 'an enragement.' 'In all your reading, true or false,' he asks Montagu, 'have you ever heard of a young earl, married to the most beautiful woman in the world, a Lord of the Bedchamber, a general officer, and with a great estate, quitting everything, resigning wife and world, and embarking for life in a packet boat with a miss ?'"—LESLIE AND TAYLOR'S *Life of Sir Joshua*, vol. i., pp. 206, 207.

"There is another picture of the lady, very beautiful, and the face younger than in Mr. Crawfurd's picture, which may have been the picture for which a Miss Hunter sat in 1758. This picture is now (December, 1861) in the possession of Beriah Bodfield."—TOM TAYLOR, vol. i., p. 208, note.

HUNTINGDON, Francis, 10th Earl of, F.R.S.

Three-quarter length, canvas 49¼ × 38¼ in.

Born April 5, 1729 ; Master of the Horse, November, 1756, and carried the sword of state at the coronation of George III., September 22, 1761 ; succeeded to the earldom, October 13, 1745 ; died October 2, 1789, suddenly, while sitting at table in the house of his nephew, Lord Rawdon.

Standing, three-quarter face to left ; wears a small wig, with black ribbons hanging down behind, blue waistcoat, black necktie, and wrist frills ; ornamented coat with deep cuffs ; left hand on hip, hat in right ; gilt column and red curtain in background.

Sat in 1754. Paid for, July, 1754, Lord Huntingdon, £21. Frame to half length of Ld. Huntn. that was sent to Ireland, £6 6s.

R. B. Parkes, 1874, 5¼ × 4¼ in.

The picture belonged to the Marquess of Hastings, and passed from him to his sister, the Countess of Loudoun, who owned it in 1874. It was afterwards bought from the family by Mr. McLean, who sold it to M. Charles Sedelmeyer, of Paris, from whom it passed to M. Ed. André, of Paris, the present owner.

"The barony of Hastings was originally created by King John. The ancestor from whom he inherited it was executed by Richard III. They were descended from the Plantagenets, and the family was most unfortunate. The Duke of Gloucester was strangled at Calais; the Duke of Clarence was put to death in the Tower; the Countess of Salisbury, his daughter, was beheaded, as was also her son, Lord Montacute; Henry, Duke of Buckingham, was beheaded by Richard III.; and Robert, Earl of Essex, died on a scaffold. The founder of the Huntingdon family, William, Lord Hastings, lost his head in the Tower by order of Richard III. . . .

"The late earl was a man whose virtues would reflect honour on his ancestors, had they been, if possible, more noble than they were. . . . His remains were interred with great pomp in the family vault at Ashby-de-la-Zouche, Lord Rawdon acting as chief mourner."—*Gentleman's Magazine*, 1789, p. 961.

HUNTINGDON AND STORMONT, Lords.

Whole length.

Sat in 1753 and 1754.

"The young Lords Huntingdon and Stormont, just arrived from their travels, sat to him for two whole lengths on one canvas; and here his merit in drawing complete figures and setting them well on their legs, in the attitude most natural to them, was equally conspicuous."—TOM TAYLOR, vol. i., p. 109. *See* STORMONT.

"There are new young lords, fresh and fresh: two of them are much in vogue, Lord Huntingdon and Lord Stormont. I supped with them t'other night at Lady Caroline Petersham's. The latter is most cried up; but he is the more reserved, seems shy, and to have sense, but I should not think extreme, yet it is not fair to judge a silent man at first. The other is very lively and agreeable."—WALPOLE to MONTAGU, December 6, 1753.

The Earl of Mansfield writes, December 5, 1898, that he has not got this picture.

HURRELL, Miss Phillis, afterwards Mrs. Froude.

Half length, canvas 35¼ × 27¼ *in.*

Mother of Archdeacon Richard Hurrell Froude, who died in 1836.

Full face, seated; blue dress, quilted, with bows in front; white satin mantle trimmed with lace over her shoulders; playing a mandoline; dark high hair with no ornaments.

Sat in 1762 as Miss Hurrell. Paid for, June 9, 1762, Miss Hurrell, £15 15s.

EXHIBITED.

Royal Academy, 1876, No. 237, as Miss Phillis Hurrell (Mrs. Froude), by W. Froude. *Scr* *.....* *.. .. 400*

The picture belongs to Charles J. Wertheimer.

HURRELL, Miss Margaret, afterwards Mrs. Bridge.

A portrait described as Miss Margaret Hurrell, daughter of Allen Hurrell, of Harston, Cambridgeshire, in a blue dress, married John L. Bridge, died 1778, 29½ × 24 in., sold at Christie's, February 29, 1896, Lot 72 (owner's name not given), for £22 1s., to Osborne.

Mr. Bridge was probably of the firm of Bridge and Rundell, silversmiths to George III.

HURST, Miss.

Sold at Greenwood's, April 14, 1796, Lot 26, for £1, to Bacon.

HUSSEY, Mrs.

Sat in 1760. Paid for before 1760, Mrs. Hussy, £21.

HUTCHINSON, Right Hon. John Hely.

Three-quarter length, canvas 50 × 40 in.

Son of Francis Hely, of Gertrough ; born 1715 ; educated at Trinity College, Dublin ; called to the Bar, 1748 ; assumed the name of Hutchinson ; Provost of Trinity College ; Secretary of State for Ireland and Keeper of the Privy Seal ; Lord of the Privy Council, and held besides several minor appointments. He was always obtaining lucrative positions for his family and friends, and his importunity was such that it was said Lord North, on his applying for some new place, observed, " If England and Ireland were given to this man, he would solicit the Isle of Man for a potato garden." He married, June 8, 1751, Christiana, daughter of Lorenzo Nickson, of Munny, co. Wicklow, and niece and heiress of Richard Hutchinson, of Knocklofty, co. Tipperary. She was created Baroness Donoughmore, October 18, 1783. He died September 5, 1794.

Seated, in scarlet robes, at a table covered with green cloth.

Paid for, May, 1779, Hely Hutchinson, Provost of Dublin, £75.

EXHIBITED.
National Portrait Exhibition, 1867, No. 768, by the Countess of Donough-more.

ENGRAVED.
James Watson, 1778, 16 × 12⅞ in.
S. W. Reynolds, 3¼ × 2¼ in.
G. H. Every, 1866, 5¼ × 4 in.

"In Dublin, aged seventy-nine, Right Hon. John Hely Hutchinson, M.P. for the city of Cork, Provost of Trinity College, Dublin, and LL.D., one of the most extraordinary characters, perhaps, that ever existed."—*Gentleman's Magazine*, 1794, p. 867.

The above notice contains a long account of his adventures in connection with the society of "Celibacy of Fellows."

A portrait of John Hely Hutchinson was bought in at Christie's, January 2, 1869, Lot 114, by the owner, S. Midgley, for £3.

The picture belongs to the Earl of Donoughmore.

HUTCHINSON, Right Hon. John Hely.

Head size, canvas 30 × 25 *in.*

A replica of the head of the previous portrait.

EXHIBITED.
Dublin, 1872, No. 161, by Trinity College, Dublin.

HUTCHINSON, Mrs., afterwards Baroness Donoughmore.

Three-quarter length, canvas 49¼ × 39¼ *in.*

Christiana, daughter of Lorenzo Nickson, of Munny, and heiress to her uncle, Richard Hutchinson, of Knocklofty; she married, June 8, 1751, John Hely, who upon his marriage assumed the additional surname of Hutchinson. She was created Baroness Donoughmore of Knocklofty, October 16, 1783, and died June 24, 1788. She was succeeded by her son, Richard, afterwards created Earl of Donoughmore.

Standing, with right arm leaning on a pedestal; white dress with dark sash; ermine-trimmed cloak held by left hand; column and green curtain in background.

Sat in November, 1766, as Mrs. Hutchinson. Paid for, October 21, 1770, Mrs. Hutchinson, £70.

EXHIBITED.
National Portrait Exhibition, 1867, No. 769, by the Countess of Donoughmore.

ENGRAVED.
G. H. Every, 1866, 5¼ × 3⅞ in.

The picture belongs to the Earl of Donoughmore.

The originals of the last two portraits were sold at Christie's, June 10, 1899 (Earl of Donoughmore, owner), John Hely Hutchinson, Lot 92, for £1,312, to Agnew; Mrs. Hutchinson, Lot 93, for £2,415, to Tooth.

HUTCHINSON, Richard Hely.

Three-quarter length, canvas 50 × 40 in.

Born January 29, 1756; succeeded his mother as Baron Donoughmore, June 24, 1788; was created Viscount Donoughmore on November 7, 1797, and Earl of Donoughmore, December 29, 1800. He was a Lieutenant-General in the army, and Governor of Tipperary, and one of the peers elected for life to represent the Irish peerage in the British House of Lords. He was created a peer of the empire as Viscount Hutchinson of Knock-lofty, June 14, 1821. He died, unmarried, August 22, 1825.

Full face; standing in a red uniform; right hand extended; left hand holding the hilt of his sword; wearing a black stock; tree to the left.

Painted about 1778. Diary missing for that year.

The picture was sold by the Earl of Donoughmore to Charles John Wertheimer, the present owner.

HUTCHINSON, John Hely.

Three-quarter length, canvas 50 × 40 in.

Born May 15, 1757; Major of the 77th regiment of Foot, September 21, 1781; Lieutenant-Colonel of the same regiment, March 21, 1783; Major-General, August 5, 1799; Lieutenant-General and Commander-in-Chief in Egypt, in May, 1801; created a Knight of the Bath, May 28, 1801. He was M.P. for the county of Cork. On the death of Sir Ralph Abercromby at the battle of Aboukir the chief command fell to General Hutchinson. Under him the French were driven from Rosetta, and, finally, from Alexandria, on September 2, 1801. For these services Sir John Hutchinson was created Lord Hutchinson of Alexandria, December 5, 1801. He succeeded as 2nd Earl of Donoughmore, August 22, 1825. He died June 29, 1832, and was succeeded by his nephew.

In a red uniform, with a white waistcoat and black stock; pointing to the right; holding a gun in his left hand; wearing a sword and bayonet; a black busby is on a pedestal, with a vase behind; sky background.

Painted about 1778. Diary missing for that year.

The picture was sold by the Earl of Donoughmore to Charles John Wertheimer, the present owner.

HYNDFORD, John, 3rd Earl of, K.T.

Born March 15, 1701; Lord-Lieutenant, county of Lanark, 1739; Envoy Extraordinary in 1741 to the King of Prussia; was successful in negotiating the peace between that monarch and the Queen of Hungary and Bohemia, signed at Breslau, 1742, for which he received several distinctions; Ambassador to the court of Vienna from 1752 to 1764; married, first, 1732, Elizabeth, daughter of Sir Cloudesley Shovel, and widow of Robert, 1st Lord Romney, and, secondly, in 1756, Jean, daughter of Benjamin Vigor. He died July 19, 1767.

Sat in April, 1757.

Memo., 1757: " Send home Lord Hyndford in Savil Row with a receipt."

On the death of the 6th and last Earl of Hyndford in 1817 the great family estates of Carmichael devolved on Sir John Anstruther, Bart., the heir-general of the house of Carmichael.

The picture belongs to Sir Windham Carmichael-Anstruther, Bart., at Carmichael House, Thankerton, Lanarkshire.

HYNDFORD, Jean, Countess of.

Three-quarter length, canvas 29¼ × 24¼ in.

Only daughter of Benjamin Vigor, of Fulham, co. Middlesex; second wife of John, 3rd Earl of Hyndford; married, December, 1756; died at Carmichael House, in Scotland, February 8, 1807, aged eighty.

Sitting; pearl earrings, with a bow at the back of the neck; dress trimmed with lace, and large lace sleeves; she is holding a shuttle, on which she is winding thread from a ball in her lap.

Sat in 1757.

ENGRAVED.

J. McArdell, 1759, 10⅞ × 8⅞ in.

The picture belonged to Mons. Jules Porges, of Paris; it was purchased from him in 1890 by M. Charles Sedelmeyer, who sold it to David H. King, of New York.

There is a portrait of the Countess of Hyndford in the possession of Sir Windham Carmichael-Anstruther, Bart., but it is uncertain whether it is by . Sir Joshua Reynolds.

ILCHESTER, Stephen, 1st Earl of.

Half length, canvas 36 × 30 *in.*

Son of Sir Stephen Fox; born about 1704; was M.P. for Shaftesbury, April, 1726; created Lord Ilchester and Baron Strangways, May 11, 1741, and Earl of Ilchester, June 5, 1756. He was constituted, June 23, 1747, one of the two Comptrollers of the Accounts of the Army, and was made a member of the Privy Council, April 22, 1763. He married, March, 1736, Elizabeth Horner, only daughter and heiress of Thomas Strangways Horner, of Mells Park, co. Somerset, and on his marriage assumed the additional surname and arms of Strangways. He died September 26, 1776.

Sat in 1762. Paid for, April 16, 1762, Lord Ilchester, £21.

The picture belongs to the Earl of Ilchester at Melbury, Dorchester.

ILCHESTER, Maria Theresa, Countess of, and Children.

Whole length, canvas 83 × 58 *in.*

Mary Theresa, daughter of Standish Grady, of Cappercullen, co. Limerick, Ireland; married, August 26, 1772, Henry Thomas, 2nd Earl of Ilchester. She died June, 1790.

Elizabeth Theresa Fox Strangways, born November 16, 1773; married, first, April 17, 1796, William Davenport Talbot, and secondly, April 24, 1804, Captain Charles Fielding, R.N. She died 1840.

Mary Lucy Fox Strangways, born February 11, 1776; married, February 1, 1794, Thomas Mansel Talbot; secondly, April 28, 1815, Sir Christopher Cole, Captain R.N., K.C.B. Died February 3, 1855.

Seated, facing the spectator; the two children stand one on each side of her, playing across her knees with a skein of wool; all dressed in white; landscape seen through open window to the right.

Sat in March, 1779.

British Institution, 1861, No. 84,
National Portrait Exhibition, 1867,
    No. 847,
Royal Academy, 1884, No. 16,
Grafton, 1895, No. 139,
} by the Marquess of Lansdowne.

Bought in at Greenwood's, April 16, 1796, Lot 56, for £92 8s., by Marchi, and sold at Christie's, May 18, 1821, Lot 72 (Thomond sale), for £74 11s. (Lady Ilchester, sitting between her two children, size of life), to the Marquess of Lansdowne.

G. H. Every, 1868, 7¼ × 5 in.

The picture belongs to the Marquess of Lansdowne, and is No. 54 in the Lansdowne catalogue. *See also* STRANGWAYS.

Lady Louisa Fox Strangways, the fifth daughter of the Earl of Ilchester, married the 3rd Marquess of Lansdowne.

INCHBALD, Mrs. Elizabeth.

Head size, canvas, oval, 27 × 22 in.

Actress, dramatist, and novelist.

Elizabeth Simpson, daughter of a respectable farmer at Stanningfield, Suffolk ; born 1753. She came to London at the age of sixteen to adopt the stage as a profession ; married Mr. Inchbald, the actor, and performed with him in Scotland and York ; after his death she joined the Covent Garden company, and retired in 1789. She wrote numerous comedies and farces, and her "Simple Story" and "Nature and Art" rank high as works of fiction. She died in 1821.

In a black dress and Vandyke cuffs, with a large white veil ; leaning on her right arm, with a letter in her left hand, in a contemplative attitude.

Sold at Christie's, March 16, 1850, Lot 44 (Winstanley, owner), for £53 11s., to Lord Normanton.

The picture belongs to the Earl of Normanton, and is No. 54 in the Somerley catalogue.

INCHIQUIN, Mary, Countess of, afterwards Marchioness of Thomond. *See* MISS MARY PALMER.

Supposed to have sat for "Hope nursing Love." *See* MISS MORRIS.

INGLETT, Rev. Mr.

Took the name of Fortescue. Date and initials on the picture : " J. R. 1754."

INGRAM, Mr.

Probably William Ingram, of Wakefield.

Sat in March, 1762.

Mem., 1759 : " Mr. Ingram, Wakefield, to be sent to 'Swan with Two Necks,' Ladd Lane."

INGRAM, Mrs.

Sat in April, 1759.

INGRAM, Miss.

Three-quarter length, canvas 50 × 40 in.

Daughter of William Ingram, of Wakefield, co. York ; born 1733 ; died, unmarried, 1785.

Walking towards the left on a terrace ; her left hand extended and resting on a large vase, right hand on her hip ; dressed in long-waisted dress fastened with pearls, with large pearl brooch ; long train supported under right hand ; lace and pearls in high, dark hair ; veil hanging over both shoulders ; column to right ; sky and flowers to left.

Sat in 1757.

EXHIBITED.

British Institution, 1863, No. 108, as " Portrait of Lady," by H. F. Ingram.

ENGRAVED.

G. H. Every, 1864, 5¼ × 4 in.

The picture belonged in 1864 to Hugh Francis Meynell Ingram, of Paulett House, Lyme, Dorsetshire.

INGRAM, Miss Isabella. *See* LADY BEAUCHAMP, *ante*, page 67.

INGRAM-SHEPHERD, Hon. Frances, afterwards Lady William Gordon.

Head size, canvas, oval, 24 × 18 in.

Hon. Frances Ingram-Shepherd, second daughter of Charles Ingram, 10th Lord Irvine ; married, March 6, 1781, Lord William Gordon, second son of Cosmo George, 3rd Duke of Gordon. She was the mother of the child who sat for the " Angels' Heads."

Full face ; black mantilla ; white cap.

Painted 1779 (Grosvenor Catalogue).

Sat in 1780. Paid for, December 1, 1781, Hon. Miss Ingram, Lady G. Gordon, £52 10s. This is an error, as Lord G. Gordon died unmarried ; it should have been Lady W. Gordon.

EXHIBITED.

Grosvenor, 1884, No. 35, as Lady William Gordon, by the Marquess of Hertford.

ENGRAVED.

J. R. Smith, 1780, 13¼ × 11 in.
S. W. Reynolds, 3¼ × 2¼ in.

A First State by Smith sold in the Buccleuch Collection in 1887 for £44 2s.

The picture belongs to the Marquess of Hertford.

INNES-NORCLIFFE, Sir James, Bart., afterwards 5th Duke of Roxburghe.

Half length, oval.

Sir James Innes-Norcliffe, Bart., born January 10, 1736 ; married, first, in 1769, Mary, daughter of Sir John Wray, Bart. He took the name of Norcliffe on Lady Innes inheriting the estates of her maternal ancestors by the will of Thomas Norcliffe. He married, secondly, July 28, 1807, Harriet, daughter of Benjamin Charlewood, of Windlesham. Sir James established his claim to the dukedom of Roxburghe, and became 5th Duke in 1812. His grace died July 19, 1823.

In square border, looking to left ; coat with fur collar.

1763, Sir James Innis, three payments each of £21 (erased) ; April 14' 1770, Sir James Innis, £105.

ENGRAVED.

Val Green, 1807, 14 × 11¼ in.

INNES, Lady Mary.

Mary, daughter of Sir John Wray, Bart.; married, 1769, Sir James Innes-Norcliffe, Bart., afterwards 5th Duke of Roxburghe. She died in 1807.

Sat in November, 1767, as Miss Wray, and April, 1769, as Lady Innis.

These two pictures are not in the possession of the Duke of Roxburghe.

IRBY, The Hon. Frederick, afterwards 2nd Lord Boston.

Head size, canvas 30 × 25 in.

Born June 9, 1749; was at Eton under Dr. Foster, who was Head Master from 1765 to 1773; he married, May 15, 1775, Christiana, only daughter of Paul Methuen; he died March 23, 1825.

The picture, which was presented to Dr. Foster, is now in the Provost's Lodge, Eton College.

IREMONGER, Mr.

Probably Lascelles Iremonger.

Sat in 1758.

IREMONGER, Mrs.

Sat in 1757.

IRVINE, Charles, 10th Viscount.

Charles Ingram, 10th Viscount Irvine; chosen one of the representative peers of Scotland in 1768; married, 1756, Miss Shepherd; died at Temple Newsham, June 27, 1778, when the peerage became extinct.

Sat in 1765 and 1771 as Lord Irwin. Paid for, June 17, 1772, Lord Irwin, £36 15s.; Do. for a shepherd boy, £52 10s.

Mem., June 29, 1772: "Lord Irwin, Temple Newsham, near Leeds, Yorkshire. His Lordship's picture and the Shepherd boy to be sent."

509

IRVINE, Frances, Viscountess.

As a shepherdess.

Miss Shepherd, a lady of fortune, married, in 1756, Charles Ingram, 10th Viscount Irvine.

No sitting recorded for this picture.

" Lord Hertford afterwards gave it (Baretti's portrait) to Henry Richard, Lord Holland, in exchange for a portrait of Lady Irwin, Lord Hertford's grandmother."—*Holland House*, by PRINCESS LIECHTENSTEIN, vol. ii., p. 43.

A picture of Frances, Viscountess Irvine, belongs to Sir John Ramsden, Bart., at Bulstrode.

IRWIN, Colonel John, afterwards Sir John Irwin, K.B.

Colonel of the Third Regiment of Horse on the Irish establishment ; Governor of Gibraltar in 1762, when Major-General ; General, February 19, 1783 ; K.B., December 15, 1775 ; died at Brussels, 1788.

Sat in 1761. Paid for, 1761, Coll. Erwin, £10 10s.; February 23, 1764, Coll. Erwin, £10 10s.

IRWIN, Mrs.

Half length, oval.

Wife of General, afterwards Sir John Irwin, Governor of Gibraltar ; died August 12, 1767.

Front face, leaning on her arms, which are crossed in front ; hair combed back and tied with black ribbon ; white sleeves ; nosegay in dress.

Sat in 1761. Paid for, 1761, Mrs. Erwin, £10 10s.; February 23, 1764, Mrs. Erwin, £10 10s.

ENGRAVED.

J. Watson, 10¼ × 8¼ in.
    „   6 × 4¼ in.
S. W. Reynolds, 3⅞ × 3¼ in.

JACKSON, Mr.

Sat in 1757.

JACKSON, Mrs.

Sat in 1757.

JACOBS, Miss.

Kitcat, three-quarter length, canvas 36 × 27¼ in.

The Blue Lady.

Sitting in a chair, face nearly profile, looking down to left; hair turned up with pearls; a single row of pearls as a necklace; bouquet of flowers in her lap, left hand supporting them, right elbow on arm of chair; wide sleeves.

Painted in 1761. *See scale rec IV p. 1396.*

EXHIBITED.

Royal Academy, 1872, No. 50, "A lady in a blue dress," } by the Marquess of Hertford.
Grosvenor, 1884, No. 79, as Miss Jacobs, }

Sold at Greenwood's, April 15, 1796, Lot 14, as Miss Jacobs, Kitcat, for £12 12s., to the Marquess of Hertford.

ENGRAVED.

J. Spilsbury, 1762, 17¼ × 13¼ in.
R. Houston, 5¼ × 4¼ in., small octavo.

The Spilsbury print obtained the highest premium at the Society of Arts, and a First State of it, Buccleuch Collection, sold at Christie's in 1887 for £60 18s.

Her father was a medallist.

The picture was sold by the Marquess of Hertford to Charles John Wertheimer, from whom it passed to C. Whitney, of New York.

JAMES, William.

Three-quarter length, canvas 50 × 40 in.

In light coat, embroidered lapels and cuffs; lace cuffs; velvet waistcoat, embroidered; white necktie and lace frill; looking to the right; left hand leaning on a pedestal.

Supposed to be the costume of the Dunstable Hunt, but this is very doubtful. For the costume of this Hunt, *see* MARQUESS OF TAVISTOCK.

Sold at Christie's, December 6, 1884, Lot 238, "portrait of a Mr. James, described by Tom Taylor, painted 1758" (William Russell, owner), for £39 18s., to Lesser.

The picture was afterwards purchased, about 1891, for the Dresden Gallery. It is No. 798c in the Dresden Catalogue of 1896.

Memo., November, 1759: "Mr. James, white coat, bath cloth, blue lapels, blue waist-coat, embroidered button holes."
"A portrait with this dress was in the possession of William Russell, of Chesham Place." —TOM TAYLOR, vol. i., p. 178.

JAMES, William.

Sat in 1757 and 1759. 1762, Mr. James, and for drapery to a half length, £21.

The picture belonged to C. T. C. James, The Grove, Langley, Slough.

JAMES, Mrs.

Head size, canvas 30 × 25 in.

As a Madonna.

Looking over her left shoulder; a veil over the back of her head.

Sat in June, 1759.

ENGRAVED.

T. Blackmore, 14¼ × 11 in.
S. W. Reynolds, 4 × 3¼ in.
Unknown, etching for the Grosvenor Gallery, 23 × 18 in.

The picture belonged to C. T. C. James, The Grove, Langley, Slough.

There seems to have been two pictures of this subject. The etching was made from the second picture, then in Earl Grosvenor's gallery. *See* HARTLEY, *ante*, p. 447.

The pocket-book of 1759 gives Mrs. James (as a Madonna), said to be

painted for Ed. Burke, but the picture in his sale at Christie's, June 5, 1812, Lot 77, is described "A female head," bought by Earl Grosvenor for £32 11s.; in the British Institution, 1813, No. 117, First Catalogue, Earl Grosvenor exhibits, "Mrs. Hartley as a Madonna."

JAMES, William.

The picture described at the top of page 512 was bought in at Christie's, March 6, 1863, Lot 86 (William Russell, owner), as "a gentleman in a drab coat and blue waistcoat, leaning on a pedestal, perhaps Mr. James," for £17 1s.

JAMES, Sir William, Bart., F.R.S.

Three-quarter length.

The hero of Fort Goriah; a commodore in the East India Company's navy; conqueror of Angria, the great Indian pirate; created a baronet, 1778; Fellow of the Royal Society; one of the Governors of Greenwich Hospital; one of the Elder Brethren and Deputy Master of the Trinity House; one of the directors and deputy chairman of the East India Company, 1778 and 1781; chairman, 1779; M.P. for West Looe, 1774 and 1781; died December 16, 1783.

In naval uniform; right hand on anchor, holding a scroll; left hand on his side; white cravat and frill; ruffles at his wrists.

Sat in April, 1780. Paid for, February, 1782, Sir William James, £105.

EXHIBITED.
British Institution, 1861, No. 211, by Sir Richard Levinge, Bart.

ENGRAVED.
J. R. Smith, 1783, 15¼ × 12⅞ in.
S. W. Reynolds (S. Cousins, R.A.), 3¼ × 2¼ in.
Ridley, small oval.

The print by Smith, dedicated to Trinity House, was described as from the picture belonging to the Corporation.

JAMES, Sir William, Bart.

Paid for, July, 1784, Lady James, for a copy of Sir William, £52 10s.

This is probably one of the two pictures described above.

JEFFRIES, Mr.

Sat in March, 1759.

513   3 U

JEKYLL, Colonel. *See* GEAKLE, *ante,* page 354.

JENKINSON, Charles, afterwards 1st Earl of Liverpool.
Three-quarter length, canvas 50 × 40 *in.*

Eldest son of Col. Charles Jenkinson ; born May 16, 1727 ; educated at the Charterhouse ; married, first, Amelia, daughter of William Watts, Governor of Fort William in Bengal (she died in 1770) ; secondly, in 1782, Catherine, daughter of Sir Cecil Bisshopp, Bart., relict of Sir Charles Cope, Bart., and mother of the Duchess of Dorset and the Countess of Aboyne. He died December 17, 1808. *See also* BUTE, *ante,* p. 135.

The picture at one time belonged to M. Charles Sedelmeyer, of Paris, and was sold by him to Ogden Goelet, of New York.

JENKINSON, Charles.

One of the Under Secretaries of John, 3rd Earl of Bute, whose full-length picture Sir Joshua painted, which represents the Earl in a suit of blue velvet, richly laced with gold, receiving papers from one of his Under Secretaries, Charles Jenkinson. *See* BUTE, *ante,* p. 135.

JENISON, Ralph.

Master of the Buckhounds to George III. ; M.P. for Northumberland, February 20, 1723 ; August 29, 1727 ; May 16, 1734 ; and M.P. for Newport, Isle of Wight, July 2, 1747, and April 18, 1754. The name in 1747 is spelt Jennison.

Paid before 1760, Mr. Jennison, for P. Fisher, £18 18*s.*

Lord Granby also gave his portrait to P. Fisher at the same time. *See* GRANBY, *ante,* p. 381.

JENYNS, Soame.
Half length.

Only son of Sir Roger Jenyns ; born 1704 ; M.P. for Cambridge from 1741 to 1780 ; supported Walpole and every other minister for the time being ; he was for a short time M.P. for Dunwich in 1754 ; author of the " Origin of Evil " and other works ; a shrewd, witty man ; died 1787.

Left elbow resting on a table, the hand up to the face ; white cravat ; lace ruffles ; books on table to his left.

Sat in 1757 as Mr. Jennings.

"Died, July 30, 1753, wife of Soame Jenyns, member for Cambridgeshire."—*Gentleman's Magazine,* 1753, p. 392.

W. Dickinson, 1776, 12¼ × 10 in.

W. Angus, 1791, 3⅞ × 3¼ in.

S. W. Reynolds, 2¼ × 2 in.

Dr. Hamilton names George Jenyns as the owner of the picture. It belongs now to Lord Robartes at Lanhydrock, Cornwall.

JERMAN, Mr.

Sat in May, 1760, as Mr. Germain. Paid for before 1761, Mr. Jerman, £21. Frame paid, £3 3s.

Sold at Chancery Lane, July 24, 1895, by Morris and Co., in bankruptcy (the Rev. W. T. Kevill-Davies, owner), no price given.

JERMAN, Mrs.

Sat in May, 1760, as Mrs. Germain. Paid for before 1761, Mrs. Jerman, £21. Frame paid, £3 3s.

Sold by Morris and Co., Chancery Lane, London, July 24, 1895, in bankruptcy (the Rev. W. T. Kevill-Davies, owner), no price recorded.

"Died, November 23, 1761, Lady of Geo. German, of Soho."—*Gentleman's Magazine*, 1761, p. 539.

JERMAN, Miss Anna.

Sat in May, 1760, as Miss Anna Germain. Paid for before 1761, Miss Jerman, £21. Frame paid, £3 3s.

Sold at Christie's, July 9, 1887, Lot 145 (Davies, owner), for £168, to Agnew.

JERSEY, George, 4th Earl of. *See* LORD VILLIERS, page 1009.

JERSEY, Frances, Countess of.

Frances, only daughter and heiress of the Right Rev. Philip Twysden, D.D., Lord Bishop of Raphoe in Ireland; married, in March, 1770, George Bussey, 4th Earl of Jersey; died, July 25, 1821.

Sat in December, 1777, December, 1786, and January, 1787.

There were evidently two portraits of this lady.

A portrait of Lady Jersey, with three others, in the Lot 12, was sold in the Thomond sale, May 26, 1821, for £11 2s. 6d., to Robertson and Rutley; the lot was divided into two, fetching sums of £3 5s. and £7 17s. 6d. respectively.

The Countess of Jersey writes, December 5, 1898: "Some years ago a picture of Frances, Countess of Jersey, was sold at, I think, a sale of a son of Lady William Russell's effects, and subsequently passed into the hands of Mr. Lesser, in New Bond Street. We heard of it too late to make any effort to obtain it at the sale. It was called a Sir Joshua. As one of Lady Jersey's daughters married the old Lord William (uncle of the one whose son's things were sold) it is quite possible that this picture was one of those to which you refer."

Lady Jersey's eldest daughter, Charlotte, married, in 1789, Lord William Russell, and died in 1808.

This picture was sold by Mr. Lesser to Charles Sedelmeyer, of Paris, in 1888, from whom it passed to Maurice Kann, of Paris, who has since parted with it.

JERVIS, Captain. See St. Vincent, page 863.

JODRELL, Mrs.

Vertue, eldest daughter and co-heiress of Edward Hase, of Sall, co. Norfolk, and niece of Sir John Hase, Bart.; married, May 19, 1772, Richard Paul Jodrell, F.R.S., M.P.

Probably sat in 1774 and 1775. The pocket-books of 1774, 1775, and 1776 are missing. Paid for, June 25, 1775, Mrs. Jodderell, £18 7s. 6d.; February, 1776, Mrs. Jodrell, £18 17s. 6d. The entry of the latter is palpably *Mr.* Jodrell; but it is evidently a mistake, as the two amounts make the price of a 30 × 25 portrait. Reynolds did not paint Mr. Jodrell, but a picture by Gainsborough of him was sold at Christie's, June 30, 1888, Lot 71, for £640 10s., to Agnew.

Sold at Christie's, June 30, 1888, Lot 70 (Jodrell, owner), for £451 10s., to Samuels.

"August 15, 1774, Mrs. Joddrel. Head oil, cereta, varnisht with ovo, poi varn(isht) con Wolf (Wolf's varnish) panni cera senza olio, vermisciato con ovo, poi con Wolf. Prima (*i.e.*, first painting) umbra e biacca, poco di olio, secondo, umbra, verm: e biacca thick occasionally thinned with turpentine. (This has cracked, as might be expected.)"—Tom Taylor, vol. ii., p. 98.

JOHNSON, Dr. Samuel.

One of the most eminent literary characters of the last century; the son of a bookseller; born at Lichfield, 1709; educated there and at Stourbridge, and went from thence to Pembroke College, Oxford; opened an academy near Lichfield, which was unsuccessful; came to London in 1735, accompanied by his pupil, David Garrick, and soon found literary work. He published his satirical poem, "London," in 1738; "Life of Savage," 1744; "Vanity of Human Wishes," 1749, and after a labour of seven years his "Dictionary of the English Language," followed by "Rasselas," "The Idler," "Lives of the Poets," etc. In 1762 he received a pension from George III., in 1765 the degree of LL.D. from Dublin, and M.A. from Oxford in 1755. Died 1784, and was buried in Westminster Abbey. "Johnson in appearance was in all respects massive. His exterior was unwieldy, his manners without polish, but he had a tender heart."

Sat in January, 1757, September, 1761, March, 1762, January, 1767, and March, 1772.

"Doctor Campbell, a clever and kindly, if somewhat blunder-headed Irish clergyman, whose curious little manuscript diary of his visit to London in 1775 turned up so oddly in 1854, behind an old press in the Supreme Court of New South Wales, dined with Johnson and Baretti at Thrale's on the 16th (March, 1775). The Doctor was not favourably impressed with Johnson on this their first meeting. 'Johnson is the very man Chesterfield describes—a Hottentot indeed—and though your abilities are respectable, you never can be respected yourself. He has the aspect of an idiot, without the faintest ray of sense gleaming from any feature, with the most awkward garb, and unpowdered grey wig on one side only of his head; he is for ever dancing the devil's jig, and sometimes he makes the most drivelling effort to whistle some thought in his absent paroxysms. His awkwardness at table is just what Chesterfield describes, and his roughness of manners kept pace with that. He said he looked upon Burke as the author of 'Junius,' and though he would not take him *contra mundum*, yet he would take him against any man. Baretti was of the same mind, though he mentioned a fact which told against his opinion.'"—LESLIE AND TAYLOR'S *Life of Reynolds*, vol. ii., pp. 112, 113.

"It was in this year, 1763, that Madame de Boufflers paid that memorable visit to Johnson at his chambers, Middle Temple. No one who has read Beauclerc's account of it, as given by Boswell, can ever forget the scene : The purblind scholar, in his rusty-brown morning suit, old shoes by way of slippers, a little shrivelled wig sticking on the top of his head, the sleeves of his shirt and the knees of his breeches hanging loose, rolling down his staircase and rushing between the dainty figures of the English beau and the French belle to repair his oversight in not attending the lady to her coach."—LESLIE AND TAYLOR'S *Life of Reynolds*, vol. i., p. 220, note 1.

"Johnson was born in an age of scepticism, when minds were all afloat in a miserable state of unrest, and their language indicating their belief that the world was like a water-mill working up the stream without a miller to guide it. His youth was one of extreme poverty ; yet when a person who knew of his condition had a pair of old shoes placed in his lodging, as soon as Johnson discovered them he flung them out of the window. This incident is an expressive type of the man's conduct through life; he never would stand in another's shoes ; he preferred misery when it was his own, to anything derivable from others. He was in all respects a ponderous man, strong in appetite, powerful in intellect, of Herculean frame, a great passionate giant. There is something fine and touching, too, if we well consider it, in that little, flippant, vain fellow, Boswell, attaching himself as he did to Johnson, before others had discovered anything sublime. Boswell had done it, and embraced his knees when the bosom was denied him. Boswell was a true hero-worshipper, and does not deserve the contempt we are all so ready to cast at him."—From CAROLINE FOX'S *Memoirs of Old Friends*, published by Smith, Elder, and Co., 1882, giving an account of Carlyle's lecture on men of letters.

"Among the memorable sitters of this year was Johnson. It was after Sir Joshua's return from his round of autumn visits to Blenheim and the camps, October 15, 1778, that Johnson writes in his diary to Mrs. Thrale : 'I have sat twice to Sir Joshua, and he seems to like his own performance. He has projected another, in which I am to be busy ; but we can think on it at leisure.' And again, October 31 : 'Sir Joshua has finished my picture and it seems to please everybody ; but I shall wait to see how it pleases you.' Note.—I am in doubt which of his pictures of Johnson is the one referred to. I think it can hardly be the one painted for Malone, now in the possession of Rev. T. Roper, with the book held close to his eyes; that I think must be the second, 'in which I am to be busy.' It could not have been one of the several repetitions of the Thrale picture, which was itself a repetition of the one painted for Bennet Langton. There is a picture at Pembroke College, Oxford. Can this be it?"—LESLIE AND TAYLOR'S *Life of Sir Joshua*, vol. ii., p. 223.

JOHNSON, Dr. Samuel.

Full length, canvas 25 × 18 in.

An imaginary picture of the "Infant Johnson."

An infant, life size, the two hands crossed in front; the head bent forward, and the eyes downcast, with a solemn expression; landscape background.

EXHIBITED.

British Institution, 1823, No. 28, as "Infancy," } by the Marquess of
Grafton, 1895, No. 155,   }   Lansdowne.

"No portrait, imaginary or otherwise, is less known than that which is called 'The Infant Johnson.' This work, which is a small one, is preserved in the drawing-room at Bowood. . . . Dr. Johnson, whom we have seen to be not insensitive with regard to his personal defects, need not have been annoyed by this good jest; and, if he ever saw it, must have laughed with the rest of his friends at the spirit and humour of the little picture of himself as Reynolds imagined him to have been in childhood. There is something of the true nature of wit in the way with which the heavy brow of the adult doctor is hinted at by that of the meditative babe, who sits before us Brahmin-like and quiescent."—F. G. STEPHENS'S *English Children by Sir J. Reynolds*, 1884, p. 47.

ENGRAVED.

George Zobel, 1858.

Sold at Greenwood's, April 16, 1796, Lot 59, as "Study of a naked boy," for £50 8s., to Farrington, and by Phillips, in 1813 (Westall, owner), for £126.

It was photographed for a set of Reynolds's children by Cundall about 1875.

The picture, which belonged to John Graves, was sold by him, through Mr. Hickman, to the Marquess of Lansdowne for 100 guineas, and is No. 106 in the Lansdowne catalogue; it hangs at Bowood.

JOHNSON, Dr. Samuel.

Three-quarter length, canvas 48¼ × 39 in.

Sitting in an armchair covered with a chequered stuff, pen in right hand, table before him, left hand on a paper; on the table an inkstand and a volume of his dictionary; wearing a wig.

Painted in 1756. The first portrait.

Note to the 1757 sitting: "Dr. Johnson—the first portrait—with a pen in his hand; in a chair covered with chequered stuff."—TOM TAYLOR, vol. i., p. 155.

EXHIBITED.

National Portrait Exhibition, 1867, No. 557, } by Charles Morrison.
Grosvenor, 1884, No. 97,   }

James Heath, 1791, 7¼ × 5¼ in.

T. Baker, 1793, 4¼ × 3¼ in.

Robert Graves, A.R.A., 4¼ × 3¼ in.

Richard Josey, 1880, 5¼ × 4¼ in.

This portrait was presented to James Boswell by Sir Joshua Reynolds, and was in his possession in 1793. Bought by John Graves, a hop merchant of Southwark, at the sale of Boswell's library, June 3, 1825, for 73 guineas, and sold by him to Charles Morrison, the present owner.

JOHNSON, Dr. Samuel.

Head size, canvas 30 × 25 *in.*

Showing both hands, held up in front; profile to left; books in background; without his wig.

Exhibited at the Royal Academy in 1770, No. 150.

British Institution, 1843, No. 54,

      ,,   ,,   1846, No. 40,   } by the Duke of Sutherland.

National Portrait Exhibition, 1867, No. 564,

"Sir Joshua had presented the picture of Johnson exhibited in 1770, or a duplicate of it, to Johnson's step-daughter, Lucy Porter. At her house Johnson found the picture on his visit to Lichfield this year. In July, 1771, he wrote to Reynolds from Ashbourne (Tom Taylor, vol. i., p. 412):

                                        'Ashbourne, July 17, 1771.

'DEAR SIR,

    'When I came to Lichfield, I found that my portrait had been much visited and much admired. Every man has a lurking wish to appear considerable in his native place, and I was pleased with the dignity conferred by such a testimony of your regard. Be pleased, therefore, to accept the thanks of, sir,

                    'Your most obliged and humble servant,

                      'SAM. JOHNSON.

—Compliment to Miss Reynolds.'"

Painted for Miss Lucy Porter, of Lichfield, Dr. Johnson's stepdaughter.

The picture belongs to the Duke of Sutherland, No. 238 in the Trentham catalogue.

JOHNSON, Dr. Samuel.

Head size, canvas 30 × 25 *in.*

Standing arguing, with his two hands half clutched, in one of his most characteristic attitudes; shows his head with no wig; a profile to left; bookcase behind. The figure of Tiresias in the "Infant Hercules" picture is modelled upon this pose of Johnson's.

"1769, first olio, after capivi, with colour, but without white; 1770, the Knole portrait exhibited."

British Institution, 1817, No. 98, by the Duchess of Dorset.

Guelph, 1891, No. 205, by Lord Sackville.

J. Watson, 1770, 16¼ × 13 in.

S. W. Reynolds, 3¼ × 3¼ in.

On the plate by S. W. Reynolds it says, "painted for Mr. Langton, now at Gunby, near Spilsby." This is probably an error, as it was a full face that belonged to Bennet Langton.

The picture belongs to Lord Sackville, at Knole.

JOHNSON, Dr. Samuel.

Half length, canvas 30 × 25 *in.*

Replica.

Sold at Christie's, May 18th, 1821, Lot 11 (Lady Thomond, owner), and described as Dr. Samuel Johnson, from original by Sir Joshua at Knowle, Kent; bought by Sharp for £11 2s. 6d.

"Cunningham is no doubt wrong in stating that Mr. Thrale's portrait of Dr. Johnson was bought by Richard Sharp, as the portrait in his possession was purchased at Lady Thomond's sale as from the original at Knowle."—COTTON, 1856, p. 195.

According to the Streatham Park Catalogue, May, 1816, Mr. Sharp only bought Lot 61, Sir J. Reynolds, and Lot 67, E. Burke.

The picture, which is an original and as fine as possible, was purchased by Richard Sharp at the Marchioness of Thomond's sale in 1821, and was bequeathed by him to Mrs. Drummond, from whom it passed to her daughters, Mrs. Kay and Miss Emily Drummond, the present owners; it hangs at 18, Hyde Park Gardens.

JOHNSON, Dr. Samuel.

Half length, canvas 29¼ × 25 *in.*

In a powdered wig and brown suit, nearly full face, and showing his left hand.

The Streatham picture. Painted in 1772.

British Institution, 1813, No. 120, by Mrs. Piozzi.

     ,,   ,,   1820, No. 28, by G. Watson Taylor.

     ,,   ,,   1833, No. 46, by Sir Robert Peel, Bart.

Sold by Squibb at Streatham for £378 to G. Watson Taylor. At Christie's, June 13, 1823, Lot 46, bought in for the owner, G. W. Taylor, for £493 10s., by Major Thwaites. Sold at Mr. Taylor's sale by Robins at Earl's Stoke for £157 10s. to Smith, for Sir Robert Peel, Bart.

ENGRAVED.

William Doughty, 1784, 15¾ × 13 in.
T. Cook, 1786, 6¼ × 4¾ in.
W. Holl, 1814, 5 × 4 in.
G. W. Hutin, 1822, 5¼ × 4 in.
R. Graves, A.R.A., 1829, 2¾ × 2 in.
S. W. Reynolds (S. Cousins, R.A.), 3¼ × 3 in.
E. Finden, 4 × 3¼ in.

A First State of Doughty's print, Buccleuch Collection, sold at Christie's in 1887 for £60 18s.

Purchased with the Peel pictures in 1871 by the National Gallery.

In a letter from Johnson to Mrs. Thrale he says : " I have twice sat to Sir Joshua, and he seems to like his own performance. He has projected another in which I am to be busy, but we can think of it at leisure." In a subsequent one he observes : " Sir Joshua has finished my picture, and it seems to please everybody, but I shall wait to see how it pleases you."

JOHNSON, Dr. Samuel.

Half length, canvas 29¼ × 24¼ in.

Full face ; hands not showing ; aged ; head and shoulders somewhat stooping ; wig ; snuff-coloured suit ; red curtain at back.

The picture was painted for Johnson's schoolfellow and friend, Canon Taylor, who lived at Ashbourne, and was bought at his death by Jesse Watts Russell, of Ilam Hall, near Ashbourne. On the sale of that place the picture was removed to Biggen Hall, where it now is, the property of A. E. Watts Russell.

JOHNSON, Dr. Samuel.

Half length, canvas 29 × 24 in.

Nearly full face ; left hand showing ; brown coat and waistcoat ; with dark background.

EXHIBITED.

Royal Academy, 1884, No. 207, by John Murray.

Sold at Christie's, April 14, 1864, Lot 277 (Bishop of Ely, owner), to Henry Graves and Co., who disposed of it to John Murray, of Albemarle Street.

JOHNSON, Dr. Samuel.

Half length, canvas 30 × 25 in.

Full face ; left hand showing ; brown coat and waistcoat ; in wig ; dark background.

521　　　　　　　　　　3 X

Sold at Messrs. Foster's, 1849, from the Reynolds sale, for £39 18*s*., to Farrer.

It was probably this picture that afterwards belonged to Henry Graves and Co., and was sold by them to the Earl of Rosebery, the present owner.

JOHNSON, Dr. Samuel.

Half length, canvas 30 × 25 *in.*

The picture belongs to Lord Burton.

JOHNSON, Dr. Samuel.

Half length to waist, canvas 12 × 10¼ *in.*

Showing left hand; full face; brown reddish claret-coloured coat.

EXHIBITED.

British Institution, 1861, No. 190, ⎫
National Portrait Exhibition, 1867, No. 574, ⎬ by Wynn Ellis.
⎭

Sold at Christie's, May 6, 1876, No. 88 (W. Ellis, owner), described as a small copy, for £46 4*s*., to Sir W. Stirling.

Sir Walter George Stirling, Bart., writes to say that he does not possess the portrait of Dr. Johnson, neither has he any trace of what became of it.

JOHNSON, Dr. Samuel.

Half length, canvas 12 × 10 *in.*

Full face; showing left hand; brown coat; waistcoat unbuttoned at the top.

EXHIBITED.

National Portrait Exhibition, 1867, No. 567, by McLeod of McLeod.

Sold at Christie's, July 19, 1890, Lot 121 (Hall, owner), and described as having been in the possession of Bennet Langton and lent to the National Portrait Exhibition by McLeod in 1867, for £30 9*s*., to Gooden.

JOHNSON, Dr. Samuel.

Head size, canvas, oval, 30¼ × 25¼ *in.*

Both hands showing, holding up a book close to his face; wig; red coat; dark background.

Painted in 1775 for his friend, Edmund Malone.

EXHIBITED.

National Portrait Exhibition, 1867, No. 556, ⎫
Royal Academy, 1883, No. 217, ⎬ by Rev. W. H. Rooper.
⎭

In the National Portrait Exhibition it is stated that it was painted in 1784, and at the Royal Academy that it was painted in 1775.

ENGRAVED.

John Hall, 1787, 3¼ × 3¼ in.

A. N. Sanders, 1865, 5 × 4 in.

The picture descended from Malone, together with his own portrait, to the Rev. William Henry Rooper. (The Rev. Thomas Richard Rooper, the father of the late owner, was the nephew of Lady Sunderlin (who sat to Reynolds in June, 1788), and inherited the portrait from her.) It was afterwards sold to Messrs. T. Agnew and Sons, from whom it passed to the Earl of Rosebery. It now belongs to Lord Iveagh.

"In the year 1775 Sir Joshua painted this portrait of Johnson, in which he is represented as reading and near-sighted. The expression of this peculiarity so much displeased the Doctor that he remarked, 'It is not friendly to hand down to posterity the imperfections of any man.' But Reynolds, on the contrary, says Northcote, esteemed it a circumstance in nature to be remarked as characterizing the person represented, and therefore as giving additional value to the portrait. In allusion to this picture Mrs. Thrale says, 'I observed that he would not be known to posterity by his defects only. Let Sir Joshua do his worst.' And when she adverted to Reynolds's own portrait, in which he introduced the ear-trumpet, and which he painted for Mrs. Thrale, the Doctor is said to have answered : 'He may paint himself as deaf as he pleases, but I will not be *blinking Sam.*'"—NORTHCOTE, vol. ii., pp. 3 and 4.

JOHNSON, Dr. Samuel.

Paid for, February, 1779, Mr. Beauclerc, for a copy of Mr. Garrick and Dr. Johnson, half payment, £26 15s. November, 1779, Mr. Beauclerc for Johnson and Garick, £26.

On the frame of his (Johnson's) portrait Mr. Topham Beauclerk had inscribed :

————"At ingenium ingens
Inculto latet hoc sub corpore."

("Under that exterior, rough though it be, a giant mind lies hid.")

"After Mr. Beauclerk's death, when it became Mr. Langton's property, he made the inscription be defaced. Johnson said complacently, 'It was kind in you to take it off;' and then, after a short pause, added, 'and not unkind in him to put it on.'"—CROKER'S *Boswell's Life of Johnson*, p. 718.

The originals were in the possession of P. Massingberd, but were removed from his house by Sir Gregory Lewin for cleaning, and by some accident were sold at Sir G. Lewin's sale, May 16, 1846, Lots 50 and 51, at Christie's, where Johnson was bought by Mr. Norton for 41 guineas.

The Garrick was described as painted at the *request* of Bennet Langton. See ante, p. 349.

The present ownership of these pictures has not been traced.

JOHNSON, Dr. Samuel.

Half length, canvas 29¼ × 25 *in.*

Similar to the National Gallery portrait.

The Bursar of Pembroke College writes, December 13, 1898 : " The picture was painted for Johnson's great friend, Andrew Strahan, the Queen's Printer, and is believed to be the original of which the National Gallery portrait and others are replicas. The picture remained in the same position in the house—10, Little New Street, Gough Square—from the day it was finished until the year 1850, when it was most graciously presented to the College by Andrew Spottiswoode, Printer to the Queen. It has absolutely escaped all attempts at cleaning or restoration. There is also a portrait of Johnson, the property of the College, which hangs in the Master's House, and which has been commonly reputed to be by Reynolds. . . . It is similar in size and pose to the portrait in the Senior Common Room. It was presented to the College, in 1804, by Panton Plymley."

The picture belongs to Pembroke College, Oxford, and hangs in the Senior Common Room.

JOHNSON, Dr. Samuel.

Head size, canvas.

Leaning on a book.

ENGRAVED.

J. J. Chant, 1854, 9⅝ × 8⅛ in.

The picture was then in the possession of the Bishop of Ely.

Sales of other Portraits of Doctor Johnson :

	Lot.	Owner.		£	s.	d.	
1846, May 16.	58.	Christie's. Lewin.	Doctor Johnson . .	43	1	0	Newton.
1856, May 20.		Phillips. Bannister.	Doctor Johnson . .	21	10	0	
1864, April 9.	729.	Christie's. Brett.	Doctor Johnson, right hand resting on a table and holding a letter in his left .	9	10	0	Waters.

Copies of Johnson sold at Christie's :

	Lot.	Owner.		£	s.	d.	
1821, June 9.	125.	Davis.	A close copy . . .	15	15	0	Vernon.
1842, Feb. 5.	95.	Miss Patterson.	By Patterson . . .	1	5	0	Anthony.
1845, June 24.	881.	Rice.	By Marchi	2	5	0	Fuller.
1868, Mar. 23.	34.	Rev. A. Sellet.	By Doughty . . .	5	0	0	Noseda.

JOHNSON'S (Dr.) BLACK SERVANT.

Frank Barber, Dr. Johnson's servant, the " Dear Francis" of his letters, was the lexicographer's affectionate friend. Barber was born in Jamaica, brought to England in 1750 by Colonel Bathurst, who sent him to school, and gave him his freedom. He entered Johnson's service, and, two short intervals excepted, continued with him from 1752 till his death, attending his master in his last moments. Boswell, in his "Life of Johnson," often mentions Frank Barber. It was he who received Miss Morris, who sat for "Hope nursing Love," when she called on the Doctor, and, finding him on the point of death, heard his last words, when he turned his face to the wall, saying, "God bless you, my dear." *See* FRANK BARBER.

EXHIBITED.

Manchester, 1857, No. 58, as a negro (F. Barber), ⎫
Royal Academy, 1877, No. 290, as a negro,   ⎪ by Sir George Beau-
Grosvenor, 1884, No. 42, as a negro, said to be   ⎬   mont, Bart.
   Frank Barber,   ⎭

Sold at Greenwood's, April 15, 1796, Lot 53, "Head of a Black Man," for £18 18s., to Sir George Beaumont, Bart.

The picture belongs to Sir George Beaumont, Bart.

This picture was copied in miniature by Henry Edridge, A.R.A., head only finished, and is No. 32 in the collection of his works in the Print Room, British Museum.

JOHNSON, William.

William Johnson was the son of the Rev. Samuel Johnson, M.A., Ch. Ch., Oxford, who was vicar of Great Torrington, and grandson of Samuel Johnson, of Reading. He was born in 1720, resided at Torrington, and married (about 1747) Elizabeth Reynolds, the younger of Sir Joshua's two married sisters. He was Mayor of Torrington in 1757, 1764, and 1771. His elder son died shortly after getting a scholarship at Exeter College in 1777. His third son, William Johnson (died 1799), was for many years Clerk of the Crown in Calcutta, and to him Sir Joshua left his watch and seals.

Sat in September, 1761, March, 1762, and January, 1767, as Mr. Johnson.

JOHNSON, Colonel William.

A portrait of Colonel William Johnson was sold at Christie's, July 3, 1875, Lot 76 (Nobleman, owner), for £105, described in gorget and uniform.

JOHNSON, Mrs. William.

Head size, canvas 30 × 25 *in.*

Elizabeth, fourth daughter of the Rev. Samuel Reynolds, and sister to Sir Joshua; born 1719; married (about 1747) William Johnson, of Torrington; she died in 1792. Elizabeth Reynolds was a handsome and sensible woman,

525

but had not the same force of character which her elder sister Mary (Palmer) possessed. She lived all her married life at Torrington, and was greatly beloved.

Full face; in brown dress, with wide sleeves, ornamented with pearls round shoulders and down the front of the dress; dark lace tippet; a turban on her head; pearl necklace and earrings.

Sat in 1758 as Mrs. Johnson.

" Probably painted on her marriage."—COTTON, 1856, p. 272.

EXHIBITED.

National Portrait Exhibition, 1867, No. 553, ⎫ by the Rev. William John-
Royal Academy, 1883, No. 280, as Miss ⎬ son.
   Elizabeth Reynolds, ⎭

The Rev. William Johnson was her great-grandson.

ENGRAVED.

George H. Every, 1864, 4¼ × 4 in.

The picture belonged in 1864 to the Rev. William Johnson, who died in 1884, and previously to his sister, Frances, wife of the Rev. Robert C. Kitson. On the death of the Rev. W. Johnson, his widow, who was an American, returned to the United States, and took the portrait with her. *See* MISS ELIZABETH REYNOLDS.

JOHNSON, Miss.

Sat in 1761 and 1762. Paid for March 10, 1761, Miss Johnson, £10 10s.; Ditto, £10 10s.; and before 1762, Miss Johnson, £21; Miss Johnson, £21.

These entries evidently refer to two Kitcat portraits.

JOHNSON, Miss Elizabeth.

Three-quarter length.

Elizabeth Johnson was the third daughter of Elizabeth Reynolds, the younger of Sir Joshua's two married sisters. Frances, the eldest daughter, married William Yonge (*see* YONGE, *later*), Chancellor and Archdeacon of Norwich, whose father, the Rev. Henry Yonge, lived at Torrington. Jane Johnson, the second daughter, married Philip Yonge, of Calcutta, brother of William Yonge, who married Frances. Jane died at Calcutta before she was seventeen years of age. Mary Johnson, the youngest daughter, married the Rev. Peter Wellington Furse, the 'squire of Halsdon House and Dolton, near Torrington. Elizabeth Johnson, the subject of this picture, married the Rev. William Deane, sometime Fellow of All Souls' College, Oxford, who was the 'squire of Webbery, a pretty seat to the north of Torrington; she had one son, Anthony

526

William Johnson Deane, of Webbery. Mrs. Elizabeth Deane was a very handsome woman, and stood to Sir Joshua for his very striking figure of "Fortitude" in the New College window. She lived a quiet country life near Torrington, and died in 1841. Her husband died in 1818.

A girl sketching; standing, leaning against a slab; in profile; left hand holds a sketch-book, which is supported by her waist; in right hand a pencil.

EXHIBITED.

British Institution, 1813, No. 38, as Girl drawing, by the Marchioness of Thomond.

British Institution, 1823, No. 32, as Girl sketching, } by Henry Rogers.
      "   "   1831, No. 151, as Girl drawing, }

Manchester Art Treasures, 1857, No. 56, as Girl sketching, by Miss Burdett-Coutts.

Bought in at Greenwood's, April 16, 1796, Lot 14, for £25 4s.; sold at Christie's, May 18, 1821, Lot 66 (Lady Thomond, owner), as a female drawing, for £106 1s., to Rogers; sold in the Rogers sale, May 2, 1856, No. 591, as a Girl sketching, at Christie's, for £367 10s., to Radcliffe, for the Baroness Burdett-Coutts.

ENGRAVED.

J. Grozer, 1794, 9¼ × 8 in., as Design.
S. W. Reynolds (S. Cousins, R.A.), 5¼ × 4 in., as Design.

Henry Rogers was youngest brother to Samuel Rogers; the picture seems to have passed from one to the other.

The picture belongs to the Baroness Burdett-Coutts.

JOHNSON, Miss.

Sketch.

Sold at Greenwood's, April 16, 1796, Lot 20, unfinished study of Design, to Sheldon, for £22 1s.; this was probably bought in at Christie's, March 29, 1851, Lot 60, by Capt. Knocker (owner), as "a young lady sketching, very elegant engraved," for £4 10s.; March 23, 1868, Lot 39, Mrs. Seymour (owner), a Girl sketching, for £22 1s.; May 10, 1873, Lot 107, J. Heugh (owner), Girl sketching, 30¼ × 24 in., to Patriccis, for £110 15s.; July 6, 1872, Agnew (owner), Girl sketching from nature, bought in for £152 5s.

Mr. P. L. McDermott (secretary to the Baroness Burdett-Coutts) writes, August 12, 1898: "There is a copy, either a sketch of the picture begun by Sir Joshua, or else a copy made in the master's studio, and under his eye, in the possession of Mr. Joseph Ellis, the poet, formerly of Eccleston Square."

JOHNSTONE, Lady Charlotte.

Half length, canvas 35¼ × 27¼ *in.*

Daughter of Geo. Montagu, 1st Earl Halifax; married Colonel Johnstone; died 1762.

Head turned over right shoulder; long plait of hair over the same; dress trimmed with ermine; pearl necklace; two pearls as an earring; right arm bent to hip; sash round waist; curtain to her right.

Sat in 1758, 1759, 1760, and 1761. The sittings of 1758, 1759, and 1760, are Lady Charlotte Johnston; 1761, Lady Johnstone.

Sold at Greenwood's, April 15, 1796, Lot 45, as Lady Charlotte Johnson, for £10 10s., to Cribb.

ENGRAVED.

James Watson, 12¼ × 9¾ in.
C. Corbutt, 12¼ × 9¾ in.
S. W. Reynolds, 2¼ × 2 in.

The picture was sold by Mr. Cribb to the 2nd Earl of Normanton. It now belongs to the Earl of Normanton, and is No. 21 in the Somerley catalogue.

JOHNSTONE, Lady Charlotte.

Head size, canvas 25¼ × 21 *in.*

Three-quarter face to the right; no necklace or earrings; white dress, with dark cloak lined with ermine; dark background.

Painted in 1760.

Sold at Christie's, January 23, 1897, Lot 23 (Fullerton, owner), for £110 5s., to Asher Wertheimer, who sold it in 1897 to M. Charles Sedelmeyer, of Paris, the present owner.

JOHNSTONE, Mrs.

Sat in 1786.

JOHNSTONE, Master.

Sat in 1786.

JONES, Sir William.

Half length, canvas 30 × 25 *in.*

Born September 28, 1746; Orientalist; educated at Harrow and University College, Oxford; called to the Bar, 1774; Judge of the Supreme Court of Judicature at Port William in 1783; founded the Asiatic Society

George Spencer Cowper

while in India; a digest of the Hindoo and Mahometan laws was compiled under his superintendence; translated from the Persian the life of Nader Shah into French for the King of Denmark. His commentaries on Arabic poetry were published in 1774. Among his other works are a Persian grammar, 1771; translations of the Sanskrit drama, 1789, and the Laws of Manu, 1794. He was tutor to George John, 2nd Earl Spencer, and was knighted about 1783. He died in Calcutta, April 27, 1794.

" I shall close this account with an extract of a letter from him some time ago now lying before me, in which he says :

" ' I have ever been since my seasoning, as they call it, perfectly well, notwithstanding incessant business seven hours a day for four and five months in the year, and unremitted application during the vacation to a vast and interesting study, a complete knowledge of India, which I can only attain in the country itself, and which I mean to leave with the eighteenth century.'

" Owing, however, to the ill-health of his lady, and her being obliged to leave India last year, Sir Wm. Jones was preparing to return to England when he was cut off, to the great regret of his friends and the public."—*Gentleman's Magazine*, 1795, p. 112.

White cravat; coat with fur collar; full face, looking to the right; right arm leaning on a chair.

Sat in 1760, 1761, 1767, 1768, and 1769. All the sittings as Mr. Jones. Paid for, June 5, 1769, Mr. Jones, £36 15s.

EXHIBITED.
British Institution, 1846, No. 58, by Earl Spencer.

ENGRAVED.
J. Cochran, 1832, 5 × 4 in., for " Lodge's Portraits."
Another plate, half length, right arm resting on a table, holding a book in his hand, by J. Heath, 1779, 5¼ × 4¼ in.

The picture was presented by Lady Jones to Earl Spencer the day before she died, and is No. 414 in the Althorp catalogue. There is a monument to him in St. Paul's.

JONES, Sir William.

ENGRAVED.
J. Hall, 1782, 3¼ × 3¼ in.

The picture belonged in 1782 to W. B. Sumner, and it was recorded that it belonged to University College, Oxford; but Dr. James Franck Bright writes, on December 18, 1898, that he does not know of any picture of Sir William Jones by Reynolds in the College, the only portrait being Flaxman's bust.

JONES, Mrs.

Sat in 1761.

JONES, Miss.

As Melancholy.—NORTHCOTE, p. 350.

Sat in 1755 and 1765.

JONES, Miss.

Sat in 1784 and 1786.

Note to the 1784 sitting : "A model; her address, 4, Cross Court, Bow Street, Covent Garden."

JORDAN, Mrs. Dorothea, Actress.

Maiden name, Bland; born 1762; died in great distress in Paris, 1816. She appeared in Dublin at the age of fourteen, under Daly's management, in the character of Phœbe in "As You Like It;" next in Tate Wilkinson's company in Leeds and York, where she became a favourite, and this led to her engagement at Drury Lane to play second to Mrs. Siddons; but she preferred to be first in comedy, and accordingly made her *début* on October 18, 1785, in the "Country Girl," "Priscilla Tomboy" in 1786, "Rosalind" in 1800, "Lady Teazle" in 1812, and also in a round of characters, including Viola, Ophelia, Helena, The Romp, Hypolita in "She Would and She Would Not," etc., etc.

She was painted by Romney, half length, in the "Country Girl," a fascinating picture, engraved by Ogborne, 1788; also by Hoppner, and engraved by J. Jones, 1791, and by Barber, oval, and engraved by Ridley for the "Monthly Mirror," 1804.

At Christie's, a portrait of Mrs. Jordan when young, May 26, 1843, Lot 139, bought in for £5, by the owner, Sir J. Pringle; bought in again, same rooms, June 10, 1844, by the owner, Gritten, for £4.

The dates now given do not support the authenticity of the picture bought in at Christie's, for when Mrs. Jordan arrived in London in 1785 she was twenty-three, and this would not be regarded by painters or fine art dealers as "when young." In Sir Joshua's diary it is recorded that Mrs. Jordan called upon him about three the 23rd March, 1789, but whether the visit was one of courtesy or for a sitting is not mentioned.

JUBB, Mr.

Sat in 1757.

A Joseph Jubb, of Greenwich, died in 1768.

JUBB, Mrs.

Sat in 1757.

"October 22, 1771 : Mrs. Jubb, Lady of Robert Jubb, of York, a near relation of Dr. Herring, late Archbishop of Canterbury."—*Gentleman's Magazine*, 1771, p. 475.

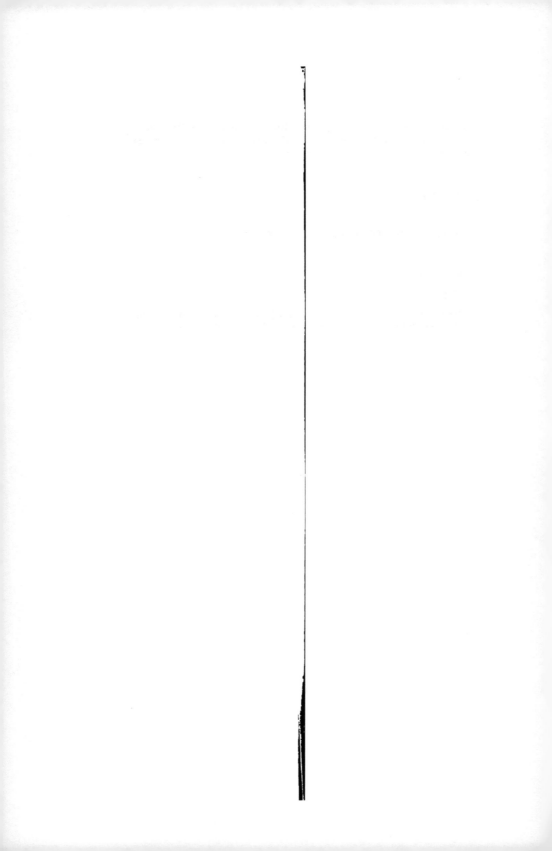

KAUFFMAN, Angelica Maria Catherine.

Half length, canvas, oval, 29 × 24 in.

History and portrait painter; daughter of John Joseph Kauffman, portrait painter; born 1740; came to London in 1765; was elected one of the foundation members of the Royal Academy in 1769, and was a contributor up to 1797. In 1780 she married the Venetian painter, Antonio Zucchi, and settled with him at Rome, where she resided till her death in 1807.

Sitting; a string of pearls and tiara in her hair; a lock of hair falls over each shoulder; she is holding a drawing in her right hand, and a crayon pencil in her left hand; a buckle on her right shoulder; the dress trimmed with fur.

Sat in 1766, 1769, and 1777.

ENGRAVED.

F. Bartolozzi (oval), 1780, 9¼ × 8 in.
E. Morace (in part), 13¼ × 10¼ in.

The picture belongs to Earl Spencer, No. 282 in the Althorp catalogue.

"The pocket-book calls up a pleasanter recollection by its frequent entries of 'Miss Angelica.' This is the pretty and graceful Angelica Kauffman, whose pictures, feeble as they are, were thought wonderful in her own time, and procured her a place in the original roll of Academicians in 1768. Her name in the pocket-book is sometimes contracted to 'Miss Angel,' and once has the suggestive addition, 'Fiori.' Had Reynolds been reminding himself to buy her flowers? She had come to London the year before, under the protection of Lady Wentworth, and had appeared as an exhibitor for the first time in 1765 among the Associate Painters at 'Mr. Moreing's great room in Maiden Lane,' with that never-failing contribution of this date, a portrait of Mr. Garrick. This year she had sent to the same exhibition a 'Shepherd and Shepherdess of Arcadia moralizing at the side of a sepulchre, while others are dancing at a distance,' a subject used originally by Guercino, and imitated from him by Sir Joshua in his picture of Mrs. Bouverie and Mrs. Crewe a few years later, of which there is a sketch in his Roman note-book. Angelica Kauffman was painted twice by Sir Joshua, and she painted his portrait.

"The picture, now at Saltram, is likely to be pronounced weak and uncharacteristic by most critics nowadays, but the poet of the 'Advertiser' sings of it:

> "'When the likeness she hath done for thee,
> O Reynolds, with astonishment we see,
> Forced to admit, with all our pride we own
> Such strength, such harmony, excelled by none,
> And though unrivall'd by thyself alone.'

Meaning, I suppose, that Sir Joshua's portrait by Angelica Kauffman could be equalled only by Sir Joshua himself. The report was, that Reynolds, who had placed her on the list of Academicians, admired the woman as well as the artist. He was her steady friend, and had lately aided her in procuring the dissolution of her marriage with a swindler—the valet of Count Horne, who, arriving in London with his master's stolen wardrobe and credentials, had figured successfully for a time in the character of the count, and as such had wooed and won the fair Angelica."—LESLIE AND TAYLOR'S *Life of Sir Joshua*, vol. i., pp. 259, 260, and 326, note 4.

KAUFFMAN, Angelica Maria Catherine.

Whole length, canvas 84 × 62 *in.*

In a landscape; holding a crayon in her right hand; white brocaded dress; red drapery.

EXHIBITED.

Grosvenor, 1884, No. 180, by E. Façon Watson.

KAUFFMAN, Angelica Maria Catherine.

Bust, 25¼ × 22 *in.*

Showing right hand, in which she holds a porte-crayon; three-quarter face to left; low cut red dress; landscape background; painted, 1777.—R.A. Cat.

Sat in 1777.

EXHIBITED.

Royal Academy, 1885, No. 2, by D. Thwaites.

Mrs. Thwaites writes, December 11, 1898, that the picture was either sold to Messrs. T. Agnew and Sons, or exchanged for another picture.

A portrait of Angelica Kauffman sold at Christie's, March 3, 1832, Lot 79 (Andrews, owner), for £3 5s., to Hind; February 16, 1850, Lot 134 (Gritten, owner), for £3 3s. Bought in at Christie's, April 27, 1860, Lot 94, portrait of Angelica Kauffman—this picture was bequeathed to the uncle of the late proprietor, Mr. John Kauffman, by the will of Angelica Kauffman, who always asserted that it was painted by Sir Joshua in her own studio—by the owner (Fairholm, Leamington), for £78 15s.; November 30, 1890, Lot 448 (Howell, owner), for £98 14s., to Renton.

KELLY, Mr.

Sat in 1761.

"Died February 3, 1777, Hugh Kelly, counsellor at law."—*Gentleman's Magazine*, 1777, p. 95.

KELLY, Miss.

Sat in 1761.

KEMBLE, Miss Fanny.

Half length, canvas 29 × 24¼ in.

Daughter of Roger Kemble and younger sister of John Kemble and Mrs. Siddons; born 1759; became an actress, and performed at Drury Lane; married Francis Twiss, and retired from the stage; died October 1, 1822. She was the mother of Horace Twiss, M.P.

Hair dressed with a ribbon; frilled lapel; black dress; in a mountainous landscape.

ENGRAVED.

J. Jones, 1784, 13¼ × 10⅞ in.

First State, with Miss Kemble in etched letters, sold at Christie's, Buccleuch Collection, 1887, for £32 11s., Huth Collection in 1895 for £71 8s., and Bessborough Collection, 1897, for £50 8s.

The picture formerly belonged to Colonel Clifford.

KEMBLE, Miss Fanny.

Half length.

A replica of the above picture, but varied by the introduction of a spray of honeysuckle lying on the ledge behind which Miss Kemble stands.

ENGRAVED.

J. Jones.

KEMBLE, Miss Fanny.

Half length, canvas 29 × 24¼ in.

To left; three-quarter face; white dress with blue sash; grey background; standing behind a plain ledge; hair more raised from the forehead; double frill to dress.

Sat in 1783. Exhibited in the Royal Academy, 1784, No. 183.

"Very good and simple."—WALPOLE.
Morning Chronicle, 1784: "No. 183. Miss Kemble wants resemblance."
Morning Herald: "No. 183. Portrait of Miss Kemble, a flattering likeness of the lady for whom it is meant, finished in Sir Joshua's best manner."

EXHIBITED.

Royal Academy, 1890, No. 49, by the Right Hon. G. C. Bentinck.

Afterwards sold to Messrs. T. Agnew and Sons, from whom it passed to Bradley Martin.

J. Jones, 1786, 14⅞ × 10⅞ in.

C. Smith, 15 × 11 in.

S. W. Reynolds, 3¼ × 3⅛ in.

A proof before the name sold at Sotheby's in 1895 for £34, and a First State at Christie's in 1897, Bessborough sale, for £84.

KEMBLE, Miss Fanny.

Head size, canvas 16¼ × 11¼ *in.*

This picture was sold at Christie's, May 11, 1896, Lot 25 (Hawkins, owner), as Miss Kemble, head, 16¼ × 11¼ in., for £215 5s., to Charles John Wertheimer, who sold it to M. Charles Sedelmeyer, of Paris, in 1896, who has since parted with it to Walter Gay, of Paris, the present owner.

KENDALL FAMILY.

A series of seven portraits.

Painted in 1744.

"Six, if not seven, portraits of this period, bearing the date 1744, are in the possession of Mr. Kendal, of Pelyn, M.P. for East Cornwall. I have not seen them, but I am informed by Mr. Kendal that they are in excellent condition. They represent his great-grandfather, his great-grandmother (the latter twice over), his grandfather, and his great-uncle, and have on the back, 'Joshua Reynolds, pinxt. (Etatis suæ 21) 1744.'

"By his receipt he had £7 for the two portraits of Mrs. Kendal."—TOM TAYLOR, vol. i., p. 27, note.

Bought in at Christie's, July 14, 1883, Lot 94, Mrs. Mary Kendal (R. Gill, owner), for £3 3s.

They belonged in 1865 to Nicholas Kendall, M.P.

The Rev. J. Kendall writes from Lostwithiel, January 3, 1898, giving the size of the pictures as 36 × 30 in., with the following names for five of the pictures: Mrs. Mary Kendall, Master N. Kendall, Master C. Kendall, Walter Kendall, and Miss Mary Kendall.

KENNEDY, Miss Polly.

Three-quarter length, 49¼ × 39 *in.*

She was "one of the Phrynes of the day," and was of an Irish family.

Sitting; in a rich dress trimmed with ermine; a Persian sash and flowered underskirt; her right hand and arm raised, holding a handkerchief; pearl earrings; curtain and architectural background.

Sat in 1770 and 1771. Paid for, 1771, Sir Charles Bunbury, £70.

"DEAR SIR,

"I have finished the face very much to my own satisfaction. It has more grace and dignity than anything I have ever done, and it is the best coloured. As to the dress I should be glad it might be left undetermined till I return from my fortnight's tour. When I return I will try different dresses. The cashmere dresses are very rich and have one sort of dignity in comparison of the simplicity of the antique. The impatience I have to finish it will shorten my stay in the country, I shall set out in an hour's time.

"I am, with the greatest respect,
"Your most obliged Servant,
"J. REYNOLDS.

"Sir Charles Bunbury, Bart."

EXHIBITED.

British Institution, 1841, No. 98, as Mrs. Kennedy, by Sir H. Bunbury, Bart.

British Institution, 1861, No. 202, as Mrs. Kennedy, by Sir C. J. F. Bunbury, Bart.

Royal Academy, 1879, No. 173, by Sir Charles Bunbury, Bart.

    "   "   1891, No. 132, by Sir E. H. Bunbury, Bart.

ENGRAVED.

T. Watson, 1771, 17¼ × 14 in.

S. W. Reynolds, 5 × 4 in.

A noted beauty in her time. An interesting story is told in Leslie and Taylor's "Life of Reynolds" of her efforts to save her brothers from being hanged for murder in 1770, vol. i., pp. 394-397.

The picture was sold by Sir Henry Bunbury, Bart., to William Waldorf Astor, the present owner.

A Miss Kennedy sold at Christie's, June 15, 1838, Lot 49 (Rochard, owner), for £1, to Lord Radstock; Miss Kennedy, same rooms, May 10, 1844, Lot 77, bought in by the owner, M. Rochard, for £8 8s.

KENT, Mrs., afterwards Mary, Lady.

Whole length, 40 × 39 *in.*

Mary, daughter and co-heiress of Josiah Wordsworth, of Wordsworth, co. York, married Sir Charles Egleton Kent, Bart., and died September 17, 1817.

Description in the Royal Academy Catalogue, 1893: "Seated in front on the ground; head turned to right; three-quarter face; fair hair, dressed on the top of her head with muslin and pearls, and falling in curls on her neck; yellow dress open in front, and fastened with a jewel; her right arm rests upon a rock, over which is thrown a mantle; in her left hand she holds the end of a gold sash which is round her waist; landscape background."

Sat in 1777 as Mrs. Kent, and in June, 1786, as Lady Kent. Paid for, February, 1777, Mrs. Kent, £36 15s.; May, 1779, Mrs. Kent, £36 15s.

Royal Academy, 1893, No. 135, by Sir J. H. Thorold, Bart.

ENGRAVED.

J. Dean, 1778, 18 × 13¼ in.

First State, sold in the Palmerston Collection at Christie's, 1890, for £14 3s. 6d.

Her daughters, Mary and Louisa, were painted by Romney. The elder married, October 1, 1811, Sir John Hayford Thorold, Bart., the grandfather of Sir John Henry Thorold, Bart., the present owner.

On the death of Sir Charles Kent the picture became the property of his sister, the late Mrs. Litchford, of Brokeby Hall, Grantham, and passed from her to her sister, Mrs. Childers, of Doncaster, who left it to Sir J. H. Thorold, Bart.

The picture is now the property of E. J. Wythes, of Copt Hall, Essex.

KEPPEL, Admiral the Hon. Augustus.

Whole length, 94 × 58 in.

Second son of William, Earl of Albemarle; born 1725; entered the service when young; accompanied Anson round the world, 1740-45; Commodore, 1752; Rear-Admiral of the Blue, 1761; Lord of the Admiralty, 1765; Admiral, 1778; fought the indecisive battle against the French at Ushant same year, when he was accused of incapacity by Sir Hugh Palliser, January 7, 1779, but acquitted February 11, 1779; M.P. for Surrey, 1780; one of the Elder Brethren of Trinity House; received the thanks of both Houses of Parliament for his services; created Viscount Keppel, April 22, 1782; twice First Lord of the Admiralty, March 30, 1782; died, unmarried, October 3, 1786.

In naval uniform; bareheaded; walking on the seashore; right arm and hand extended; left hand on his sword; a stormy sea on his left; high rocks on his right. The latter portion of the picture was an illustration of his escape from the wreck of the "Maidstone," lost in 1747 on the coast of France whilst under his command.

Painted in 1753.

EXHIBITED.

British Institution, 1832, No. 84,
    "   "   1852, No. 137,
    "   "   1864, No. 161, } by the Earl of Albemarle.
Royal Academy, 1873, No. 199,
Grosvenor, 1884, No. 181,

ENGRAVED.

Edward Fisher, *1759*, 18¼ × 14 in.
James Scott, 1863, 7¼ × 4¼ in.
Anonymously (stipple), 5⅞ × 3¼ in.

The picture was sold by the Earl of Albemarle to Messrs. T. Agnew and Sons in 1888 ; they sold it to the Earl of Rosebery, the present owner.

"But the portrait which tended most to establish Sir Joshua's reputation was a whole length of Captain Keppel, on a sandy beach, the background a tempestuous sea. A figure so animated, so well drawn, and all its accompaniments so perfectly in unison with it, I believe never was produced before by an English pencil. His business increased rapidly upon it, and chiefly among persons of the first rank."—MASON, p. 80.

"'With this picture,' says Farrington, 'he took great pains, for it was observed at the time that, after several sittings, he defaced the work and began it again. His labours were not lost. The excellent production was so much admired that it completely established the reputation of the artist. Its dignity and spirit, its beauty of colour, and the fine general effect, occasioned equal surprise and pleasure. The public, hitherto accustomed to see only the formal tame representations which reduce all persons to the same standard, were captivated with this display of animated character, and the report of its attraction was soon widely circulated.'"—BEECHEY, 1852, vol. i., p. 119.

"In the conception of the picture he availed himself of an event which had occurred before the commencement of his acquaintance with the commodore. Keppel, when but twenty-one years of age, had been appointed to the command of the 'Maidstone,' a fifty-gun ship, and in the following year was wrecked in her on the coast of France, while in the pursuit of a large French vessel. By great exertion he saved most of his crew, and on his return to England was honourably acquitted of all blame by the unanimous resolution of a court-martial that 'the loss of his Majesty's ship "Maidstone" was in no manner owing to Captain Keppel or any of his officers, but to the thickness of the weather at the time the "Maidstone" was chasing in with the *land*, and the ledge of rocks she struck upon being under water, and therefore not perceived, and trusting to the ship the "Maidstone" was chasing, which had the appearance of being a large one, and drawing as much water as the "Maidstone."'

"In the picture Keppel appears on a rocky shore, the breakers are round him, and he is stepping forward to give his orders with an energy and an expression that tell the story, though no other figure is seen. Light, spare, and active, with a quick eye of great intelligence, he looks the very beau ideal of a sailor."—LESLIE AND TAYLOR'S *Life of Sir Joshua*, vol. i., pp. 105, 106.

KEPPEL, Admiral the Hon. Augustus.

Three-quarter length, 52¼ × 45 in.

Standing, facing the spectator, with his right hand on a stick ; in a blue coat, with white and gold-laced waistcoat ; cocked hat under his left arm ; lapel of his uniform turned over on the left side and buttoned to waistcoat ; left arm bent ; hand resting on hip ; the waistcoat not embroidered ; the sea in the right distance ; rock and stormy sky to the left.

Sat in 1759.

E. Fisher, 1760, 13¾ × 11 in.
Anonymous, 12¼ × 9⅞ in.
S. W. Reynolds, 3½ × 2¼ in.
J. Scott, 1864, 4⅞ × 3¼ in.

The picture belongs to the Duke of Bedford at Woburn Abbey, and is No. 257 in the Woburn catalogue.

KEPPEL, Admiral the Hon. Augustus.

Replica of the previous picture.

British Institution, 1846, No. 51, by Lord Falmouth.

The picture belongs to Lord Falmouth, and hangs at 2, St. James's Square.

KEPPEL, Admiral the Hon. Augustus.

Sat in 1764. Paid for, August 27, 1764, Admiral Keppell, in full, £100, *for his own two pictures and the Bishop of Exeter's ;* January 23, 1764 (? 1765), General Keppell, in full, £117 ; February 8, 1768, Admiral Keppell, given to the Bishop, 35 guineas.

The above entry is not clear ; the note printed in italics comes between the payments of the admiral and the general, but from the final entry it appears that the note refers to the admiral, although from the colour of the ink it seems to have been written at the time of the entry of the general.

The Bishop of Exeter from 1762 to 1778 was the Hon. Frederick Keppel, fourth son of the 2nd Earl of Albemarle, and brother to Admiral and General Keppel ; he might have had presentation portraits from both.

KEPPEL, Admiral the Hon. Augustus.

Sat in 1765. Paid for, February 23, 1770, Mr. Brett, for Admiral Keppell, £26 5s. *See* BRETT, *ante,* p. 113.

KEPPEL, Admiral the Hon. Augustus.

Half length, canvas 29½ × 24¼ in.

Nearly full face ; head turned slightly to the right ; the lips parted as if about to speak ; the eyes looking out to the right ; his own hair powdered; admiral's uniform; dark blue coat with white lapels and braided with gold; white vest gold-laced, and white lace cravat; pale grey background.

Grosvenor, 1889, No. 40, by Lord Burton.

W. Doughty, 1779, 16 × 13 in.
S. W. Reynolds, 3¼ × 2⅞ in.

This picture in 1835 was in the possession of Edward Wright, of Newark; it now belongs to Lord Burton.

Letter from Reynolds to Keppel, February, 1779: "I have taken the liberty of lending your picture to an engraver to make a print from it."

KEPPEL, Admiral the Hon. Augustus.

Half length, 49 × 39 *in.*

To left, in naval uniform; blue coat and white waistcoat, both gold-laced; lace tie and ruffles; right hand rests on his sword; left upon his hip; sky and landscape background, with sea to the right.

Sat in 1779. Paid for, September, 1779, Admiral Keppel, for four half-lengths, £400.

British Institution, 1867, No. 205, by C. B. Lee-Mainwaring.
Royal Academy, 1884, No. 50, } by the Hon. W. F. B. Massey-Main-
Guelph, 1891, No. 98,   }   waring.

After the admiral's trial by court-martial and acquittal at Plymouth, he presented a banknote for £1,000 to each of his counsel for their professional assistance. John Lee, known as Honest Jack Lee, returned the money, and wrote: "Will you make me a present of your picture painted by Dance, who takes excellent likenesses, that I may keep it, and my family after me." Admiral Keppel also presented Mr. Lee with his own portrait, the same size.

James Scott, 1863, 5¼ × 4¼ in.

The picture was in 1863 the property of Charles Benjamin Lee-Mainwaring, who bequeathed it to his nephew, the Hon. W. F. B. Massey-Mainwaring, M.P., the present owner.

KEPPEL, Admiral the Hon. Augustus.

Three-quarter length, canvas 49 × 39¼ in.

Similar to the last.

Paid for, September, 1779, Admiral Keppel, for four half-lengths, £400.

EXHIBITED.

British Institution, 1833, No. 23, by Lady Ashburton.

National Portrait Exhibition, 1868, No. 843, by the National Portrait Gallery.

The picture was presented by Keppel to his friend John Dunning, afterwards Lord Ashburton, in acknowledgment of his legal services during the Portsmouth trial, in lieu of a banknote for £1,000, which had been returned. It was purchased by the National Portrait Gallery in June, 1864, and is No. 179 in the catalogue.

KEPPEL, Admiral the Hon. Augustus.

Three-quarter length, canvas 49 × 39 in.

Naval uniform ; turned to left ; right hand resting on his sword ; background of sea and stormy sky.

Similar to the last.

Paid for, September, 1779, Admiral Keppel, for four half-lengths, £400.

EXHIBITED.

Grosvenor, 1884, No. 44, by the Earl of Albemarle.

The picture was sold by the Earl of Albemarle to Messrs. T. Agnew and Sons in 1888, and by them to Lord Iveagh, the present owner.

KEPPEL, Admiral the Hon. Augustus.

Three-quarter length, canvas 50¼ × 40¼ in.

Similar to the last.

Paid for September, 1779, Admiral Keppel, for four half-lengths, £400.

The picture was presented by Lord Keppel to Burke, who writes to Lord Keppel :

"'The town, and my house there, will be the more pleasant to me for a piece of furniture I have had since I saw you, and which I owe to your goodness. I shall leave it to my son, who is of a frame of mind to relish that kind of honour, the satisfaction of knowing that his father was distinguished by the partiality of one of those who are the marked men of all story, by having the glory and reproach of the times they live in, and whose services and merits, by being above recompense, are delivered over to ingratitude. Whenever he sees this picture, he will remember what Englishmen and what English seamen were in the days when name of nation, and when eminence and superiority in that profession, were one and the same thing.

"'I assure you, my dear sir, that though I possess the portraits of friends highly honoured by me, and very dear to me on all accounts, yours stands alone, and I intend that it shall so continue to mark the impression that I have received of this most flattering mark of your friendship.' The picture was preserved with reverence at Beaconsfield while Burke lived. His widow left it to Earl Fitzwilliam."—TOM TAYLOR, vol. ii., p. 236.

The picture now belongs to the Hon. George W. Fitzwilliam at Milton, Peterborough.

In 1796, Burke, old and broken-hearted, wrote of this picture to the Duke of Bedford, nephew of the man it represented :

" It was but the other day that I looked over some fine portraits, most of them of persons now dead, but whose society, in my better days, made this a proud and happy place. Amongst them was the picture of Lord Keppel. It was painted by an artist worthy of the subject, the excellent friend of that excellent man from his earliest youth, and a common friend of us both, with whom we lived for many years without a moment of coldness, of peevishness, of jealousy, or of jar to the day of our final separation. I ever looked on Keppel as one of the greatest and best man of his age ; and I loved and cultivated him accordingly. He was much in my heart, and I believe I was in his to the very last beat. It was at his trial at Portsmouth that he gave me the picture," etc.—BURKE'S *Works*, vol. vii., p. 433.

KEPPEL, Admiral Augustus, Viscount.

Three-quarter length, canvas 49 × 39 in.

In a claret-coloured suit ; right hand resting on his sheathed sword ; left on his hip ; a view of the sea in the background.

Sat in 1780. Paid for, after 1782, and before 1786, Lord Kepell, given to Mr. Erskine, £100. *See Scale Vol III. p. 1008*

EXHIBITED.

British Institution, 1849, No. 126, by Sir Robert Peel, Bart.

This picture, which was given to Erskine several years after it was painted (1780), fetched 1,000 guineas at Erskine's sale ; bought by Peacock. It afterwards became the property of Thomas Wright, and was sold at his sale. At Christie's, June 7, 1845, Lot 52, described as " Admiral Keppel. This picture was presented by the admiral to the late Lord Erskine for his defence against Admiral Palliser. Sir Joshua considered it one of his most perfect pictures." It was sold for £535 10s. to Stephenson, for Sir Robert Peel, Bart. It was purchased by the nation in 1871 with the Peel Collection, and now hangs in the National Gallery (No. 886).

Postscript to a letter from T. Erskine, from Serjeant's Inn, to Sir Joshua Reynolds, dated January 26, 1783 : "I hope you will let me have Lord Keppel's picture soon."

KEPPEL, Admiral Augustus, Viscount.

Whole length, canvas 93 × 57 *in.*

Holding in his hand the order for the relief of Gibraltar.

Standing, full face, in a blue coat with gold facings buttoned by one button, with lace cuffs; left hand on sword; right arm leaning on a rock, holding a paper in the hand; high rock to right; low sea horizon to the left.   Sec *..... ....*

Sat in 1780. Paid for, August, 1786, Lord Keppel, given to the Prince of Wales, 200 guineas.

EXHIBITED.

British Institution, 1813, No. 111, by the Prince Regent.
        „   „   1833, No. 21, by William IV.
        „   „   1843, No. 22, by Her Majesty the Queen.
The picture belongs to Her Majesty the Queen at St. James's Palace.

This picture has for some time had a label on the frame describing it as Lord Barrington.

KEPPEL, Admiral Augustus, Viscount.

Three-quarter length, canvas.

A picture belongs to Lord Fitzhardinge at Cranford House, Hounslow.

KEPPEL, Admiral Augustus, Viscount.

EXHIBITED.
British Institution, 1847, No. 139, by Rev. R. F. Elwin.

KEPPEL, Admiral Augustus, Viscount.

EXHIBITED.
British Institution, 1832, No. 158, by Earl Brownlow.

KEPPEL, Admiral Augustus, Viscount.

Half length, canvas 30 × 24¼ *in.*

EXHIBITED.

British Institution, 1845, No. 60, }
      „   „   1858, No. 141, } by the Hon. Mrs. Ramsden.

The picture was painted for Lord Rockingham, and given by him to Lady Rockingham; it was left by her to her half-sister, Mrs. Weddell, from whom it passed to the father of Sir John Ramsden, Bart., the present owner; it hangs at Bulstrode, Gerrard's Cross, Bucks.

The last four portraits have been placed at the end, under Lord Keppel, although they may belong to earlier periods. The compilers have not seen these pictures.

Sales of other portraits of Admiral Keppel at Christie's and elsewhere:

	Lot.			£	s.	d.	
1813.		Phillips.	Sir J. Craig, owner. Captain Keppel, afterwards Admiral	5	15	6	
1814, April 2.	14.	Christie's.	Belli, owner. Small portrait of Admiral Keppel . .	1	13	0	Colnaghi.
1818, May 2.	88.	„	Rising, owner. An original of Admiral Keppel, when young	9	19	6	Bought in.
1821, „ 26.	4.	„	Thomond Collection. Admiral Keppel, with others . .	7	7	0	Wansey.
„ „ „	10.	„	Thomond Collection. Admiral Keppel, and the late Duchess of Devonshire. Sketches .	5	10	0	Turner, R.A.
„ „ „	24.	„	Thomond Collection. Admiral Keppel, Counsellor Dunning	2	6	0	
1830, March 12.	74.	„	Paine, owner. Whole length of Admiral Keppel. Sketch	2	0	0	Qualsh.
1832, „ 3.	4.	„	Andrews, owner. Admiral Keppel when Captain. Painted at Rome. . .	4	8	0	Tiffin.
1882, May 27.	129.	„	D. Macheath, owner. Admiral Keppel. Collection of Turner	55	13	0	Robinson.

Messrs. Henry Graves and Co. sold in 1883 a portrait of Admiral Keppel for £20 to Admiral the Hon. Sir Henry Keppel, G.C.B.

KEPPEL, The Hon. General William.

Three-quarter length, canvas 67¼ × 56 *in., oblong.*

Fourth son of William Anne, 2nd Earl of Albemarle, made captain of the first regiment of Foot Guards, December 21, 1752; on July 21, 1760, made major of the same; in January, 1762, he had the command of the 56th regiment of infantry, with which he embarked in March following in the fleet fitted out against the Havannah. He conducted the storming of

Moro Castle; was left commander of La Punta after the departure of his eldest brother. He re-delivered the city of Havannah to the Spanish troops, July 7, 1763, according to the articles of peace signed at Paris in February. In December, 1773, he was made commander-in-chief, and was M.P. for Windsor. He died March, 1782, unmarried.

In uniform; landscape background, with Fort Moro in the distance, towards which he points with his left hand; right hand in the breast of his coat.

Sat in 1758, 1759, 1762, as Colonel Keppel; 1764, as General Keppel; 1765, as Colonel Keppel. Paid for, 1763, General Keppell, £21; January 23, 1764, General Keppell in full, £117. Before this last entry and after that of Admiral Keppel is written, "*for his own two pictures and the Bishop of Exeter's*"; it is uncertain to which entry it refers.

See picture the C. 11 . p 464

EXHIBITED.

Grosvenor, 1884, No. 28, by the Earl of Albemarle.

The picture was sold by the Earl of Albemarle in 1888 to Messrs. T. Agnew and Sons, from whom it passed to the Earl of Rosebery, the present owner. It hangs at 38, Berkeley Square.

KEPPEL, Colonel, afterwards General.

Three-quarter length, canvas 29 × 24 in.

Sketch.

Face turned to the right; red coat with black and gold facings; sash over right shoulder.

EXHIBITED.

Grosvenor, 1884, No. 14, by the Earl of Albemarle.

Sold at Christie's, in 1893, as General Keppel, to Messrs. Tooth and Sons, from whom it passed to Timothy Hopkins, of San Francisco, the present owner.

KEPPEL, Lady Caroline, afterwards Lady C. Adair.

Half length, 29 × 24¼ in.

Daughter of William Anne, 2nd Earl of Albemarle; born August 20, 1737; married, 1759, Robert Adair, the eminent surgeon; died September 11, 1769.

Dr. Robert Adair, a surgeon of considerable eminence, attended George III. and other members of the royal family, and at the time of his death was Inspector of Hospitals and Surgeon to the Royal Hospital at Chelsea. The marriage was regarded somewhat in the light of a mésalliance. Horace Walpole, in a letter to Lord Hertford, dated April 12, 1764, laments the marriage of Lady Susan Fox with O'Brien the actor. He adds: " I could not have believed Lady Susan would have stooped so low; she may, however, still keep good company, and say, *Nos memori sumus* Lady Mary Duncan, Lady Caroline Adair, Lady Betty Gallini—the shopkeepers of the next age will be mighty well born." The son of Lady Caroline Adair was, however, not a shopkeeper but a celebrated diplomatist. His mother died when he was a boy. She accompanied her brother, Captain Keppel, on the voyage to Lisbon, which was undertaken in a last hope of saving the life of her sister, who died in 1768. She nursed her with the utmost care and devotion. She herself died the following year, having been married only ten years. A marble bust commemorates the spot where she was buried, and where her husband was also interred in 1790.

Full face; the arms crossed, resting on a table; white dress, with black mantilla; a band of black ribbon and a string of pearls round her neck.

Sat in 1755 and 1757.

EXHIBITED.

British Institution, 1852, No. 126, ⎫
Royal Academy, 1873, No. 139, ⎬ by the Earl of Albemarle.
Grosvenor, 1884, No. 123, ⎭

This picture was sold by the Earl of Albemarle in 1888 to Messrs. T. Agnew and Sons.

KEPPEL, Lady Caroline, afterwards Lady C. Adair.

Half length, canvas 29 × 24 in.

To the waist; in a pink dress with bows of a slaty colour, and a dull blue drapery passing over her left shoulder; the figure turned somewhat to the left, and the face seen in three-quarters looking away to the right; the hair is dark brown of a natural colour; a black velvet ribbon encircles her neck; plain dark grey background.

The picture belongs to the Duke of Bedford, and is No. 251 in the Woburn catalogue.

KEPPEL, Lady Elizabeth, afterwards Marchioness of Tavistock.

Three-quarter length, canvas 29 × 24½ in.

Fifth daughter of William Anne, 2nd Earl of Albemarle (thirteenth child); born November 15, 1739; married, June 9, 1764, Francis Russell, Marquess of Tavistock, son of John, 4th Duke of Bedford, who was killed March 10, 1767. She died November 2, 1768.

547

Horace Walpole in one of his letters to Lord Hertford thus alludes to her engagement to Lord Tavistock :

"I dined with her at M. de Guerchy's. . . . Mde. de G. said she perceived I would let nobody else tease her. . . . Yesterday all went well at Woburn, and to-morrow the ceremony is to be performed."

Her marriage was one of unclouded happiness. Two little sons were born. Her youngest, William, was born after the terrible accident which ended so fatally for her husband, in 1767. Up to the time of his birth she struggled on bravely, but from that time she drooped and pined away. As a last hope a voyage to Lisbon was agreed upon, and her brother, Captain Keppel, conveyed her there in a frigate ; but she survived the voyage only a few days, and died of grief and decline in October, 1768.

Seated, turned to the right ; white dress, with lace cross over, and a rose in her bosom ; pearl necklace and earrings ; hands in lap ; red chair.

Sat in 1755, 1757, 1758, and 1759, as Lady Elizabeth Keppel. Paid for (no date), Lady Elizabeth Keppell. Paid in full by the Admiral, £15. Exhibited in the Society of Artists, 1760, No. 41.

EXHIBITED.

British Institution, 1852, No. 147,
Royal Academy, 1873, No. 88, } by the Earl of Albemarle.
Grosvenor, 1884, No. 111,

Grosvenor, 1889, No. 3, } by E. L. Raphael.
Royal Academy, 1893, No. 21,

The picture was sold by the Earl of Albemarle in 1888 to Messrs. T. Agnew and Sons, from whom it passed to E. L. Raphael, of 4, Connaught Place, the present owner.

KEPPEL, Lady Elizabeth, afterwards Marchioness of Tavistock.

Whole length, canvas 93 × 57¼ in.

"Represented in the dress which she wore as a bridesmaid at the marriage of Queen Charlotte, decorating the statue of Hymen with flowers, attended by a negress ; she raises with both hands a garland to decorate the statue on the left. Her face is seen almost in profile, looking towards the right. The negress kneeling behind her holds up another massive garland. A rich curtain suspended from the branches of a tree behind the statue affords a solid background for the principal figure ; a tripod altar with pale red flame before the figure of Hymen is on the extreme left-hand side in front, and the terminal statue holds a royal crown in one hand and a lighted torch in the other. The dress of the negress is spotted white, and open at the neck to display three rows of pearls and pearl earrings. The sky behind is dazzlingly bright, and the folds of the long white satin dress are most cleverly arranged. Inscribed on the side of the step beneath her feet :

"'Cinge Tempora Floribus
Suaveolentis Amaraci :

548

Adsis, o Hymenæe Hymen!
Hymen, o Hymenæe!'

from Catullus, on the marriage of Julia and Manlius. On the lower step in the deep shade are also traces of an obliterated inscription to the following effect :

"' Elizabeth, Countess of Albemarle, Daughter of Admiral Keppel, 1761.'

(No reason can be assigned for this obviously incorrect description.)

"The accessories were painted by Peter Toms. In Reynolds's book of sitters we find that Lady Elizabeth Keppel sat to him in September, 1761, and a 'negro,' probably for the same picture, was several times employed in December of the same year.

"The picture was presented by William Charles, 4th Earl of Albemarle, who died in 1849, to the Duke of Bedford ; see a letter from Lady Augusta Noel, dated March 17, 1884."

The above description is taken from the "Biographical Catalogue of the Pictures at Woburn Abbey," by Adeline Marie, Duchess of Bedford, and Lady Ella M. S. Russell.

Sat in 1761 and 1762 as Lady Elizabeth Keppel. Paid for (no date), Lady Eliz^{th}. Keppel—paid by Lord Albermarle, £42. July 4, 1765, Lady Eliz. Keppell, now Lady Tavistoke, £42. Exhibited in the Society of Artists, 1762, No. 87, as Lady Elizabeth Keppel, as one of Her Majesty's bridesmaids, whole length.

Edwards mentions : "Among whole lengths of Sir Joshua's, to which Toms had painted the draperies, the Woburn whole length of the Marchioness of Tavistock, when Lady Elizabeth Keppel. For this Toms only received 12 guineas."

ENGRAVED.

E. Fisher, 1761, 23½ × 14½ in.
S. W. Reynolds (S. Cousins, R.A.), 6¼ × 3⅞ in.

A First State of the Fisher plate, in the Buccleuch Collection, sold at Christie's in 1887 for £63.

The picture belongs to the Duke of Bedford, and is No. 248 in the Woburn catalogue.

KEPPEL, Lady Elizabeth, afterwards Marchioness of Tavistock.

Half length, canvas 29 × 24½ in.

The face is turned in profile to the left and slightly drooping ; her dress is quilted blue silk, with bows of the same colour, covered by a black lace shawl ; her dark hair is set off by a small white lace cap and a blue knot in the centre over the forehead ; a blue ribbon and white lace encircle the neck, and she wears handsome diamond earrings ; white lace sleeves ; the tall back of a crimson chair rises behind her to the left ; mellow grey background.

The picture belongs to the Duke of Bedford, and is No. 250 in the Woburn catalogue. *See* TAVISTOCK.

549

KEPPEL, Miss Anna Maria.

Daughter of the Rev. Lord Frederick Keppel; consecrated Bishop of Exeter in 1762; married, September, 1758, Laura, daughter of Sir Edward Walpole, and sister of Maria, late Duchess of Gloucester. She was born June 17, 1759, and married in 1790 the Hon. General G. Chetwynd Stapleton.

Sat in September, 1764.

"Sir Joshua was present (1772) at the supper and ball given by the newly-installed knights at the Opera House; when Sir Charles Hotham and Lady Bridget Lane opened the dance; after which Miss Hotham and Miss Keppel, the Hon. H. Hobart and Captain Corbet danced a minuet and *allemand à quatre*—composed for the occasion—so gracefully that it was repeated again and again at the desire of the company."—TOM TAYLOR, vol. i., p. 448.

KEPPEL, Miss, afterwards Mrs. Thomas Meyrick.

Three-quarter length, canvas 50 × 40 in.

A natural daughter of Admiral Viscount Keppel; married, October 16, 1787, Captain Thomas Meyrick, who afterwards became General, and died June 5, 1830.

Walking in a park; to the left; in a white dress, with black mantle; drawing on her right glove; muslin frill round neck, with bows in front; large hat with black feathers; narrow ribbon round neck.

Sat in May, 1782, as Miss Keppel. Paid for before 1786, Lord Keppell, for Miss Kepell's picture, £50.

EXHIBITED.

British Institution, 1858, No. 180, as Mrs. Colonel Meyrick, by F. Grant, R.A.

Sold at Christie's, May 18, 1810, Lot 97 (J. Hoppner, R.A., owner), as Mrs. Meyrick, for £11 0s. 6d., to Owen; June 27, 1863, Lot 31 (Grant, owner), Mrs. Meyrick, in a white dress, putting on her gloves, black scarf and hat, £55 13s., to Smith; April 24, 1869, Lot 76 (George E. Seymour, owner), as Mrs. Meyrick, in a white dress, exhibited at the British Institution, £94 10s., to D. Colnaghi.

ENGRAVED.

S. W. Reynolds, 1820 (S. Cousins, R.A.), 5¼ × 4¼ in., as Mrs. Merrick.

"October 16, 1787. Capt. Meyrick of the 66th Regiment to the Hon. Miss Keppel, dau. of the late Lord Visc. Keppel."—*Gentleman's Magazine*, 1787, p. 1022.

"June 5, 1830. At the house of his son in Berkeley Square, after three days' illness, of dyspepsia, aged sixty-six, Thomas Meyrick, General in the Army, and Lieutenant-Colonel of the 21st Regiment of Foot. . . . His more active military career commenced in the year following; for in December, 1782, Captain Meyrick embarked with General Prescott for the relief of St. Kitts, and was present in the three engagements off that island between Sir Samuel Hood and the fleet of Admiral the Comte de Grasse. He afterwards landed with the

First Payment

Admiral Keppell given to the Bishop [?]   22

Feb 1st   Capt King Howll —
1777   Mrs Kent _____ [?] for four half lengths   15
Sept.   Admiral Keppell for four half lengths   40
1779   Do   for Samuel   do   £
          His majestys and the Queen —   420
          Lord Keppell for miss Keppell 50
          Lord Kepell — given to her brother   100

august   Lord Keppell given to the
1786   Prince of Wales — 200 G.

troops, and was present in all the actions that took place until the re-embarkation. After his return home, in consequence of an attack of yellow fever, he married the natural daughter of the celebrated Admiral Lord Keppel, a very pretty woman, who, being her father's sole heir, brought him a handsome acquisition of fortune. She died June 19, 1821. The issue of that marriage was one son, William Henry Meyrick, born in 1790, now Lieutenant-Colonel in the 3rd Regiment of Foot Guards. . . . He was uncle to Dr. Meyrick, of Goodrich Court, Herefordshire, etc., etc."—*Gentleman's Magazine*, vol. c., p. 87.

KERRY, Anastasia, Countess of.

Anastasia, second daughter and co-heiress of Peter Daly, of Queensbury, co. Galway; married, March 24, 1768, Francis Thomas, 3rd Earl of Kerry. Upon the deaths of her sisters, the Countess of Louth and Viscountess Kingsland, she inherited the whole of Mr. Daly's very great estates. She died April 9, 1799, and her remains were deposited in St. Andrew's Chapel, Westminster Abbey, on April 19, where her husband was also buried, July 4, 1818, when his title became merged in that of the Marquess of Lansdowne.

Sat in September, 1769, as Lady Kerry.

KILDARE, James, Earl of, afterwards Duke of Leinster.

James, third son of Robert, 19th Earl of Kildare; born May 29, 1722; succeeded as 20th Earl, February 20, 1743; created Viscount Leinster of Taplow, February 21, 1747; Marquess of Kildare, March 3, 1761, and Duke of Leinster, November 26, 1766; married, February 7, 1747, Lady Emilia Lennox, daughter of Charles, 2nd Duke of Richmond. He died November 19, 1773.

Standing in peer's robes; left hand holding a scroll; right hand pointing to landscape, seen through window on the right; left elbow leaning on a pedestal.

Painted in 1754.

ENGRAVED.

J. McArdell, 1754, 12¼ × 9¾ in.
S. W. Reynolds, 3 × 2¼ in.

KILDARE, James, Earl of, afterwards Duke of Leinster.

Three-quarter length, canvas 49 × 38¼ in.

Standing figure, turned to the right; face seen in three-quarters; hair powdered; right hand slightly raised; left elbow resting on a pedestal; left hand holding his hat; he wears a blue coat trimmed with gold.

Lady Rayleigh writes, December 14, 1898: "The McArdell print of the 1st Duke of Leinster in peer's robes is *not* taken from our Sir Joshua portrait of him. I do not know where the original of the print is, nor do I know when or how the painting we have got came here. It was *not* at the same time as that of the Duchess, which was given by her second husband, and which is evidently the original of McArdell's print of her. The description I gave you of our painting of the Duke is correct. It has very little resemblance to the print (except as to face)."

The picture belongs to Lord Rayleigh, at Terling Place, Witham, Essex.

KILDARE, Emilia Mary, Countess of, afterwards Duchess of Leinster.

Three-quarter length, canvas 49 × 38¼ *in.*

Lady Emilia Mary Lennox, daughter of Charles, Duke of Richmond and Lennox; born October 6, 1731; married, first, February 7, 1747, James, 20th Earl of Kildare, created Duke of Leinster in 1766; on his death, November 19, 1773, he left Carton to her for life, or until she married again; she married, secondly, William Ogilvie, fifth son of Sir James Ogilvie, of Deskford and Findlater. She died in March 27, 1814. A long tribute to her worth is to be found in the "Gentleman's Magazine," 1814, page 417.

Seated, her right elbow leaning on a red-covered table, with her head resting on her right hand; a veil on her head; pearl earrings; bracelets of the same; a row of pearls falling across her bosom from right to left; her left hand holds a book in her lap; she wears a low grey-green dress, showing a white underskirt embroidered with gold, with undersleeves gathered up with pearls; from a window a view of trees in a landscape; curtain on her right.

Sat in June, 1755.

ENGRAVED.

J. McArdell, 1754, 12¼ × 9¼ in.
S. W. Reynolds, 3 × 2¼ in.
R. B. Parkes, 1876, 5¼ × 4¼ in.

The picture was given by William Ogilvie, who married Emilia Mary, Duchess of Leinster, in 1776, as her second husband, to Colonel Joseph Holden Strutt, who married her daughter Charlotte, by the 1st Duke of Leinster, in 1789. Lady Charlotte Strutt was afterwards created Baroness Rayleigh.

The picture belongs to Lord Rayleigh, at Terling Place, Witham, Essex. *See* LEINSTER, page 575.

A picture described as the Duchess of Leinster was exhibited at Suffolk Street in 1832, No. 2, by Major Beauclerc. This picture is a copy (49 × 40 in.) by J. Payne in 1824. It was purchased from his son, A. Beauclerc, of Ardglass, in 1885, by the Duke of Leinster. It hangs at Kilkea Castle, co. Kildare, Ireland.

Her daughter, Emily Charlotte, by William Ogilvie, born May 12, 1778, married, April 29, 1799, Charles G. Beauclerc, only son of Topham Beauclerc.

KILDARE, Emilia Mary, Countess of, afterwards Duchess of Leinster.

Half length, canvas 30 × 25 *in.*

Three-quarter face to the right; her right elbow resting on a table, with her right hand to her face; wearing a low quilted body, with lace fichu round her neck and black cloak over the shoulders; large lace sleeves; pearls in her hair, and pearl bracelet and earrings.

The picture belongs to Earl Bathurst, at Cirencester House, Cirencester.

The Countess of Dysart

KILDARE, Bishop of. *See* R. ROBINSON.

KILLALA, Bishop of.

Sat in December, 1758, as Bishop of Killala. *See* R. ROBINSON.

KILWALIN, Lord.

Sat in 1755.

This name must have been misspelt by the artist. The compilers have in vain endeavoured to discover who it is intended for.

KING, Dr. James, afterwards Dean of Raphoe.

Appointed Dean of Raphoe, October 25, 1776; died 1795.

"April 24, 1795, at Woodstock, in his eighty-first year, the Rev. James King, D.D., Dean of Raphoe in Ireland, formerly chaplain to the House of Commons in England, and Canon of Windsor."—*Gentleman's Magazine*, 1795, p. 441.

Sat in December, 1781, as Dean of Raphoe. Paid for, December 26 1781, Dean of Rapho, £52 10s.

KING, Mr.

Sat in 1757 and 1771.

KINGSLEY, Lieut.-General William.

Half length, oval, canvas 30 × 25 in.

Made Lieut.-General, February 22, 1760; Governor of Fort William, N.B.; died 1768.

In uniform with a breastplate; three-quarters length; turned to the left.

Sat in 1760 as General Kingsley. Paid for, 1760, General Kingsley, £21.

ENGRAVED.

R. Houston, 1760, 13¼ × 10¾ in.
S. W. Reynolds, 1¼ × 1¼ in.

"Of Kingsley's Foot; was distinguished in the campaign of 1759, and one of the commanders of the secret expedition assembled at Portsmouth this year, which disbanded without action."—TOM TAYLOR, vol. i., p. 187.

KINGSMILL, Captain.

Paid for, 1776, Capt. Kingsmill, £20; July 2, 1776, Capt. Kingsmill, £16 15s.

Probably the following: "November 23, 1805, at his seat at Sidmonton, Hants, aged seventy-four, Admiral Sir Richard Kingsmill, Bart. He is succeeded in his title and Hampshire estates by his nephew Robert, son of the late Edward Kingsmill of Belfont."—*Gentleman's Magazine*, 1805, p. 1087.

He was made admiral, February 1, 1793.

"May 3, 1776: Naples; Cinibar; red lead; Cologne earth; black."
"June 3, 1776: Blue; light red; verm.; white; black."

KINGSTON, Elizabeth Chudleigh, Duchess of. *See* CHUDLEIGH, *ante*, page 175.

KINGSWELL, Captain.

Sat in November, 1766.

KIRKLEY, Ralph.

At Christie's, March 19, 1812, Lot 85 (Paul Sandby, owner), Mr. Ralph, who formerly lived with Sir Joshua, for £2 5s., to Thane.

"Between cards and conversation the guests sat late, and twelve has struck before steady Ralph Kirkley has lighted the last of the party out, and barred and bolted the house."—TOM TAYLOR, vol. ii., p. 7.

"Reynolds then determined to make a temporary exhibition of his own master pictures in a room in the Haymarket. He hoped by this Exhibition to promote the sale of the pictures (after offering them to the Royal Academy), but he gave the profits to his old servant, Ralph Kirkley, and in the catalogue called it 'Ralph's Exhibition,'" etc.—TOM TAYLOR, vol. ii., p. 604.

KIRKMAN, Miss.

"October 2, 1772.—Miss Kirkman, gum dr. et whiting, poi cerata, poi ovata, poi verniciata e retouched. Cracks."—"A picture begun with whitening and gum tragacanth, then covered successively with wax, white of egg, and varnish, could hardly escape cracking and separating."—COTTON, p. 245.

"October, 1772. Miss Kirk(man), Gum Dr. (gum tragacanth) and whiting, poi cerata, poi orata, poi verniciata e retoccata. Cracks."

Haydon notes on this: "Beechey says: 'This manner is the most extraordinary.' It is insanity; he had at his elbow a mocking fiend! Gum and whiting—then waxed, then egged, then varnished, and then retouched! No wonder it cracked."—COTTON, 1856, p. 248.

KNAPP, Mr.

Sat in 1758 and 1759 as Mr. and Mrs. Knapp. Paid for, 1760, Mr. Knap, £15 15s.

"Died, July 21, 1766, Mr. Knapp, head clerk in the chamberlain's office."—*Gentleman's Magazine*, 1766, p. 343.

KNAPP, Mrs.

Paid for, 1760, Mrs. Knap, £15 15s.

KNAPP, Mr.

Sat in 1773 as Mr. Knapp.

KNAPPER, General.

Sat in April, 1761, as General Knapper.   Paid for, 1760, General Knapper, £10 10s.; 1763, General Knapper, £10 10s.   *See* NAPIER.

KNAPPER, Miss.

Sat in 1771.

Tom Taylor adds, " Query Napier ? "   *See* NAPIER.

KNIGHT, Ralph.

Half length, canvas 30 × 25 in.

Full face ; looking to the right ; in plum-coloured coat and lace cravat ; own hair ; plain background.

Sat in March, 1755.

The picture belongs to the Rev. Sir Richard Fitzherbert, Bart., at Nettleworth Manor, Mansfield.

KNIGHT, Miss.

Half length, canvas 29¼ × 24¼ in.

Seated in front at a table ; head turned over her left shoulder ; low cut dress ; blue, fur-trimmed cloak ; both hands concealed in a large ermine muff.

EXHIBITED.

Royal Academy, 1882, No. 263, by Sir F. E. Drake, Bart.

ENGRAVED.

S. W. Reynolds, 1823, 5 × 4 in.

Lady Drake writes, December 16, 1898 : " The portrait was painted for Sir Francis Henry Drake at a time when he was engaged to be married to Miss Knight ; she fell ill and died of consumption before the date of her intended wedding.   Sir Francis seems to have known Reynolds well in his early painting days.   An old family letter written to Sir Francis, dated Buckland Abbey, January 3, 1753, says : ' Mr. Reynolds, your painter, is gone to town.

He has drawn several pictures at Plymouth I think very well. He intends to wait on you. It looks as if he would turn out a Vandyke, at least, as to family pieces : could not you trust him as to a copy of your ancestor?'"

KNIGHT, Miss E. Cornelia.

Sold at Christie's, July 1, 1858, Lot 32, Miss E. Cornelia Knight, daughter of Admiral Knight. Painted by Miss Frances Reynolds, Sir Joshua's sister, holding a dog painted by Sir Joshua (Mrs. Hicks, owner), for £28 17s. 6d., to Ruy Webb.

KNOWLES, Admiral Charles.

Born 1699 ; was made Vice-Admiral, 1747 ; fought the Spanish fleet under Reggio at Havannah, but not being sufficiently victorious, was tried by court-martial in 1749 and acquitted ; Governor of Jamaica, from 1752 to 1756 ; Rear-Admiral, 1765 ; created a baronet, October 31, 1765 ; married, first, Mary, daughter of John Alleyne, of Barbadoes, and, secondly, Maria, daughter of Ferdinand, Comte de Bouget. Probably owing to the attacks made on him by the press he entered the Russian service, and was appointed in 1770, by the Empress of Russia, Chief President of Her Majesty's Admiralty, with a seat in the Russian Council. His only son by his first wife was lost in H.M.S. "Peregrine" in a storm, about 1763. He returned to England in 1774, and died December 9, 1777.

"December 9, 1777. Sir Charles Knowles, Bart., Admiral of the White Squadron, in Bulstrode Street, in the seventy-fourth year of his age."—*Gentleman's Magazine*, 1777, p. 612.

Sat in 1757 and 1759.

There is no portrait of him by Reynolds at present in the family. There is an engraving of him, in naval uniform, by Ridley (3⅞ × 3¼ in.), but it bears no painter's name. It has, however, the appearance of being after a picture by Reynolds, and the hair is dressed in the style of 1756, and is very similar to that in a portrait after Hudson, and engraved by J. Faber, of him in armour, as Governor of Jamaica.

KNOX, Mrs.
Three-quarter length.

Sold at Greenwood's, April 14, 1796, Lot 10, Mrs. Knox, three-quarters, for £1 18s., to Silvestre.

KYNASTON, Mr. or Mrs.

Sat in January, 1760, as Mr. Kynaston. Paid for, March 10, 1763, Mrs. Kinaston, £21.

LADE, Sir John, 2nd Baronet.

Three-quarter length, canvas 39 × 35¼ *in., oblong.*

Born August 1, 1759; posthumous and only child of John Lade, of Warbledon, who was created a baronet, 1757; married Mary, daughter of Ralph Thrale, and died by a fall from his horse on April 21, 1759.

"April 21, 1759. Sir John Lade, Bart., member for Camelford, of a mortification by cutting off his leg, which was lately broke by a fall from his horse, a-hunting."—*Gentleman's Magazine*, 1859, p. 194.

"August 1, 1759. Relict of Sir John Lade, Bart., of a son and heir, who is immediately entitled to a very large estate."—*Gentleman's Magazine*, 1859, p. 392.

The 2nd baronet during his minority was under the guardianship of his uncle, Henry Thrale, for many years M.P. for the borough of Southwark; came under the notice of Dr. Johnson, who wrote some satirical verses on his coming of age, alluding to the folly and extravagance to which he gave himself up, that proved prophetic of the spendthrift course he pursued. He married in 1825 a Mrs. Smith, and died on February 10, 1838, when the baronetcy became extinct.

The following is an extract from an old letter, August 5, 1760, from Miss Agnes Smith, of Lee, near Deptford, Kent ("Tockenham Letters"): "I suppose you see by the papers that Sir John Lade is gone at last. 'Tis said he has left the present baronet twenty shillings a week, to be paid him every Monday morning, and the little girl you have seen, £10,000; his sister £200 a year for life, and £8,000 a year to the new adopted heir, a boy of eight years old."

Seated on a bank; leaning on his left elbow; holding cocked hat in left hand; right hand on the back of a dog, who has his paw on his lap; in a red coat.

Painted about 1778.

Put up at Christie's, June 13, 1813, Lot 83* (Mitchell, owner), and passed. Bought in at Christie's, May 8, 1897, Lot 74, by the owner, Mrs. Rice, for £220.

ENGRAVED.

F. Bromley (oblong), 1862, 4¼ × 4¼ in.

In 1862 the picture belonged to the Rev. H. M. Rice, rector of South Hill, Cornwall, whose great-grandmother was another daughter of Ralph Thrale.

The picture belonged recently to Mrs. C. L. Rice, who disposed of it to George Harland Peck, of 9, Belgrave Square, London, the present owner.

LADE, Lady.

Three-quarter length, canvas 52 × 38 in.

Formerly Mrs. Smith, a mistress of Sir John Lade, 2nd Baronet, whom he afterwards married, in 1825.

Standing ; drawing a glove on her left hand ; white dress ; pink sash ; black mantle ; white and blue hat looped up at the side, surmounted with white and red feathers ; hair powdered and flowing down the neck ; landscape background.

Exhibited at the Royal Academy in 1785, No. 71, as a " Portrait of a Lady."

Tom Taylor, vol. ii., p. 472, says : " Mrs. Smith, mistress of Thrale's nephew."

The numbers on Reynolds's pictures at this year's Academy seem to have been changed, and it is evidently from this cause that Walpole and others gave different names to the portraits. No. 23 is called both Mrs. Smith and Lady Hume, and No. 71 the same, whereas No. 18, which was really the full-length of Mrs. Musters as Hebe, elicits the following criticisms :

A newspaper of 1785 says : " No. 18. Sir John Lade's lady, whole length, by Sir J. Reynolds. Capital, though some captious critic would complain of want of relief in the figure. No. 23. Lady Hume, by Sir J. Reynolds. Rather flat in its effects, but otherwise pleasing."

Morning Herald, April 28, 1785 : " No. 18. Portrait of a lady, evidently the Mrs. Smith of Sir John Lade. It is a full-length, but destitute of the graceful attitude which generally marks his portraits of that dimension ; a want of animation pervades the colouring as well as the design. No. 23. Portrait of a lady ; a good likeness of Lady Hume, but from her fine figure she should have sat for a full length. No. 212. Portrait of a lady ; Mrs. Musters, in the character of Hebe. The design possesses great elegance, the drapery, sky, and foreground are coloured in a tender style, but the face of Hebe has neither the animation, youth, nor beauty of the original."

In the above criticisms No. 18 pretty correctly describes Mrs. Musters, No. 23 Mrs. Smith, and No. 212 another lady altogether, for the description does not tally with Mrs. Musters as Hebe.

The following criticism on Mrs. Smith correctly describes the picture :

General Advertiser, May 2, 1785 : "Sir John Lade's Mrs. Smith stares West's sermon (No. 153) in the face. This is not the best of Sir Joshua's pencil work. There is somewhat of a stiffness in the contour. The absence of loveliness, of grace, of dignity and elegance, are natural enough when we consider the subject ! and the evident paint upon the cheek are excellently picturesque of the demirep disguised in the dress of the fashionable woman. That she should be opposite to St. Paul is well, and that she should be in full view of the Prince of Wales is better. Her back is of course turned to the clergy in an undress, but that she should be putting on her glove and seemingly taking a walk towards 'The Last Supper' is totally improper. The picture should have been placed under Maria Cosway's 'Deluge,' that it might share the common fate of the wicked."

West's "St. Peter's Sermon" was No. 153, Reynolds's "Prince of Wales" No. 155, and would have been on the opposite wall to No. 23, Mrs. Smith, in the Great Room.   There was a clergyman near her, No. 8.

EXHIBITED.

British Institution, 1856, No. 128, as Lady Ladd, by W. J. Broderip.
Royal Academy, 1884, No. 213, by Baron Ferdinand de Rothschild, as
    "Lady Lade."

Sold at Christie's, February 11, 1854, Lot 82 (Adams, owner), for £82 10s., to Broderip ; same rooms, June 11, 1859, Lot 84 (Broderip, owner), for £58 16s., to Graves.

ENGRAVED.

F. Bromley, 1861, 5¼ × 3⅞ in.

The picture was for many years in the possession of Sir John Lade's coachmaker ; it afterwards belonged to W. J. Broderip, at whose sale it was purchased by Henry Graves and Co., who sold it some years after to Wilbraham Tollemache, of Dorford Hall, from whom it passed to Baron Ferdinand de Rothschild, who sold it to Messrs. T. Agnew and Sons.

LA LIPPE, Count Schomberg.

Whole length, canvas 96 × 81 *in.*

Commander of the troops sent to Portugal to aid that country against the Spaniards and French, 1762.

"Died September 9, 1777, Count William de la Lippe Buckeburg."—*Gentleman's Magazine*, 1777, p. 507.

In a green coat and buff leggings.

He stands on an eminence with a soldierly erectness, his hands crossed over the head of his long walking cane ; near him a mortar and a white flag, and a negro orderly reins in his horse.   The face is long and grave, and the pose firm and commanding (Tom Taylor, vol. i., p. 236).

Sat in 1764 and 1767.   Paid for, August 12, 1767, Count La Lippe, £25 ; Ditto, for General Burgoig's picture, to Mrs. Calliand, £70.

EXHIBITED.

British Institution, 1813, No. 122 (third catalogue), by H.R.H. the
    Prince Regent.
British Institution, 1826, No. 133, }
    „   „   1827, No. 128, } by George IV.
    „   „   1843, No. 47, by Her Majesty the Queen.

ENGRAVED.

S. W. Reynolds, 1833, $7\frac{1}{4} \times 6$ in.

In Sir Joshua's note of practice, 1767, Count La Lippe, " Count Lippe senza olio."

"In November, 1764, as appears by the entries in the pocket-book, Reynolds painted his whole length of Count Lippe Schaumberg (Lippe Buckebourg he is called in the books of the time). For a military portrait he never had a nobler subject. The Count, though born in London, was the sovereign of a German principality. He was every inch a soldier, and he stands forward on the canvas of Reynolds,

> 'No carpet knight so trim,
> But in close fight a champion grim,
> In camps a leader sage.'

"To illustrate his entire character, however, would require another and very different picture, in which he should be surrounded with books, objects of science, pictures, and statues, for he cultivated the arts of peace as well as war, not from ostentation, but from love. At the head of an English army he had saved Portugal from a combined attack of France and Spain. As a statesman, also, he had conferred many political benefits on that country, and these things done, he turned his attention, as Washington did, to the improvement of agriculture among his people."—LESLIE AND TAYLOR'S *Life of Reynolds*, vol. i., pp. 235, 236.

"It is to be hoped, for the credit of George III., that it was a royal commission. This would do something towards relieving the memory of that king from the reproach of having neglected the greatest of English painters."—TOM TAYLOR, vol. i., p. 236.

"This year (1767) Reynolds has two engagements at the Queen's house (on July 26 and 28). These appointments may have been connected with the portrait of Count La Lippe, whose picture seems to have been a royal order."—TOM TAYLOR, vol. i., p. 273.

LA LIPPE, Count Schomberg.

Three-quarter length, canvas.

Sold at Christie's, May 23, 1846, Lot 40, La Lippe, the Count Schomberg, Marshal of the Portuguese Electorate and Field-Marshal of the British troops (Braddyl, owner), for £69 6s., to Lord C. Townshend ; May 13, 1854, Lot 46, Count La Lippe, leaning on his baton, a gun and flag behind him, half length (Lord Chs. V. Townshend, owner), bought in for £84 ; June 16, 1860, Lot 91 (Lord Chs. Townshend, owner), bought in for £21 ; June 17, 1864, Lot 41 (Lord Chs. Townshend, owner), £131 5s., to Smith, Bond Street.

The picture is described in Christie's catalogue of 1864 as a "half length from the Thomond sale," but in that sale no name was given ; Lots 48 and 50, on 19 May, 1821, are catalogued as " Portraits of General Officers."

LAMB, Elizabeth, Lady, and Child. *See* MELBOURNE.

560

Henry Earl of Pembroke and Son.

Page 270

LAMB, Master Peniston. *See* MELBOURNE.

Sat as Master Melbourne in 1770 and as Master Lambe in 1771.

LAMB, The Hon. Peniston, William, and Frederick James.

Whole lengths, canvas 94 × 57¼ *in.*

Children of Peniston, 1st Lord Melbourne. The eldest, Peniston, born May 3, 1770, was M.P. for Herts, and died, unmarried, January 24, 1805.

William, born March 15, 1779 ; M.P. for Portarlington ; married, June 3, 1805, Lady Caroline Ponsonby, only daughter of Frederick, 3rd Earl of Bessborough ; he became Secretary of State to the Home Department from 1830 until 1834, when, as Lord Melbourne, he became Prime Minister. He became 2nd Lord Melbourne, January 24, 1805. He died November 24, 1848.

Frederick James, born April 17, 1782 ; he attained considerable distinction as a diplomatist, and was Envoy Extraordinary to Vienna in 1831 ; he was made K.C.B. and created Baron Beauvale in 1839 ; he married, February 25, 1841, the Countess Alexandrina, daughter of the Count of Maltzau ; succeeded as 3rd Lord Melbourne in 1848, and died January 29, 1853.

The eldest boy sitting supporting his youngest brother, who wears a hat with a feather ; the second boy is helping to support his baby brother.

EXHIBITED.

British Institution, 1813, No. 138 (third catalogue),
    „   „   1843, No. 33,
Royal Academy, 1881, No. 136,
                       } by Earl Cowper.

ENGRAVED.

F. Bartolozzi, 1791, 13¼ × 9¼ in., as " The Affectionate Brothers."
S. W. Reynolds, 1836, 6¼ × 4¼ in.

Artist's Proof in brown by Bartolozzi sold at Sotheby's in 1894 for £16 5s. 6d.

The picture belongs to Earl Cowper, at Panshanger, Herts.

A picture called " The Three Brothers " was sold at Greenwood's, April 16, 1796, Lot 45, for £105, to the Rev. R. Dodge.

LAMBERT, General.

Sat in 1761.

LAMBTON, William.

Three-quarter length, canvas 50 × 40 in.

Third son of Ralph Lambton; died, unmarried, January 2, 1774, at Lambton Hall.

Seated at a writing-table, with his right hand upon it; in his lap he holds a hat, gloves, and cane with the left hand; dressed in a plum-coloured coat and breeches, with a wig.

Sat in 1767. Paid for, May 16, 1767, William Lambton, Esq., £36 15s.; 1770, Mr. Lambton, £36 15s. Frame paid.

The picture, which is signed and dated " J. Reynolds, pinx. 1768," belongs to the Earl of Durham at Lambton Castle.

Memo. 1768 : "Mr. Lambton, Princes Street, Hanover Square, to be sent there packed up."

LANE, The Hon. Robert.

Robert Fox Lane, the only son of George, Lord Bingley; born August 5, 1732; married, first, Mildred, daughter of John Bourchier, and secondly, in 1761, Lady Bridget Henley, eldest daughter of Robert, 1st Earl of Northington. He died May, 1768, in the lifetime of his father, who died February 22, 1773.

Sat in 1762. Paid for, 1762, Hon. Mr. Lane, £21.

LANE, Mr.

Sat in 1764. Paid for, August 22, 1764, Mr. Lane, £50.

This payment may refer to a second portrait of the Hon. Robert Lane, who died in 1768.

LANGTON, Bennet, LL.D.

Three-quarter length, canvas 50 × 40 in.

Born 1737; married, in 1769, Mary, Dowager Countess of Rothes; friend of Johnson; professor of ancient literature at the Royal Academy; died December 8, 1801.

Seated to left; resting head on right hand; large book on table beside him.

Sat in 1759, 1761, and 1762. Paid for before 1761, Mr. Langton, £21.

National Portrait Exhibition, 1868, No. 829, by J. H. Hollway.
Royal Academy, 1885, No. 52, by C. L. Massingberd.

"Bennet Langton, LL.D., succeeded Dr. Johnson in the professorship of ancient literature in the Royal Academy. To him the Doctor bequeathed his polyglot bible, and once speaking of him to Mr. Boswell with an affectionate regard, exclaimed : 'The world does not bear a worthier man than Bennet Langton !'"—*Gentleman's Magazine*, 1801, p. 1207.

LANGTON, Miss Diana.

Only surviving daughter of Bennet Langton, senr., by Diana, daughter of Edmund Turner, and sister to Bennet Langton ; married the Rev. Robert Uvedale, D.D., rector of Langton, who died in 1799.

Sat in January, 1764. Paid for, January 1, 1764, Miss Langton, £15.

LANSDOWNE, William, 1st Marquess of. *See* LORD ASHBURTON, *ante*, p. 34, and SHELBURNE.

Sat in April, 1788, and July, 1789, for the group with Lord Ashburton and Colonel Barré.

LANSDOWNE, Louisa, Marchioness of.

Head size, canvas 29¼ × 24¼ in.

Lady Louisa Fitzpatrick, second daughter of John, 1st Earl of Upper Ossory ; born 1755 ; married, July 8, 1779, as his second wife, William, 2nd Earl of Shelburne ; created 1st Marquess of Lansdowne, November 30, 1784. She died August 7, 1789. *[handwritten annotation]*

Head and shoulders ; profile turned to the right ; hair powdered and dressed in the style of Marie Antoinette ; large white cap ; blue dress trimmed with fur ; landscape background.

Paid for, March, 1786, Lady Landsdown, £52 10s.

The picture belongs to the Marquess of Lansdowne, and is No. 17 in the Lansdowne catalogue.

A picture described as the late Marchioness of Lansdowne was exhibited at Suffolk Street in 1833, No. 206, by Mr. Swabey.

LA RENA. *See* RENA.

LASCELLES, Edwin, afterwards 1st Lord Harewood.

Whole length, canvas.

Edwin Lascelles, born February 5, 1713; M.P. for Scarborough, North-allerton, and York; created, July 9, 1790, Lord Harewood of Harewood Castle, co. York; married, first, Elizabeth, sole daughter and heiress of Sir D'Arcy Dawes; secondly, March 29, 1770, Jane, daughter of William Coleman and relict of Sir John Fleming, Bart.; died January 25, 1795.

Sat in June, 1765, May, 1766, and June, 1768, as Mr. Lascelles. 1764, Mr. Edwin Lascells and Mrs. Hale, £157 10s. 1770, Mr. Edwin Lascells and Mrs. Hale, £157 10s. May 1, 1781, Mr. Lascelles (remaining half payment for his own and Mrs. Hale), £157 10s.

The picture belongs to the Earl of Harewood.

LASCELLES, Mrs. Edwin, formerly Jane, Lady Fleming, and afterwards Lady Harewood.

Whole length, canvas 93 × 57 in.

Jane, daughter of William Coleman, of Garnhey, co. Devon (by Jane, sister of Edward, 8th Duke of Somerset), married, first, July 4, 1753, John Fleming, afterwards Sir John Fleming, Bart., of Brompton Park, who died November 6, 1763, and secondly, March 29, 1770, Edwin Lascelles, who was created Lord Harewood, July 9, 1790, as his second wife. She survived her husband, who died January 25, 1795, and died in March, 1813.

In a light brown dress; with light green mantle; sitting with her left arm round a large vase, out of which water is pouring, and the other resting on her left knee, holding her dress away from the water; the background is a dark landscape, with trees.

The costume of this picture points to its having been painted in 1779, the same year as the second picture of her daughter, to which it forms a companion. The third payment made by Mr. Lascelles shown in the previous entry was probably entered Mrs. Hale in error. The payments in full evidently refer to three whole lengths.

The picture, which was probably left by Lady Harewood to her daughter, the Countess of Harrington, in 1813, belongs to the Earl of Harrington at Elvaston Castle, Derby.

See also FLEMING, *in Addenda.*

LASCELLES, Edward, afterwards 1st Earl of Harewood.

Fourth son of Edward Lascelles, who died at Barbadoes, October 31, 1747; born at Barbadoes, January 17, 1740; M.P. for Northallerton, 1761,

1768, and 1790; he succeeded to the estates of Lord Harewood (Edwin) in 1795, and was created Baron Harewood, June 18, 1796, and Earl of Harewood, September 7, 1812. He married, May 12, 1761, Anne, daughter of William Challoner, and died April 3, 1820.

Sat in December, 1762, and February, 1764, as Mr. and Mrs. Lascelles. Paid for, 1764, Mr. and Mrs. Lascels and child, £65 2s., and before 1772, Mr. Lascell's, brother (? cousin) to Edwin Lascells, 62 guineas, being the remaining half payment for his own and Mrs. Lascell's pictures and for prints of Mrs. Hale, 5 guineas.

The picture belongs to the Earl of Harewood.

LASCELLES, Mrs. Edward, afterwards Countess of Harewood, and Child.

Three-quarter length, canvas 48 × 38 *in.*

Anne, daughter of William Chaloner, of Guisborough, and sister of Mrs. Hale, " Euphrosyne ; " married, May 12, 1761, Edward Lascelles, created Earl of Harewood, 1796; died February 22, 1805, after a lingering illness of nearly two years.

The child is Frances; born June 11, 1762 ; married, October 4, 1784, the Hon. John Douglas, uncle to the Earl of Morton. She died March 31, 1817.

Seated to left, nearly full face, with the child in her lap, holding his left foot in her right hand; blue and red dress; architectural and curtain background; landscape on the left.

Sat in 1762 and 1764 as Mr. and Mrs. Lascelles. For payments, *see* EDWARD LASCELLES.

EXHIBITED.

British Institution, 1823, No. 62,
     "   "   1851, No. 142,
National Portrait Exhibition, 1868, No. 897, } by the Earl of Harewood.
Royal Academy, 1886, No. 155,

ENGRAVED.

James Watson, 17¼ × 14 in.
C. Corbutt, 13¼ × 10⅞ in.
S. W. Reynolds, 1835, 5¼ × 4 in.

First State, by Watson, Buccleuch Collection, sold at Christie's, 1887, for £16 16s.

Copied in 1823, full size, by Wright, Simpson, Say, Onion, Wilkin, Sharland, Howard, and Miss Kearsley; small, by Shepperson, Scanlan

Salter, and Fairland ; in miniature, by Miss Sharpe, Miss Hayter, Miss Blanchard, Miss Thomson, and Mrs. Norris.

The picture belongs to the Earl of Harewood.

LAUDERDALE, James, 7th Earl.

Whole length, canvas.

Son of the 6th Earl ; born in 1718 ; married, 1749, Mary, daughter and co-heiress of Sir Thomas Lombe, Bart. ; lieutenant in the army and Scotch representative peer ; distinguished for his services in Flanders, 1744-45, and in the Scotch campaign against the rebels in 1745-46 ; died .August 17, 1789.

Sat in 1759 and 1761. Paid for, 1761, Lord Lauderdale, £80.

The Earl of Lauderdale writes, November 11, 1898: " The two pictures of Lord and Lady Lauderdale are not the same size ; the one is full length in robes, the other half length only, or rather half the figure only. The third picture of Lord Lauderdale, which you speak of, I am not sure about, though I know there is a third of the same Earl as a younger man, but not full length."

Note to the 1759 sitting in November : " Copy of Lord Lauderdale, 4½ ft. high by 3 ft. 7 in., 20 guineas."

The picture belongs to the Earl of Lauderdale.

LAUDERDALE, Mary, Countess of.

Three-quarter length, canvas.

Daughter and co-heiress of Sir Thomas Lombe, Bart., Alderman of the City of London ; married James, 7th Earl, in 1749 ; died July 18, 1789.

Sat in 1760. Paid for before 1761, Lady Lauderdale, £20.

The picture belongs to the Earl of Lauderdale.

LAUGHTON, Mrs. Christina.

Head size, canvas 29½ x 24 in.

Widow of Colonel Stewart, afterwards wife of Rev. George Laughton, D.D.

EXHIBITED.
Grosvenor, 1884, No. 209, by Lady Erskine May.

Her son, General Richard Stewart, commanded a brigade at the battle of Talavera.

LAURIE, Richard Holmes.

Half length, canvas 38 × 24 *in.*

When a boy ; in republican dress and black hat ; left hand in bosom.

EXHIBITED.
Royal Academy, 1873, No. 231, by Miss Cecilia Laurie.

LAWRENCE, Major-General Stringer.

Whole length, canvas 92¼ × 56¼ *in.*

One of Clive's heroes; a Major-General and Commander-in-Chief of the East India Company's Forces ; born 1697 ; Major-General, December 9, 1760 ; died January 10, 1775. There is a monument to him in Westminster Abbey.

Standing by the side of his tent ; a stick in his right hand ; his sword in the left ; in the distance the view of a fortress with cavalry.

Sat in 1767. Paid for, 1767, General Lawrence, £210 ; 1760, General Lawrance (copy), £21. The payment of 200 guineas must be for two pictures.

"January 10, 1775, in Bruton Street, Major-General Lawrence. He was the first officer who introduced military discipline into India, where for twenty years he commanded the Company's troops."—*Gentleman's Magazine*, 1775, p. 47.

ENGRAVED.
E. A. Ezekiel, 1795, 19¼ × 12⅞ in.

The picture was in 1795 in the possession of Sir Robert Palk, Bart. The first Sir Robert Palk was Governor of Madras in 1763, and was created a baronet in 1772.

"One of the fellow-heroes of Clive in the East Indies ; associated with him and Admiral Pocock in the vote of thanks by the East India Company, and presented by them with £500 a year for life in the September of 1761."—TOM TAYLOR, vol. i., p. 189.

Sir Edward A. Palk, Bart., writes, December 29, 1898 : "The picture of General S. Lawrence, by Sir J. Reynolds, was at Haldon until April, 1893 ; it was after that date disposed of by Walton and Lee."

The picture was bought in at the Haldon sale, and was afterwards sent to Christie's by Messrs. Walton and Lee, and probably sold January 20, 1894, Lot 17 (Walton, owner), as a portrait of a gentleman in blue velvet costume, and bought by Lord Arran for £19 19s.

This picture was sold by Messrs. Hollender and Cremetti in 1895 to Charles Sedelmeyer, of Paris, from whom it passed to Rodman Wanamaker of Philadelphia, the present owner.

LAWRENCE, Major-General Stringer.

Half length, oval, canvas 29¼ × 24 *in.*

Nearly full face ; powdered hair ; in uniform, with breastplate.

Sat in 1760. Paid for, 1760, General Lawrence, £10 10s. ; January 26, 1761, General Laurence, £10 10s.

EXHIBITED.
Royal Academy, 1885, No. 45, by Stephen Tucker.

ENGRAVED.
R. Houston, 1761, 12¼ × 10¼ in.

R. Purcell, 11¼ × 9⅞ in.

S. W. Reynolds, 1¼ × 1¼ in.

A portrait of General Lawrence (29 × 24 in.) was purchased from Messrs. Shepherd Brothers in 1894 by Charles Sedelmeyer, of Paris, and sold by him to C. Groult, of Paris, the present owner.

Another head-sized picture is in the India Office.

LAWRENCE, Major-General Stringer.

Sat in 1761. Paid for, 1760, Captain Martyn, for General Lawrence, £21.

Note to 1761 sitting : "Captain Martyn, in Harley Street, Cavendish Square, to measure the space where General Lawrence's picture is to hang."

LAWRENCE, Major-General Stringer.

Head size, canvas.

Paid for, 1765, General Lawrence, for Mrs. Bret, £36 15s.

A portrait of General Stringer Lawrence was bought in at Christie's, February 28, 1860, Lot 113, by the owner, Tiffin, for £1 8s. ; same rooms, May 28, 1877, Lot 34 (Tiffin, owner), for £5 5s., to Smith ; January 20, 1883, Lot 36 (S. T. Smith, owner), bought in, £8 11s. 6d. ; Robinson and Fisher's, a copy, whole length, bought in.

LEE, The Right Hon. Sir George, LL.D.

Son of Sir Thomas Lee, the 2nd Baronet ; born 1700 ; took the degree of Bachelor of Laws in 1724, and was D.C.L. in 1729 ; he was returned as M.P. for Brackley in 1733, and was member for Devizes, Liskeard, and

.. L.......

S.... to ... ...

.. .. Christie's,
.. ..
....ry 20, 18..,
.. .. f.... ..

.. .. ..

LEE, ...
.. ..
.. .. .. of Laws in ....d .ve
.. P.....g .. .. we .... ..
                              .. .. .. I.... .d, and

Children of the 5th Earl of _____

Launceston successively until his death. He was treasurer to Frederick, Prince of Wales, and after his death in 1751 was treasurer to the Princess Dowager for six years. Married Judith, daughter of Humphrey Morrice (she died in 1743); Dean of Arches, 1751; Judge of the Prerogative Court, Canterbury, December 20, 1751; Privy Councillor, February 13, 1752; died December 18, 1758.

Sat in January, 1757.

There is a portrait of Sir George Lee at Hartwell House, described as painted by Hudson. It is probable that it is an early Reynolds. It belongs to Edward Dyke Lee.

LEE, Sir William, Bart.

Half length, canvas 30 × 24 in.

Son of Sir Thomas Lee, 3rd Bart., of Hartwell, who married Elizabeth, daughter of Thomas Sandys; born 1726; married, June 20, 1763, Lady Elizabeth Harcourt, eldest daughter of Simon, 1st Earl Harcourt; became 4th Baronet in 1749. He died July 6, 1799.

Profile, looking to the right; powdered hair; in a pink Vandyke dress, with slashed sleeves; a blue mantle over the left shoulder; lace neckcloth.

Paid for, before 1760, Mr. Hopkins for Sir Will. Lee's picture, £10 10s.

The picture belongs to Edward Dyke Lee, of Hartwell House, Aylesbury.

LEE, Lady Elizabeth.

Whole length, canvas 66 × 48 in.

Eldest daughter of Simon, 1st Earl Harcourt; born January 18, 1739; was one of the ten young ladies, daughters of dukes and earls, who supported the train of Queen Charlotte at her nuptials, September 8, 1761; married, June 20, 1763, Sir William Lee, Bart.; died 1811.

Sitting, left arm resting on her ermine cloak; right hand in her lap, holding some flowers; a flowing robe over her seat; trunk of tree with branches at the back.

Sat in March, 1765. Paid for, January 14, 1769, Lady Betty Lee, £105.

ENGRAVED.

E. Fisher, 19¼ × 14 in.

J. Watson, 12¼ × 9⅞ in.

S. W. Reynolds, 6¼ × 4¼ in.

A proof of the Fisher plate was sold in Paris, May, 1898, for 430 francs.

The picture, which is fitted into a large overmantel of an earlier date, belongs to Edward Dyke Lee, at Hartwell House, Aylesbury.

LEE, Mrs. William.

Head size, canvas, oval, in square, 30 × 25 in.

Philadelphia, daughter of Sir Thomas Hart Dyke, Bart., of Lullingston Castle, Kent; married William Lee, son of Lord Chief Justice Lee, who died in 1754; she became a widow in 1778; died in 1799.

Three-quarter face, looking to the left; low hair; pearl earrings; blue ribbon round neck, tied behind; white cross-over dress, embroidered with gold; a string of pearls from over her left shoulder, passing under the right arm; gold sash round waist.

Sat in February, 1761, and March, 1767. The following is a copy of the original receipt at Hartwell House:

"Received, March 19, 1761, from Mrs. Lee, the sum of ten guineas, being the first payment for her picture by me.
"£10 10s.   "J. REYNOLDS."

Paid for, March 9, 1761, Mrs. Lee, £10 10s. Copied from Reynolds's ledger.

The picture belongs to Edward Dyke Lee, at Hartwell House, Aylesbury.

LEE, Miss Anne.

Head size, canvas 30 × 25 in.

Daughter of Sir Thomas Lee, 3rd Baronet, who died in 1749; born 1721; married, December 22, 1741, George Venables Vernon (created Lord Vernon in 1762), as his second wife. She died September 22, 1742.

"September 22, 1742: The lady of George Venables Vernon, member for Lichfield."— *Gentleman's Magazine*, 1742, p. 499.

Full face, turned to the right; in black satin dress, with white puffed sleeves tied with pink ribbons at the elbow; a ruff collar, with pearl pendants at breast, from which a string of pearls passes under the left arm; a Peg Woffington hat with pink ribbons and white feathers.

This picture was copied by Reynolds for Sir Thomas Lee, Bart., from the full-length portrait of her by Thomas Hudson, then at Totteridge Park, and recently moved to Hartwell House. The costume is identical, as is also the position of the head. It may have been copied about 1757, fifteen years after her death, and at the same time as the copy of Frederick, Prince of Wales, to whom Sir George Lee was treasurer. It may, however, have been painted for her husband, who himself sat to Reynolds in 1757, after her death (the full length being the only portrait then existing of her), and found its way to Hartwell House after his death in 1807. George Venables Vernon married, for the third time, April 10, 1744, Martha, daughter of the Hon. Simon Harcourt, M.P. for Aylesbury, and aunt of Lady Elizabeth Lee.

The picture belongs to Edward Dyke Lee, at Hartwell House, Aylesbury.

LEE, John.

Three-quarter length, canvas 50 × 40 in.

A popular lawyer known as "Honest Jack Lee"; one of the counsel engaged in the defence of Admiral Keppel, 1779; Solicitor-General, 1782; Attorney-General, same year; died 1793.

Seated to right, in an armchair; in wig and gown with long lace bands; right hand on arm of chair; behind, a curtain, books, etc.

Sat in January, 1786. Paid for, January, 1786, Councillor John Lee, £105. Exhibited at the Royal Academy in 1786, No. 103.

Public Advertiser, 1786: "Mr. Lee's head is not less excellent than any of the former; it only appears so from the situation, the light is against it."

Morning Herald, 1786: "No. 103, half length of Mr. Lee; the likeness is good, but not sufficiently expressive of that spirit which constitutes the character of the well-informed original."

EXHIBITED.

British Institution, 1867, No. 193, by C. B. Lee Mainwaring.

Royal Academy, 1884, No. 46,
Guelph, 1891, No. 97, } by Hon. W. F. B. Massey-Mainwaring.

ENGRAVED.

C. H. Hodges, 1788, 18 × 13¾ in.

S. W. Reynolds, 5¼ × 4¼ in.

The picture was presented to Mr. Lee by Admiral Lord Keppel, and from him descended to J. B. Lee Mainwaring, and it now belongs to the Hon. W. F. B. Massey-Mainwaring, M.P.

LEE, John.

Three-quarter length, canvas 50 × 40 in.

Paid for, May, 1788, Mr. Lee, the councillor, for a copy, £78 15s.

Sold at Christie's, April 6, 1867, Lot 87 (Lord Ribblesdale, owner), for £52 10s., to Hollings.

LEE, Mr.

Whole length.

Sat in January, 1770.

Sold at Greenwood's, April 16, 1796, Lot 43 (Mr. Lee, whole length), for £5 5s., to Downman.

LEE, Master.

Sat in 1761.

LEEDS, Thomas, 4th Duke, K.G., LL.D., F.R.S.

Three-quarter length, canvas 50 × 40 in.

Born November 6, 1713; married, June 26, 1740, Lady Mary, daughter of Francis, Earl Godolphin; K.G., June 22, 1749; Cofferer of the Household,

January 13, 1756. He died March 23, 1789, and was succeeded by Francis Godolphin, 5th Duke.

Three-quarter face; standing, in a richly embroidered coat; wearing the star and ribbon of the Garter; facing towards the right; his left hand is holding a paper, and the right hand is in his breast; to the right is a table with a sword and hat upon it.

Sat in April, 1764. Paid for, October 12, 1764, Duke of Leeds, £52 10s. 1764, Duke of Leeds, for Lord Carmarthen and the Dutchess (copy), £52 10s.

The picture belongs to the Duke of Leeds, and is No. 152 in the Hornby catalogue.

A sketch of the Duke of Leeds was sold at the Thomond sale, May 26, 1821, Lot 27, for £3 5s., to Turner.

LEEDS, Mary, Duchess of.
Canvas.

Born 1723; youngest daughter of Francis, Earl Godolphin; married, June 26, 1740, Thomas, 4th Duke of Leeds; died, August 3, 1764.

Seated, in an embroidered dress and ermine-lined cloak; resting her right arm on a pedestal; low hair, ornamented with pearls; a tree to the left; distant landscape to the right.

The picture belongs to the Duke of Leeds, at Grosvenor Crescent.

There is an oblong replica, 34 × 24 in., and an upright one, 36 × 30 in., at Hornby Castle, Nos. 85 and 293 respectively in the Hornby catalogue.

LEESON, Mr. *See* CARICATURES, page 1229.

LEGGE, The Hon. William.
Half length, oval, canvas 24 × 18 in.

Second son of the 2nd Earl of Dartmouth; born February 4, 1757; died October 19, 1784.

As a boy, in a Vandyke dress; cloak over his right shoulder; left sleeve slashed; front of dress slashed; looking to his right; fair hair.

Paid for, October 14, 1761, Lord Dartmouth, for Master Legge, £10 10s.

EXHIBITED.

British Institution, 1824, No. 151, as the *late* Hon. William Legge when a boy,
Grosvenor, 1884, No. 131, as the Hon. William Legge,
Grafton, 1895, No. 119,
} by the Earl of Dartmouth.

ENGRAVED.

J. Spilsbury, 1764, 11¼ × 9 in.

N. Salway, 5¼ × 4¼ in.

The picture belongs to the Earl of Dartmouth.

LEICESTER, George, Earl of. *See* FERRARS, *ante*, page 301.

LEICESTER, Sir John, Bart.

Whole length.

Born April 4, 1762; succeeded his father, Sir Peter Byrne (who had taken the name of Leicester in 1744), in 1770; was raised to the peerage, July 16, 1826, as Baron de Tabley, of Tabley House; married, November, 1810, Georgina Maria, youngest daughter of Lieutenant-Colonel Cottin. Died June 18, 1827. He was distinguished as a munificent patron of the arts and a supporter of native artists.

In hussar uniform, standing by his horse; right hand holding a sword, which he is pointing to his left; landscape background, with castle and lake.

Sat in May, 1789. Exhibited at the Royal Academy, 1790, No. 232.

" Very bad."—WALPOLE.

St. James's Chronicle, 1790: " No. 232, Sir John Leicester. We are sorry to see the name of Sir Joshua to this picture ; the head has a resemblance to the original, but the figure is badly drawn. There is a poverty in the invention and execution of the background which we do not recollect in any of the president's other works : even the colouring is faulty. There is no air in the distant hills, which are of the same colour as the front of the picture, and the handling of the dock leaves, etc., is stiff and bad."

Other critics say : " Sir John Leicester is painted less by Sir Joshua than by his assistant, Mr. Marchee." " Sir J. Lester's whole length goes into Cheshire, and therefore it is in the militia uniform."

ENGRAVED.

S. W. Reynolds, 1800, 24 × 15 in.

Second State, Buccleuch Collection, sold at Christie's, 1887, for £15 4s. 6d.

There is no illustration of this picture in the " Leicester Gallery," 1821.

LEIGH, Colonel.

Sat in March, 1762, as Colonel Leigh. Paid for, March, 1762, Coll. Legh, £10 10s., and before 1763, Coll. Legh, £10 10s.

LEIGH, Mr.

Paid for, March 10, 1763, Mr. Legh, £42.

LEIGH, Miss.

23 × 17 in.

Sat in January, 1764, as Miss Leigh. Paid for, March 10, 1763, Miss Leigh, £21 ; March 2, 1764, Miss Leigh, £21.

EXHIBITED.

Royal Academy, 1870, No. 72, as portrait of Miss Leigh (a study), by Richard Newsham.

A portrait described as Miss Leigh, small whole length, sold at Christie's, June 18, 1870, Lot 63 (Agnew, owner), for £18 18s. to Johnson. *See also* MRS. LLOYD, page 589.

573

LEIGH, Miss Catherine.

Three-quarter length, canvas 50 × 40 in.

Second daughter and co-heiress of John Leigh, of North Court House, Isle of Wight; married Chaloner Arcedeckne, of Glevering Hall. She was sister to Mrs. Lloyd.

The picture belonged to Mr. Arcedeckne, and was sold in 1899 to Lord Burton, the present owner.

LEINSTER, James, 1st Duke of. *See* KILDARE, *ante*, page 551.

LEINSTER, William Robert, 2nd Duke of.

Three-quarter length, canvas 49 × 39 in.

Born March 2, 1749; succeeded November 19, 1773; married, November 4, 1775, Emilia Olivia St. George, only daughter and heiress of Usher, Lord St. George, Baron of Hatley St. George; died October 20, 1804.

Seated, full face; left arm resting on chair; the right hand pointing to a document on a table; marabu fur-lined coat; light drab vest and breeches; curtain background.

Pocket-book of 1775 missing. Paid for, May, 1775, Duke of Leinster, 70 guineas. Exhibited in the Royal Academy, 1775, No. 234, as a nobleman, half length.

A newspaper critic, 1775 : " No. 234 is the Duke of Leinster, and 236 Caleb Whiteford, both good likenesses, and finely executed."

EXHIBITED.

Dublin, 1872, No. 210,
Royal Academy, 1879, No. 44, } by the Duke of Leinster.

ENGRAVED.

John Dixon, 1775, 18¼ × 14 in.
S. W. Reynolds, 5¼ × 4 in.

There is an impression of another plate (17½ × 14 in.) by an unknown engraver, in which the thumb is extended along the forefinger, and Freemasons' emblems are on the paper on the table.

First State by Dixon, Buccleuch Collection, sold at Christie's, 1887, for £12 1s. 6d.

The picture belongs to the Duke of Leinster, at Carton, Maynooth, co. Kildare, Ireland.

A portrait of the Duke of Leinster was sold at Christie's, May 24, 1862, Lot 145 (Herries and Co., owners), for £6 5s., to Watson.

LEINSTER, William Robert, 2nd Duke of.

Three-quarter length, canvas 50 × 40 in.

The composition is identical with the last picture; in both the left thumb is turned up, and there is an inscription on the paper.

Paid for, 1777, Duke of Leinster, half length, paid (no price). May, 1782, Duke of Leinster's bill paid, £247 16s. Opposite to the 1777 entry, with no date, is written: " Duke of Leinster paid to Mr. Nixon for a miniature of His Grace 6 guineas;" also, "For two small pictures of Mr. Powel." Mr. Powell was a copyist, and is referred to in Tom Taylor, vol. ii., p. 213. *See* MARLBOROUGH FAMILY, page 628.

EXHIBITED.

Suffolk Street, 1832, No. 10, as the Duke of Leinster, by Major Beauclerc.

The picture was purchased in 1885 from A. Beauclerc, of Ardglass, by the Duke of Leinster. It hangs at Kilkea Castle, co. Kildare, Ireland.

LEINSTER, William Robert, 2nd Duke of.

Head size, canvas 30 × 25 in.

Replica of a portion of the previous pictures.

Paid for, 1777, Duke of Leinster, head, paid (no price).

The picture belongs to the Rev. Sir Talbot Baker, Bart., at Ranstone, Blandford, Dorset.

Sir Edward Baker, Bart., married, July 22, 1805, Lady Emily Mary FitzGerald, daughter of the 2nd Duke of Leinster.

LEINSTER, Emilia Mary, Duchess of.

Half length, canvas 30 × 25 in.

For biography and earlier portraits of this lady, *see* KILDARE, *ante*, p. 552.

In a white dress embroidered with gold flowers, open at the neck, with figured lace scarf tied in a bow, and gold ornament on left shoulder; red ermine-lined cloak, with six tails; dark hair, slightly grey, worn high, with red and blue ribbons and pearls.

Paid for, October, 1775, Duchess of Leinster, £36 15s.

EXHIBITED.

Royal Academy, 1879, No. 16, as Emily, wife of 2nd Duke, by the Duke of Leinster.

ENGRAVED.

Richard Josey, 1879, 9¼ × 7¼ in.

The picture belongs to the Duke of Leinster, at Carton, Maynooth, Ireland. Carton was left to the 1st Duchess for life or until she married again, which she did in 1776.

This picture was wrongly described in the Royal Academy, 1879.

LEINSTER, Emilia Mary, Duchess of.

Half length, canvas 30 × 25 *in.*

Similar to the last, but with hair hanging over right shoulder, seven tails on ermine cloak, and no pearls in the hair.

The picture belongs to Col. Gerald E. Boyle, of 48, Queen's Gate Terrace.

The Hon. John Boyle married the Hon. Cecilia De Ros, granddaughter of the Duchess of Leinster.

LEINSTER, Emilia Mary, Duchess of.

Half length, canvas 30 × 25 *in.*

In a white and gold dress; with no cloak or scarf round the neck; long curls reaching down on the neck on both sides; no pearls in the hair.

Paid for, 1788, Duchess D(owager) of Leinster, given to Lady Louisa Conolly, £36 15*s.* Lady Louisa Conolly was sister to the Duchess of Leinster.

EXHIBITED.

Dublin, 1872, No. 210A, by Thomas Conolly, M.P.

Sold at Christie's, July 7, 1894, Lot 81 (Conolly, owner), for £525, to Obach, for the executors of the late Duke of Leinster

The picture, which must have been painted about 1778, is now the property of the Duke of Leinster, at Kilkea Castle, Mageney, co. Kildare, Ireland.

For earlier portraits of this lady, *see* KILDARE, *ante*, page 552.

LEINSTER, Emilia Olivia, Duchess of.

Half length, canvas.

Daughter of St. George Usher, Lord St. George; born 1759; married William Robert, 2nd Duke of Leinster, November 4, 1775; died June 23, 1798.

Nearly profile; looking to the right; white dress, crossed over in front; gold trimming over the shoulders; full sleeves.

Sat in May, 1779. Paid for, July 4, 1779, Duchess of Leinster, £36 15*s.* 6*d.*, and Do., £36 15*s.* 6*d.* The entries, which follow each other in the second ledger, and were written at the same time, probably refer to two 30 × 25 pictures.

There is at Carton a beautiful miniature of the 2nd Duchess, signed S. (probably Shelley), 1778, on an ivory box, which, in the opinion of Mr. A. Graves, proves the engraving by Dickinson to be her portrait, and not that of the 1st Duchess, as it was hitherto believed to be.

"June 23, 1798, at Thomas's Hotel in Berkeley Square, the Duchess of Leinster. Her grace was so much affected on hearing of the fate of Lord Edward Fitzgerald that she is supposed to have died of grief."—*Gentleman's Magazine*, 1798, p. 544.

Lord Edward FitzGerald died on June 4, 1798, of the wounds he received at his apprehension for a supposed charge of high treason; he was brother of the 2nd Duke of Leinster, and was born October 15, 1763. He was visited a few hours before his death by his aunt, Lady Louisa Conolly, and his brother, Lord Henry FitzGerald.

ENGRAVED.

W. Dickinson, 1780, 13¼ × 11 in.

S. W. Reynolds, 2¼ × 2 in.

First State by Dickinson, Buccleuch Collection, sold at Christie's in 1887 for £18 18s.

"He had painted," says Northcote, "an excellent head of the Duchess of Leinster, and when Burke saw the picture he exclaimed, 'What a beautiful head you have made of this lady; it is impossible to add anything to its advantage!' But Sir Joshua was not satisfied, and replied, 'It does not please me yet. There is a sweetness of expression in the original that I have not been able to give in the portrait, and therefore cannot think it finished.'"— TOM TAYLOR, vol. ii., p. 137.

In the Carton catalogue the above description is quoted as referring to the picture of the Duchess Emilia Mary, the picture of whom is at Carton.

Neither of these pictures belongs to the Duke of Leinster, and their whereabouts is not known.

LELAND, Thomas, D.D.

Half length, oval.

Born 1722; friend and correspondent of Johnson; published a history of Ireland, 1773; librarian of Trinity College, Dublin; died 1785.

Full face; in his doctor's robes; wig and bands.

Pocket-book for 1776 missing, but mentioned in Cotton's list, p. 47.

Bought in at Christie's, June 19, 1858, Lot 89, by the owner, Farrer, for £71 8s.

ENGRAVED.

John Dean, 1777, 12¼ × 10⅞ in.

S. W. Reynolds, 2¼ × 1¼ in.

Purchased by William Dent Farrer at the sale of the pictures belonging to Leland's son in Ireland.

LENNOX, Lord George Henry.

Three-quarter length, canvas 56 × 40 in.

Son of Charles, 2nd Duke of Richmond; born November 29, 1737; entered the army, February 15, 1754; M.P. for Chichester 1761-75, and for Sussex until 1805; aide-de-camp to the Duke of Cumberland, 1757;

served as brigadier-general in Portugal in 1763 ; became general, October 12, 1793 ; married, in 1759, Lady Louisa Ker, daughter of William, Earl of Ancrum, afterwards 1st Marquess of Lothian ; his son George became 4th Duke of Richmond, December 29, 1806 ; he died March 22, 1805.

Seated, in a red uniform, with gold facings ; left hand holding a cocked hat, and right hand on a dog's head ; landscape background.

Sat in 1760, 1762, and 1764. Paid for before 1761, Lord George Lennox, £42 10s.

The picture belongs to the Earl of Ilchester at Holland House.

The eldest sister of Lord George Lennox married Henry Fox, 1st Lord Holland.

LENNOX, Lord George Henry.

Paid for June 28, 1757, Lord George Lenox, a head for his tutor, £12 12s. Frame to Lord George, for his tutor, £3 3s. ; case to ditto, 8s.

LENNOX, Lord George Henry.

Paid for before 1761, Lord George Lenox, £21.

LENNOX, Lady Anne.

Three-quarter length, canvas 49¼ × 39¼ in.

Daughter of Charles Lennox, 1st Duke of Richmond ; born June 24, 1703 ; married, February 21, 1723, William-Anne, 2nd Earl of Albemarle ; became a widow in 1754, and died October 20, 1789, in New Street, Spring Gardens.

Seated ; face nearly full ; grey hair ; dressed in a gown of blue and white brocade, with black silk mantle and hood, the latter drawn over her head ; wide sleeves, trimmed with deep lace, fall to the elbows, leaving the rest of the arms bare ; she holds a tatting shuttle in her right hand ; on her lap is a ball of thread ; she sits in an armchair, covered with crimson velvet ; by her side is a small table, with a work basket, etc.

Sat in 1757 and 1759 as Lady Albemarle. Paid for, November 18, 1760, Lady Albermarle, £42.

EXHIBITED.

Grosvenor, 1884, No. 67, as Lady Anne Lennox, by the Earl of Albemarle.

The picture was sold by the Earl of Albemarle in 1890 to Messrs. T. Agnew and Sons, from whom it passed to the National Gallery, No. 1259.

See COUNTESS OF ALBEMARLE, *ante*, p. 11.

LENNOX, Lady Emilia Mary. *See* KILDARE, *ante*, page 552, and LEINSTER, *ante*, pages 575 and 576.

LENNOX, Lady Georgina Carolina. *See* LADY HOLLAND, *ante*, page 474, and LADY CAROLINE FOX, *ante*, page 336.

LENNOX, Lady Louisa Augusta. *See* CONOLLY, *ante*, page 190.

LENNOX, Lady Sarah. *See* BUNBURY, *ante*, page 124, and FOX, page 334.

The picture described on page 124 is stated in error as belonging to William Waldorf Astor. It is still in the possession of Sir Henry Bunbury, Bart., at Barton Hall.

LENOX, Mrs. Arabella.

Three-quarter length.

Sketch, head only finished ; looking to right.

A literary lady, who had apartments in Somerset House, which she had to vacate, in 1773, to make room for Sir W. Chambers's new building.

Sat in 1761.

1773: " . . . or Mrs. Lenox, another literary lady, but less learned than Mrs. Carter—for *her* translations of the Greek are through the French—and less favoured by fortune than most about her. She is just now in great distress, as the apartments which have been granted her in Somerset House are about to be pulled down in the course of Sir William Chambers's projected rebuilding, and she will pour out her griefs and fears in Sir Joshua's sympathizing ear, etc."—TOM TAYLOR, vol. ii., p. 10.

ENGRAVED.

F. Bartolozzi, 1792, 4¼ × 3¼ in.

There is another engraving, called Lady Lenox, in the British Museum, engraved for Harding's "Shakespeare," in white dress, looking to the right, hair dressed high, a curl under the left ear.

579

LESLIE, Lady Jane.

Eldest daughter of John, 8th Earl of Rothes; born, May 5, 1750; died, unmarried, at Edinburgh, March 18, 1771.

Sat in 1764. Paid for, 1763, Lady Jane Lesly, £21; 1764, Lady Jane Lesly, £21.

LESLIE, Lady Mary.
Whole length.

Youngest daughter of John, 8th Earl of Rothes; born, August 29, 1753; married, November 5, 1770, William Charles, 3rd Earl of Portmore; died, March 21, 1799, at Kedleston, the seat of Lord Scarsdale.

Kneeling by a raised stone slab, on which is a lamb encircled by her arm; in her right hand a bouquet of flowers; sheep and lambs by her side; landscape background.

Sat in 1764. Paid for, 1763, Lady Mary Lesly, £21; 1764, Lady Mary Lesly, £21.

ENGRAVED.

J. Spilsbury, 1766, 18¼ × 14 in.

LETHBRIDGE, Mr.

Sat in 1768 and 1769. Paid for, June 20, 1768, Mr. Lethbridge, £18 7s. 6d.; frame and case paid; May 22, 1773, Mr. Lethbridge, £18 7s. 6d.

LETHULIER, Mrs.

Sat in 1757.

LEWISHAM, George, Lord, afterwards 3rd Earl of Dartmouth, K.G.
Half length, oval, canvas 24 × 18 *in.*

Born, October 3, 1755; succeeded his father as 3rd Earl of Dartmouth, July 15, 1801; called by writ to the House of Lords during the lifetime of his father, June 16, 1801; M.P. for Plymouth, 1775; Stafford, 1783; and filled important public offices; married, September 24, 1782, Lady Frances Finch, daughter of the 3rd Earl of Aylesford. He died, November 2, 1810.

As a youth; in a Vandyke dress; left sleeve slashed; cloak over right shoulder; dress not slashed; front face; dark hair over the forehead; looking to his left.

Sat in October, 1761. Paid for, October 14, 1761, Lord Dartmouth, for Lord Lewesham, £10 10s.

British Institution, 1824, No. 139, as the late Earl ⎫
    of Dartmouth when a boy,   ⎪
Grosvenor, 1884, No. 149, as the Hon. Henry ⎬ by the Earl of Dart-
    Legge (born January, 1765),   mouth.
Grafton, 1895, No. 117, as Heneage, fourth son ⎪
    (born May, 1761),   ⎭

ENGRAVED.

J. Spilsbury, 1764, 11¼ × 9 in.

The picture belongs to the Earl of Dartmouth.

As Lord Dartmouth only possesses two portraits of this character, there is no doubt this one was wrongly named in the *first* edition of the Grosvenor Catalogue, 1884, and also in the Grafton, 1895.

LEWISHAM, George, Lord, afterwards 3rd Earl of Dartmouth, K.G.

Three-quarter length, canvas 57 × 45 in.

Seated on a stone seat, left hand leaning on parapet; in a black dress; landscape background.

Sat in 1784 as Lord Leveson. Paid for, 1784, Lord Levison, £105. Exhibited at the Royal Academy, 1784, No. 139.

"Light too broke."—W.:
Morning Chronicle, 1784: "No. 139, portrait of Lord Lewisham, wants ease."
Morning Herald: "No. 139, Lord Lewisham, a striking likeness of the nobleman who is the subject. The air, the drapery, and pencilling, display the hand of a master."

EXHIBITED.

British Institution, 1813, No. 81 (third catalogue), ⎫
    as the Earl of Dartmouth,   ⎬ by the Earl of
Grosvenor Gallery, 1889, No. 95,   ⎭   Aylesford.

Withdrawn at Christie's, June 8, 1881, Lot 132, by the Earl of Aylesford.

LEWISHAM, Frances, Lady. *See* FINCH.

LIFFORD, James, 1st Viscount.

Whole length, canvas 96 × 58 *in.*

James Hewitt, born 1709; Lord Chancellor of Ireland, 1767; Baron Lifford, 1768; Viscount Lifford, 1781; married, first, Miss Williams, and, secondly, Ambrosia, daughter of the Rev. Charles Bayley. Died, October 28, 1789.

Seated; Lord Chancellor's robes; holding great seal; curtain and architectural background.

Sat in 1788. Exhibited in the Royal Academy, 1789, No. 240. Walpole says "very good." Paid for November, 1788, Lord Lifford, £105; and June, 1790, Lord Lifford, £105.

Public Advertiser, 1789: "His portrait of Lord Lifford is by far the best."

St. James's Chronicle, 1789: "No. 240, portrait of a nobleman, a very fine resemblance of Lord Lifford, Chancellor of Ireland. Sir Joshua has attended properly to the subordinate parts of the picture."

EXHIBITED.

British Institution, 1833, No. 10, } by Lord Lifford.
National Portrait Exhibition, 1867, No. 849, } by Lord Lifford.
Royal Academy, 1892, No. 100, by the Hon. Edward Hewitt.

ENGRAVED.

R. Dunkarton, 1790, 23½ × 16¾ in.
S. W. Reynolds (unpublished). Plate destroyed.

LIFFORD, James, 1st Viscount.

Half length, canvas.

Sold at Christie's, August 4, 1860, Lot 20 (Morrison, owner), Lord Lifford (not sent). June 6, 1868, Lot 39 (Haigh, owner), for £8 18*s.* 6*d.*, to Cox. May 20, 1874, Lot 126, bought in by the owner, Rev. Thomas Peake, for £15 15*s.* A copy by Andrew Martin was sold, May 14, 1846, Lot 30, for £2, to Darrell.

LIGONIER, John, Viscount, afterwards 1st Earl.

Whole length, canvas 110 × 94 *in.*

Of an ancient French family; born 1678; entered the army under Marlborough, and distinguished himself in his campaigns; Knight-Banneret at Dettingen ; Commander-in-Chief, 1757 ; Baron Ligonier, 1763 ; Earl, 1766. Died, 1770.

On a large horse ; looking to the right ; baton in right hand ; battle in the background ; castle to the right.

"The old nobleman is probably represented as at Dettingen, where he commanded a division of the army. In the management of the background the workmanship of Reynolds is sufficiently apparent, but Lord Ligonier was in his eighty-second year when the picture was painted, and this may perhaps account for the inferiority of the head. It was necessary to antedate the features, and such a proceeding could not but intimidate the painter ; for Reynolds never seems to have been truly himself when he was obliged to depart from the model before him. He could bring out all that was finest in what he saw, and could add something to it still finer ; but when it was required that he should make the head he was looking at twenty years younger, and light it up with an imaginary expression, his confidence in his own power must have been shaken, and the result that the picture presents naturally followed. The face is finished with great care, but the genius of the painter is not seen in it." —LESLIE AND TAYLOR's *Life of Reynolds*, vol. i., pp. 191, 192.

" During his residence in Newport, Sir Joshua Reynolds painted his celebrated portrait of Lord Ligonier on horseback. A noble performance, says Farrington, which may be classed with any of his after productions for grandeur of composition and force of effect. He had not attained his thirty-sixth year when he executed this fine work, which showed at once his exquisite taste and the depth of his knowledge in those parts of the art to which he had devoted his incessant attention."—BEECHEY, 1852, vol. i., p. 126.

Sat in 1760. Exhibited in the Society of Artists, 1761, No. 85. Paid for, 1764, Lord Ligonier for Sir Richard Lyttleton, £100.

EXHIBITED.

British Institution, 1827, No. 173, } by George IV.
 „ „ 1831, No. 164, }

ENGRAVED.

E. Fisher, 21¼ × 18 in.
S. W. Reynolds, 5¼ × 4¼ in.

First State by Fisher, Buccleuch Collection, sold at Christie's, 1887, for £12 12s.

Presented by King William IV. in 1836 to the National Gallery, No. 143.

A replica of this picture was in the Royal Academy, 1876, No. 143 (48¼ × 35 in.), and Guelph, 1891, No. 176 ; exhibited by the Duke of Sutherland, described, Equestrian figure, under life size, galloping to right ; looking back ; in military uniform, and Order of the Bath ; in right hand a baton ; in the background, scene of the Battle of Dettingen ; 60 × 56 in.

The Duke of Sutherland has only one picture of this subject, and it hangs at Trentham (No. 160 in the catalogue). The correct size is 67¼ × 60¼ in.

LIGONIER, John, Viscount, afterwards 1st Earl.

Sketch.

EXHIBITED.
British Institution, 1861, No. 191, by William Russell.

Sold at Christie's, May 19, 1821, Lot 39 (Thomond, owner), described as small study for the grand equestrian portrait of Lord Ligonier, to Rogers, for £21; June 16, 1832, Lot 83 (Rogers, owner), for £4, to Gilmore; March 6, 1863, Lot 75 (W. Russell, owner), described as a study for the equestrian portrait of Lord Ligonier, to Balfour, for £25; and December 6, 1884, Lot 240 (W. Russell, owner), for £22 1s., to Agnew.

Another sketch was sold at Christie's : equestrian Lord Ligonier and two other sketches, May 26, 1821, Lot 13 (Lady Thomond, owner), for £7, to Turner.

LIGONIER, John, Viscount, afterwards 1st Earl.

Three-quarter length, canvas 51 × 41 in.

Three-quarter face, looking to the right ; in uniform ; cuirass and ribbon of K.B.

Sat in 1755 and 1757.

EXHIBITED.
British Institution, 1846, No. 48, by J. A. Lloyd.
National Portrait Exhibition, 1867, No. 417, by Charles S. Lloyd.

LIGONIER, Penelope, Lady.

Daughter of George Pitt, 1st Lord Rivers; married, 1767, Col. Ligonier, afterwards Edward, 2nd Viscount Ligonier, who died 1782; divorced, December 10, 1771, and married, secondly, in 1784, Captain Smith.

Sat in February, 1771. Paid for, 1770, Lady Ligonier, £150; March 18, 1774, Lady Ligonier, paid by Mr. G. Pitt, £157 10s.; and between March, 1774, and May, 1775, Lady Ligonier, for changing the portrait, £36 15s.

The first payment is in the first ledger, and the second is evidently a repeat of this entry in the second ledger, as it appears at the top of the page. The word *changing* is ambiguous : it might mean altering, but as the picture is not to be found it might really mean changing for another picture, the original being either destroyed or sold as an unknown portrait in 1796.

584

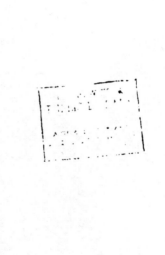

"May 4, 1784, at Northampton, Lady Ligonier, the divorced wife of Lord Ligonier, to a private in His Majesty's Regiment of Royal Horse Guards Blue."—*Gentleman's Magazine*, 1784, p. 395.

Lord Ligonier married again, December 14, 1773, Lady Mary Henley, sister to the 2nd Earl of Northington.

The marriage of. Lady Ligonier was dissolved at Doctors' Commons in 1771; the payment for the portrait by G. Pitt, and the payment for the alteration of it by her ladyship, arose, doubtless, out of that event.

There is a full-length portrait of her, by Gainsborough, belonging to General Pitt Rivers.

LINCOLN, Frances, Countess of.

Half length, canvas 24 × 18 *in.*

Lady Frances Seymour Conway, fourth daughter of Francis, 1st Marquess of Hertford; born, December 4, 1751; married, May 22, 1775, Henry Fiennes, Earl of Lincoln, second son of Henry, 2nd Duke of Newcastle, who died in his father's lifetime, October 22, 1778.

To left, three-quarter face, leaning her head on her right hand, and looking down; black dress; white sleeves and kerchief; powdered hair, falling in curls over her shoulders. Sky background.

Sat in 1781, 1782, and 1784. Paid for, 1784, Lord Hertford, for Lady Lincoln and Lady Elizabeth Conway, £110.

EXHIBITED.
Bethnal Green, 1872, No. 31, by Sir Richard Wallace, Bart.
Royal Academy, 1893, No. 28, by Lady Wallace.

The picture was bequeathed by the 4th Marquess of Hertford to Sir Richard Wallace, Bart., and by him to Lady Wallace, who left it to the nation with the Hertford House Collection in 1897.

LINDSEY, Albemarle, Earl of.

Head size, canvas 30 × 25 *in.*

When Colonel Bertie. Born, September 17, 1744; Colonel of the 89th Regiment of Foot; General, September 25, 1803; married, first, May 7, 1794, Eliza Maria, daughter of William Clay, widow of Thomas Scope, and, secondly, November 18, 1809, Charlotte, daughter of the Rev. Charles Layard, D.D.,

Dean of Bristol; succeeded as 9th Earl of Lindsey, February 8, 1809. He died September 17, 1818.

In the uniform of the Guards; with hair in powder.

Sat in 1787. Paid for, November, 1787, Coll. Bartie, £26 5s.; December, 1790, Coll. Bertie, £26 5s. Exhibited at the Royal Academy, 1788, No. 265.

The picture belongs to Lord Wimborne, and is No. 158 in the Canford catalogue. *See* BERTIE, *ante*, p. 82.

LINDSEY, Peregrine, Marquess of. *See* LADY MARY BERTIE, *ante*, page 81.

LINDSEY, Sir David.

Head size, canvas, oval, 30 × 24 in.

General, 1796; died, 1797.

Head turned to the right, looking out; dark brown hair, tied with ribbon behind; red coat edged with gold lace; white lace necktie. Blue-grey sky.

Sat in 1759 as Colonel Lindsey. Paid for before 1760, Coll. Lindsy, £21.

Sold at Christie's, June 25, 1842, Lot 325, Hon. Captain Lindsay (Collector, owner), for £4 10s., to Emery.

The picture was bequeathed by Lady Murray to the Board of Manufactures, Edinburgh, and is now in the National Gallery of Scotland.

LINDSEY, Lady Jane.

Whole length, canvas.

Jane, daughter of George, 10th Earl of Crawford; born 1757; married, March 30, 1772, as his first wife, Archibald, 11th Earl of Eglinton. She died January 22, 1778.

Seated; playing on a harp; amber dress, with dark blue robe; at her feet a book of music; landscape background beyond.

EXHIBITED.

Royal Academy, 1883, No. 213 (dimensions given, 82¼ × 58 in.), by the Earl of Crawford. Described as above.

The picture belongs to the Earl of Crawford and Balcarres. *See* EGLINTON, *ante*, p. 282, for a further account of the two pictures. They were both paid for before the Earl of Eglinton married Miss Twysden in 1783, but four years after his first wife's death. The original belongs to the Earl of Eglinton.

LINLEY, Miss Elizabeth. *See* SHERIDAN.

EXHIBITED.

Grafton, 1894, No. 124, by the Corporation of Glasgow.

Sold at Christie's, May 12, 1838, Lot 68 (Lord Northbrook, owner), sketch of Miss Linley, first wife of R. B. Sheridan, £82 19s., to Gritten. Portrait of Miss Linley sold at Christie's, June 3, 1865, Lot 127 (Colnaghi, owner), for £12 12s., to Haig.

LISBURNE, Wilmot, 4th Viscount, afterwards 1st Earl.

Half length, canvas 30 × 25 *in.*

Born 1728; M.P. for Cardigan, 1755-1796; succeeded, February 4, 1766; created Earl of Lisburne on July 18, 1776; married, first, July, 1754, Elizabeth, only daughter of Joseph Gascoyne Nightingale, who died May 9, 1755; secondly, on April 19, 1763, Dorothy, daughter of John Shafto. He died, January 6, 1800. There is a long account of him in the "Gentleman's Magazine," 1800, p. 89.

Three-quarter face to the right; head and shoulders to the waist; right hand lying across a book; books in the background; part of the robes are red, and part gold embroidery.

Sat in August, 1766.

Sold at Greenwood's, April 15, 1796, Lot 7, as Lord Lisburne, for £9 19s. 6d., to Simpson; same day, Lot 8, as Lord Vaughan (family name of the Earl of Lisburne), for £7 7s., to Collins; at Messrs. Foster's, 1849, same picture, £12 12s., to Norton.

The picture belongs to the Earl of Lisburne, at Crosswood, Aberystwith, South Wales.

LISBURNE, Dorothy, Countess of.

Three-quarter length, canvas 48¼ × 39¼ *in.*

Dorothy, eldest daughter of John Shafto; married, April 19, 1763, as his second wife, the Hon. Wilmot Vaughan, afterwards 1st Earl of Lisburne. She died 1805.

Full face; left hand clasped over right hand, which holds an open book; low bodice; white dress; black shawl over both shoulders; landscape background.

Sat in March, 1771, May, 1772, and May, 1777.

The picture belongs to the Earl of Lisburne, at Crosswood, Aberystwith, South Wales.

LISBURNE, Wilmot, 2nd Earl of. *See* Lord Vaughan.

LISLE, John, Lord. *See* Lysaght.

LISTER, Master Thomas.

Whole length, canvas 91 × 55 *in.*

Born March 22, 1752; created Baron Ribblesdale, October 26, 1797; married, 1789, Rebecca, daughter of Joseph Fielding. He died, September 22, 1826.

In a landscape; Vandyke dress; right hand raised, and leaning on a staff.

Sat in 1764. Paid for, April 7, 1764, Master Lister, £31 10s.; November 10, 1764, Master Lister, £31 10s.

EXHIBITED.

Grosvenor, 1884, No. 20, by Lord Ribblesdale.

The picture belonged to Lord Ribblesdale, who sold it to Lord Masham of Swinton Park, the present owner.

LISTER, Miss Beatrix.

Half length, canvas 31 × 25 *in.*

Daughter of Thomas Lister, M.P., and sister of Thomas Lister, 1st Baron Ribblesdale; born November 25, 1749; married, November 14, 1778, John Parker, of Browsholme, co. York.

Seated, with a dog in her lap; dark blue dress with slashed sleeves; a row of pearls round her neck.

Sat in 1765. Paid for, 1764, Miss Lister, £18 7s. 6d.; August 17, 1765, Miss Lister, £18.

EXHIBITED.

British Institution, 1817, No. 4, by T. Lister Parker.

Grosvenor, 1884, No. 91, by Lord Ribblesdale.

ENGRAVED *[handwritten annotation]*

S. W. Reynolds, 1820, 4⅞ × 4 in. ——— *[handwritten annotation]*

The picture, which probably came from Browsholme on the death of Thomas Lister Parker, belongs to Lord Ribblesdale.

LIVERPOOL, Charles, 1st Earl of. *See* JENKINSON, *ante*, page 514, and BUTE, pages 135, 136.

LIVERPOOL, Catherine, Countess of.

Whole length, canvas.

Catherine, daughter of Sir Cecil Bishopp, Bart., married, first, Sir Charles Cope, Bart., and secondly, June 22, 1782, as his second wife, Sir Charles Jenkinson, created Baron Hawksbury, August 21, 1786, and Earl of Liverpool, May 28, 1796. She was the mother of the Duchess of Dorset. The Earl of Liverpool died at the age of eighty-one on December 17, 1808, in consequence of a shock caused by an accident that occurred to the Countess, her dress having caught fire and dreadfully burnt her before the flames were extinguished. *See Illustration Vol. I, ; 48. [handwritten annotation]*

Sat in 1757 as Miss Bishop.

Bought of Martin H. Colnaghi, March 17, 1877, by Henry Graves and Co., and sold by them, November 11, 1877, to Sir H. M. Thompson, Bart.

The picture belongs to Sir Henry Meysey-Thompson, Bart.

LLOYD, Mr.

Sat in 1757 eight times, 1759 as Mr. and Mrs. Lloyd, and 1761 as Mr. Lloyd. Paid for before 1763, Mr. Loyd, £21.

LLOYD, Mrs.

Sat in March, 1757, eight times; June, 1759, Mr. and Mrs. Lloyd.

LLOYD, Mrs.

Whole length, canvas 93 × 57 in.

Joanna, daughter of John Leigh, of North Court, Isle of Wight, married first, 1775, R. B. Lloyd, of Maryland; secondly, F. L. Beckford, of Basing Park, Hants.

Standing to left, in a wood, leaning against a pedestal, inscribing her name on the trunk of a tree; white dress; sandals.

Sat in 1777. Paid for after 1772, Mrs. Loyd, £78 15s.; June, 1777, Mrs. Loyd, £78 15s. Exhibited in the Royal Academy, 1776, No. 234.

Morning Post, 1776 : "The whole-lengths of the two ladies are fine pictures (No. 233, Duchess of Devonshire ; No. 234, Mrs. Lloyd). The designs are pleasing, particularly that of Mrs. Lloyd on the left side, a beautiful figure in a loose fancy vest, inscribing her husband's name on the bark of a tree. The idea is taken from 'As you Like it.'"

"Mrs. Lloyd afterwards married F. L. Beckford, of Basing Park, Hants. The picture is in the possession of Mrs. Arcedeckne, whose family is connected with Mrs. Lloyd."—TOM TAYLOR, vol. ii., p. 155.

EXHIBITED.
British Institution, 1831, No. 80, by Andrew Arcedeckne, M.P.
Royal Academy, 1873, No. 59, by Baron Lionel de Rothschild, M.P.
       „   „   1887, No. 37, by Lord Rothschild.

Sold at Christie's, May 29, 1869, Lot 102 (Ward, owner), Miss Leigh (afterwards Mrs. Lloyd, secondly Mrs. Beckford), for £840, to Agnew. March 3, 1883, Lot 49, copy (Morris, owner), £39 18s., to Wertheimer. A study of Mrs. Lloyd sold at Christie's, March 2, 1865, Lot 64 (Lord Arran, owner), for £6 15s., to Hawkins. Sold at Foster's, March 8, 1899.

ENGRAVED.
S. W. Reynolds, 1835, 6¼ × 3¾ in.
R. Graves, A.R.A., 1867, 16¼ × 10¾ in.

The picture was left by Mrs. Lloyd to her daughter, by her second husband, who became Mrs. Ward. She was half-sister to Mrs. Arcedeckne, widow of Andrew Arcedeckne, who housed the picture until 1869, when it was sold by Mrs. Ward's children at Christie's to Messrs. T. Agnew and Sons, who sold it to Baron Lionel de Rothschild, from whom it descended to Lord Rothschild, the present owner. It hangs at Tring Park.

LOCKHART, Captain John, R.N., afterwards Admiral Sir John, Bart.

Three-quarter length, canvas 50 × 40 *in.*

Born 1721 ; succeeded his brother, 1780; admiral, 1779; distinguished himself when in command of the "Tartar"; died 1790.

In uniform ; right hand holds a staff; forefinger of left hand points to a ship in the distance.

Sat in 1760 and 1762 as Captain Lockhart, R.N. Paid for, 1761, Captain Lockard (first picture), £26 5s.

J. McArdell, 14 × 11 in.

S. W. Reynolds (S. Cousins, R.A.), 3½ × 2¼ in.

"One of the most gallant officers of his time. His action with seven French privateers in the 'Tartar' in 1757 had been rewarded with a salver by the merchants of London, and a £100 cup by those of Bristol in January, 1758."—TOM TAYLOR, vol. i., p. 186.

LOCKHART, Captain John, R.N.

Paid for before 1763, Capt. Lockart, for Lord Hindford, £42.

John, 3rd Earl of Hyndford, succeeded to the title in 1707, and was ambassador to Vienna from 1752 to 1764. He married the daughter of Sir Cloudesley Shovel. He died July 19, 1767.

LOCKWOOD, Mrs. *See* MISS MORRIS.

LONG, Harriot, Lady Tilney. *See* MISS HARRIOT BOUVERIE, *ante*, page 104.

LONG, Mrs., afterwards Lady. *See* MISS AMELIA HUME, *ante*, page 494.

LONG, Mr.

Sat in August, 1757, as Mr. and Mrs. Long.

LONG, Mrs.

Sat in August, 1757, as Mr. and Mrs. Long.

LONG, Miss.

Afterwards Mrs. Palmer, wife of John Palmer, M.P. for Bath, Comptroller of the General Post Office ; inventor of mail coaches, 1784.

Sat in September, 1777.

Sold at Christie's, February 18, 1886, Lot 58 (Colonel Palmer, owner), described as above, for £63, to E. B

LORT, Rev. Michel, D.D., F.R.S., F.S.A.

Born, 1725 ; died, 1790.

Profile to right ; in black coat ; arms folded in front ; white neckcloth ; large white wig ; curtain and sky background.

"May 14, 1791. Ended the sale of the valuable library of the late Dr. Lort . . . the produce of which amounted to £1,269."—*Gentleman's Magazine*, 1791, p. 577.

ENGRAVED.

James Stow, 1815, 4¼ × 3⅞ in.

LOTEN, Joan Gideon.

Was appointed Dutch Governor of Ceylon, September 30, 1752.

Sat in December, 1764, as Mr. Lowten. Paid for, December 8, 1764, Mr. Loten, £25 ; December 14, 1764, Governor Loten, £25.

The Portuguese settled in Ceylon in 1517, but they were ousted by the Dutch about 1658. In 1795-96 it was conquered by the British, who annexed it to the Presidency of Madras. It was formally ceded to Great Britain at the Peace of Amiens in 1801-2.

LOTHIAN, William John, Marquess of, K.T.

William John, 5th Marquess ; General in the Army ; Colonel of the 11th Regiment of Dragoons, and K.T. ; born 1737 ; married, 1763, Elizabeth, only daughter of Chichester Fortescue ; died 1815.

Sat in May, 1777. Paid for July 1, 1776, Lord Lothian, £36 15s.

The picture, which was presented to Charles, Marquess of Granby, in exchange for his own (see *ante*, p. 389), was burnt at Belvoir Castle, October 26, 1816.

LOTHIAN, Elizabeth, Marchioness of. *See* ANCRUM, *ante*, pages 20, 21.

LOUDOUN, James, 5th Earl of.

Three-quarter length, canvas 49¼ × 38¼ *in.*

Born 1726; Major-General in the Army ; assumed the name of Muir ; succeeded the 4th Earl, who commanded the British Horse at the Battle of

, , Marchioness of   *See* ANNESLEY, *ante*, pages
, 21.

LOUDOUN, James, 5th Earl of.

See ANNESLEY, ante, pages 153.

, Master ... , issue of the ... of Mear;
the 9th Earl, also ... commanded the British Horse at the Battle of

Fontenoy, April 30, 1745, where he was mortally wounded, one of his legs being taken off by a cannon-ball. He expired soon afterwards. The 5th Earl died in 1786.

In military uniform; his hands upon his hips; landscape background.

EXHIBITED.

Grosvenor, 1884, No. 154, by Lord·Donington.

ENGRAVED.

R. B. Parkes, 1874, 5¼ × 4¼ in.

This picture came into the Hastings family by the marriage of Francis, 2nd Earl of Moira, with Flora Muir (Campbell), Countess of Loudoun in her own right. It afterwards belonged to her grandson, the 4th Marquess of Hastings, and on his death became the property of Edith Maud, Countess of Loudoun, and now belongs to her son, the Earl of Loudoun.

LOUGHBOROUGH, Alexander Wedderburn, Lord.

Three-quarter length, panel 49 × 39 in.

Descended from Sir Henry Erskine and his wife, Janet, daughter of Peter Wedderburn, a Lord of Session as Lord Chesterhall; born in Edinburgh, February 13, 1733. He was called to the Scottish Bar when only nineteen years of age, but determining to seek a wider sphere for his professional pursuits, he came to London in 1753, and became a member of the Inner Temple, and took lessons in elocution from Macklin. He was called to the English Bar in 1757. He pleaded in the Douglas and Hamilton cause, and successfully defended Lord Clive; became Solicitor-General in 1771; Attorney-General in 1778; Lord Chief Justice of the Common Pleas 1780, and Lord High Chancellor of Great Britain in 1793. He was, June 14, 1780, created Baron Loughborough, and April 21, 1801, advanced to the dignity of Earl Rosslyn, county Midlothian. Married, first, 1767, Betty Anne, daughter of John Dawson; and, secondly, 1782, Charlotte, daughter of William, Viscount Courtenay. Died January 3, 1805, and his remains were interred in St. Paul's Cathedral.

Sitting in his robes; his arm resting on the arm of a chair; a paper in his left hand; on table inkstand and papers; curtain and columns.

Exhibited in the Royal Academy, 1785, No. 181.

Morning Chronicle, April 28, 1785: "His portrait of Lord Loughborough is a good likeness, but he has suffered his Lordship's *oculus eloquens* to escape him. No man's countenance was ever animated with more animated and with more sensible and piercing eyes than Lord Loughborough's, but they are not alive in the portrait."

General Advertiser, April 21, 1785: "Among those of merit are the works of Sir Joshua Reynolds; and the best picture in the room is confessedly his portrait of Lord Loughborough in his judicial robes, half length. The likeness is inimitable, and every judge of painting expressed his wish that the colouring might live as long as the canvas existed."

Morning Herald, April 28, 1789: "No. 181, Lord Loughborough, an assemblage of lines in which light and shade appear without the least harmony or design."

EXHIBITED.

National Portrait Exhibition, 1867, No. 779, } by the Earl of Sheffield.
Royal Academy, 1884, No. 42,

ENGRAVED.

J. Grozer, 1786, 18 × 13¾ in.

Another plate in line, British Museum; half length, seated; holding front of robe in left hand; right hand upon Lord Chancellor's cushion; mace on a table; robes of Chancellor, 16¼ × 13¼ in.; engraver not known.

LOVAINE, Isabella, Lady, afterwards Countess of Beverley.

Half length, canvas 30 × 25 *in.*

Isabella Susannah, second daughter of Peter Burrell, of Beckenham, Kent, and sister to the second wife of Hugh, 2nd Duke of Northumberland; married, June 8, 1775, Algernon, 2nd Lord Lovaine, who succeeded as Lord Lovaine in 1786, and was created Earl of Beverley, November 2, 1790. She died January 24, 1812.

Three-quarter face, looking towards the right; in pink dress, with black silk cloak trimmed with black lace; white fichu round neck, passing under a white bodice, tied with narrow white strings; hair powdered, worn in large curls.

Sat in June, 1789, as Lady Lovaine. Paid for, February, 1790, Lady Lovain, £52 10s.

"Lady LOUVAIN is for FAWCETT."—From a newspaper, 1789.

The picture belonged to George, 2nd Earl of Beverley, until 1865, when he became 5th Duke of Northumberland. It now belongs to the Duke of Northumberland at 28, Grosvenor Square, London.

LOWTEN, Mr.   *See* LOTEN.

LOWTHER, Sir William.

Of Swillington.

"This amiable and accomplished young millionaire had known Reynolds at Rome, and had sat to him soon after his first settlement in London. In April of this year he died of a fever at twenty-six, leaving £20,000 a year in land, of which the bulk descended to his imperious and morose cousin, Sir James, afterwards 1st Earl of Lonsdale, already enormously rich, and the tyrant of Cumberland and Westmoreland. But Sir William, generous in death as he had been in life, left out of his personal estate thirteen legacies of £5,000 each to as many friends. Most of the legatees commissioned Reynolds for copies of Sir William's portrait, and for two years afterwards he was busy with these profitable commissions, executed under his own eye, but principally painted by Marchi, Barron, and Berridge, his pupils, or by his drapery men. The original picture belongs to Mr. G. Bentinck."—LESLIE AND TAYLOR's *Life of Sir Joshua*, vol. i., p. 149.

Paid for 1754, Mr. Hopkins, paid for Sir W. Lowther, £12 12s.

    „   1754, Major Kenneer, for Sir W. Lowther's picture, £12 12s.

    „   before 1760, Mr. Bridgman, for Sir W. Lowther, £12 12s.

    „   1765, Mr. Lowther, for a copy, £26 5s.

Sold at Greenwood's, April 16, 1796, Lot 6, Sir Wm. Lowther, three-quarter length, for £5 10s., to James.

Memo., February, 1757, "Mr. Reynolds's Sir Wm. Lowther."

  „   April,   „   "To finish a copy of Sir Wm. Lowther for Mr. Wilson, to be finished beginning of June."

  „   June,   „   "Mr. Cambell in Hanover Square, to send a copy of Sir Wm. Lowther."

  „   „   „   "A copy of Sir Wm. Lowther for Major Kinnear to be ready within six weeks."

LUARD, Mr.

Sat in 1757.

LUCAN, Charles, 1st Earl.

Whole length, oval, 29 × 24 in.

Sir Charles Lucan, M.P. co. Mayo, Ireland; created, June 24, 1776, Baron Lucan of Castlebar; advanced to the earldom of Lucan, October 6, 1795; died March 29, 1799.

In the dress of the period; powdered hair; face turned to the right.

Sat in 1780. Paid for, August 30, 1778, Lord Lucan, £36 15s. 6d. Pocket-book of 1778 missing, but in the "Life of Sir Joshua," vol. ii., p. 224, Lord Lucan is mentioned thus: "Other sitters of the year were Lord Lucan, etc., etc."

ENGRAVED.

J. Jones, 1787, 13¼ × 11 in.

S. W. Reynolds, 2¼ × 2 in.

The picture, which was bequeathed in 1799 by Charles, 1st Earl of Lucan, to his daughter, Lavinia, Countess Spencer, belongs to Earl Spencer, and is No. 176 in the Althorp catalogue.

LUCAN, Richard, 2nd Earl.

Head size, canvas 30 × 24 *in.*

Richard, eldest son of Charles, 1st Lord Lucan; born 1764; married, May 26, 1794, Lady Elizabeth Belasyse, daughter of Henry, Earl of Fauconberg; died, June 29, 1839.

Sat in July, 1786, as Mr. Bingham.

EXHIBITED.

British Institution, 1861, No. 164, } by Earl Spencer.
Dublin, 1872, No. 170,

The picture belongs to Earl Spencer, and is No. 208 in the Althorp catalogue.

LUCAN, Lady, Children of.

The only evidence of the existence of such a picture rests with Walpole, who in 1786 describes a picture of two children as " Two children of Lady Lucan, natural expression ; " " At that time Lord Lucan's family were grown up—the Miss Anne Bingham and Lady Spencer, two of his daughters, being exhibited the same year."

The picture was evidently of the children of Mr. Vandergucht, who sat in January, 1786, and was paid for November, 1785 ; moreover, the criticism in the "Morning Herald" exactly describes this picture. The "Public Advertiser" calls it Mr. Vandergucht's children. *See* VANDERGUCHT.

LUCAS, Charles, M.D.

Half length.

An Irish physician ; he was compelled to leave Ireland on account of his political principles ; came to London ; was regarded as a martyr to liberty and eulogized by Dr. Johnson ; afterwards M.P. for Dublin ; a statue erected to his memory is in the Exchange, Dublin ; died in 1771.

In a wig, bands, and gown ; holding a scroll with Latin inscription (thesis for his Doctor's degree) in his hand.

Sat in 1755.

ENGRAVED.

J. McArdell, 11 × 8¼ in.
S. W. Reynolds, 1¼ × 1¼ in.

The picture once belonged to the Earl of Charlemont.

Note to the sitting : "A man of note at this moment. He was an Irishman. Originally an apothecary, became a physician, an honour of which he shows himself proud by making Reynolds put into his hand in this portrait the thesis for his Doctor's degree. Distinguished himself by his vehement opposition to the Government and Duke of Dorset the Viceroy ; was accused and compelled to leave Ireland, and was now regarded by the opponents of the administration as a martyr of liberty. Johnson, in a review of his essay on Waters, 1754, says of Lucas : 'The Irish ministers drove him from his native country by a proclamation in which they charge him with crimes of which they never intended to be called to the proof, and oppressed him by methods equally irresistible by guilt and innocence. Let the man thus driven into exile for having been the friend of his country be received in every other place as a confessor of liberty, and let the tools of power be taught in time that they may rob but cannot impoverish.' In 1758 Lucas edited 'Smith's History of the last four years of the reign of Queen Anne,' went back to Ireland, where he was returned member for Dublin, died in 1771, and was honoured by a statue in the Dublin Exchange. His portrait represents a young and handsome man, but with an unmistakable expression of vanity."—TOM TAYLOR, vol. i., pp. 146, 147.

LUDLOW, Peter, afterwards 1st Earl, and his Dog.

Whole length, canvas 93 × 57 in.

Born April 30, 1730 ; represented co. Huntingdon in Parliament ; Privy Councillor in England, 1782 ; Baron of Ardsalla, December 19, 1755, and Earl Ludlow, October 3, 1760 ; married, January 20, 1753, Frances Lumley, eldest daughter of Thomas, Earl of Scarborough. He died September 30, 1803, at Ardsalla, co. Meath.

Sat in February, 1755, as Mr. Ludlow and his dog.

Full length, standing figure, in white hussar or Hungarian uniform, with round white hat and feather. The face is seen in three quarters, turned towards the right ; the dress is white satin, embroidered with gold, and a short ermine-lined cloak over the left shoulder. He rests his right hand on the head of a magnificent dog, seated beside him. The background is a wild and dark mountainous scene.

The picture was purchased by the Duke of Bedford before 1856 ; it is mentioned in the preface of Cotton's book as having come from a seat of the former Earls of Ludlow ; it now belongs to the Duke of Bedford, and is No. 265 in the Woburn catalogue.

LUDLOW, Frances, Lady.

Frances Lumley, eldest daughter of Thomas, 3rd Earl of Scarborough ; married, January 20, 1753, Peter Ludlow, afterwards 1st Earl.

Sat in May, 1755, as Lady F. Ludlow, and April, 1758, as Lady Ludlow.

LUSHINGTON, Mrs., and Child.

Sold at Christie's, January 30, 1897, Lot 157 (owner's name not given), for £35 14s., to Frazer.

LUTHER, Mr.

Sat in January, 1770. Paid for November 4, 1763, Mr. Luther, £25; before 1769, Mr. Luther, for a copy, £26 5s.; May 30, 1770, Mr. Luther, £73 10s. These entries point to two head-size pictures and a three-quarter length.

Sold at Greenwood's, April 16, 1796, Lot 25, for £10 10s., as Mr. Luther, half length, to Hawke.

LUTHER, Mrs.

Sat in June, 1766. Paid for November 4, 1763, Mrs. Luther, £25.

LUTTRELL, Miss.

Elizabeth, second daughter of Simon Luttrell, 1st Earl of Carhampton, and sister of Colonel Luttrell. She died in August, 1799.

Sat in April, 1769. Paid for, 1770, Miss Lutterel, now Mrs. Southcot £36 15s.; frame paid, two guineas and a half.

" 1772, while facetious Mr. Southcote, in his character of a Smithfield butcher, kept feeling his ribs from time to time, and estimating his weight and value at the then high price of butchers' meat."—TOM TAYLOR, vol. i., p. 434.
Note to the sitting: "When Miss Luttrell is finished, write to Mr. Luttrell, Dunster Castle, Somersetshire."
"Miss Luttrell was the sister of Mrs. Horton, afterwards Duchess of Cumberland. They were the sisters of Colonel Luttrell, who, at the time Miss Luttrell was sitting, was in the full flush of his notoriety as the opponent of Wilkes at the Middlesex election on the 13th of April. Their father was Simon Luttrell, Lord Carhampton, an Irish peer."—TOM TAYLOR, vol. i., p. 347.

LYNE, Mrs. *See* SEAFORTH.

LYSAGHT, John, afterwards John, Lord Lisle.

Head size, canvas 30 × 24 *in.*

John Lysaght, who was descended from the ancient house of O'Bryen, born 1702, was created Baron Lisle, of Mountnorth, co. Cork, September 18, 1758; married, first, 1725, Catherine, daughter of Lord Chief Baron Deane; secondly, 1746, Elizabeth, daughter of Edward Moore; died June 15, 1781.

Paid for before 1760, Mr. Lysaght, for Capt. Walsingham, £21.

Sold at Christie's, July 9, 1888, Lot 346 (Lord Lisle, owner), for £22 1s., to Martin H. Colnaghi; sold by him to Charles Sedelmeyer, of Paris, in 1888, from whom it passed to Mons. C. Groult, of Paris, the present owner.

LYTTELTON, George, 5th Bart. and 1st Lord.

Bust, canvas 30 × 25 *in.*

Born January 17, 1709; educated at Eton and Oxford; page of honour to the Princess Royal, 1729; M.P. for Oakhampton from 1735 to 1754; opposed Walpole; secretary to the Prince of Wales, 1737; Lord of the Treasury, 1744; Chancellor of the Exchequer, 1755; litterateur, principal work, "New Dialogues of the Dead;" created Lord Lyttelton, November 19, 1757; married, first, Lucy, daughter of Hugh Fortescue; secondly, August 10, 1749, Elizabeth, daughter of Field-Marshal Sir Robert Rich, Bart.; died August 22, 1773.

Looking to the right; purplish dress; powdered wig; white necktie; right hand in waistcoat.

EXHIBITED.
National Portrait Exhibition, 1867, No. 338, by Lord Lyttelton.

ENGRAVED.
G. H. Every, 1866, 4¼ × 3¼ in.

Johnson, in his "Lives of the Poets," criticises the productions of Lord Lyttelton in a very trenchant and unsparing manner.

The picture belongs to Viscount Cobham at Hagley Hall, Stourbridge.

LYTTELTON, William Henry, afterwards Lord Lyttelton.

Created Baron Westcote, July 31, 1776, and Lord Lyttelton, August 13, 1794; married, first, June 2, 1761, Mary, daughter of James Macartney, and, secondly, February 19, 1774, Caroline, daughter of John Bristow. He died September 14, 1808, aged eighty-four.

Sat in June, 1772, as Mr. Lyttelton.

Sold by Mr. Squibb, May, 1816, at Mrs. Piozzi's sale, Lot 57, for £43 1s., to Mr. Lyttelton.

The picture belongs to Viscount Cobham at Hagley Hall, Stourbridge.

Lord Cobham succeeded as 5th Baron Lyttelton in 1876, and became Viscount Cobham on the death of the Duke of Buckingham in 1889.

LYTTELTON, Elizabeth, Lady.

Daughter of Field-Marshal Sir Robert Rich ; married, secondly, August 10, 1749, George, 1st Lord Lyttelton ; she died September 17, 1795.

Sat in August, 1759. Paid for, 1763, Lady Lyttleton, £21 ; December 6, 1763, Lady Lyttleton, £18 10s.

This picture is not at Hagley Hall.

Lightning Source UK Ltd.
Milton Keynes UK
UKHW02f0625260918
329519UK00011B/220/P